Savory Baking ···· ···· from the Mediterranean

OTHER BOOKS BY ANISSA HELOU

Lebanese Cuisine

Café Morocco

Mediterranean Street Food

The Fifth Quarter

Savory Baking

from the

Mediterranean

FOCACCIAS, FLATBREADS, RUSKS, TARTS, AND OTHER BREADS

ANISSA HELOU

wm   WILLIAM MORROW   *An Imprint of* HarperCollins*Publishers*

HarperCollins books may be purchased for educational, business, or sales promotional use. For information please write: Special Markets Department, HarperCollins Publishers, 10 East 53rd Street, New York, NY 10022.

FIRST EDITION

Designed by Mia Risberg
Photographs © by Anissa Helou

Library of Congress Cataloging-in-Publication Data

Helou, Anissa, 1952–
    Savory baking from the Mediterranean : focaccias, flatbreads, rusks, tarts, and other breads / Anissa Helou.
      p. cm.
    Includes bibliographical references and index.
    ISBN: 978-0-06-054219-1
    ISBN-10: 0-06-054219-5
    1. Bread—Mediterranean Region. 2. Baking—Mediterranean Region. 3. Cookery, Mediterranean. I. Title.

TX769.H4245 2007
641.8'15091822—dc22

                                                    2006046858

07 08 09 10 11 WBC/QWF 10 9 8 7 6 5 4 3 2 1

For Peregrine and Patricia

✦ Contents ✦

Acknowledgments

From early on in my career, I have been very lucky to have friends everywhere in the world. With each book, this circle of friends expands as I meet new people on my travels, usually friends of friends or food professionals who share the same passion and are always generous with their time and knowledge. I would like to thank the following people, in no particular order, for their help with the research and writing of this book.

In Italy: Suni Agnelli for having me to stay and asking her cooks, Teresa, Vittoria, and Vita, to bake pies and breads for me to note the recipes, see how they are done, and, of course, taste them. Franco Santasilia, author of *The Aristocratic Neapolitan Cuisine,* for showing me, one memorable morning in Suni's kitchen in Rome, how to make timballo. Franco also took me to Naples to show me different Neapolitan specialties and, of course, to have pizza at Ciro's, the best ever; and to meet Professore Massimo Ricciardi, who gave me a fascinating paper that he wrote on pizza. And Ilaria Borletti, without whose unfailing support I would probably not have become a food writer.

Everyone at Il Forno in Campo dei Fiori for letting me take pictures, giving me recipes, and explaining to me what makes their pizza and breads so superior.

Grande capo Michele Russo, owner of Pizza Rustica on Via Flaminia in Rome, who also took the time to explain the secrets of his pizza, different from that at Il Forno in Campo dei Fiori, but equally good. Angelina Gilianelli in Rome for showing me how to make piadina and letting me take photographs. Mary Taylor Simeti for wonderful advice and invaluable information on different Sicilian breads. Mrs. Fullo, and Rosa, Leone, and Francesco Licari, all bakers in Castelvetrano. Alessandra, in whose bed-and-breakfast I stayed in Siracusa, for telling me about local bakeries. Everyone at Panificio Bianca in Siracusa. Also Gea Planeta, Anna Calabro, Luigi Corti, Carlina de Villarosa, Mario Durso, Anna Sermonti, Daniela Ghisalbeit, Viviana Pecci Blunt, Seth Rosenbaum, Gabriella Becchina, Zeke Freeman, and Christine Garabedian.

In France: Jacqueline de Guithaut for finding me many interesting recipes. Beatrice Viennet for introducing me to the *petits pâtés de Pézenas;* Jean Lafont, who is a fount of knowledge in culinary matters, and everything else for that matter. And Anne-Marie and Guy de Rougemont, in whose house I always stay in the south of France. Anne-Marie is a great cook and she was always there to answer whatever question I had on French cooking and baking. Also Philip and Mary Hyman for being so generous with their encyclopedic knowledge of French food; Mary also shared with me her knowledge of and experience with *pain au levain.*

In America: Susan Friedland, who initially commissioned this book and tested recipes for me. David Black, my agent and friend, whose idea it was for me to write this book. Amy Scherber and everyone at Amy's Bread; Amy was kind enough to let me do a few days' internship at her bakery, which was invaluable in helping me understand dough and shape it far better than ever before. Ellen Rose and everyone at Cook's Library in Los Angeles. Also in Los Angeles, my friend Peter Fuhrman, who put his house at my disposal for me to test recipes in his American kitchen. Susan Reid at King Arthur Flour. Rebecca Chispa and Janice Redsie for bringing me flour and baking powder from the U.S., as did Ray and Johanna Sokolov, and my nephew and niece Andrew and Sarah Karam. Also William Rubel for information and photographs of the Sardinian Pane Carasau.

Califia Suntree, Kate Hirson, Toni Sagakuchi, Tracy West, and Julie Logue Riordan for testing recipes and commenting on them. Also Charles Perry, Nancy Harmon Jenkins, Paula Wolfert, Ellen Huxley and her family, Celia Lowenstein, Nancy Silverton, Paul Schrade, Alex Toledano, and Roberta Klugman. And finally Harriet Bell, who took over as my publisher and editor, and Dan Rosenberg, who edited the recipes. Also Janet McDonald, Mia Risberg, Stephanie Fraser, and Lindsay Condiot.

In England: Peregrine and Patricia Pollen, to whom this book is dedicated, for letting me test recipes in their kitchen. Elisabeth Luard, who also brought me flour from the U.S. and told me about Spanish breads. Adrian von Ferscht for providing me with Israeli recipes and answering my questions. Jane Levi for testing recipes, and Alex, her partner, for being a very enthusiastic taster. Also Susannah Tarbush, Daniel Young, and Jill Norman, who also tested recipes for me. Cecil Hourani, Arabella Boxer, Rai Ghoussoub, and Jeremy Lee. And finally my neighbors Don and Yoko Brown, Chris Hill, and Liz Hassell for being so willing to taste my breads and pies and commenting on them.

In Greece: Aglaia Kremezi for giving me wonderful Greek recipes and always being there, at the other end of Skype, to answer my questions on Greek baking. My friend Marina Coriolano Lykorezous for having me to stay in Athens and translating for me when bakers didn't speak English. Marilena and Alexandros Kedros for inviting me to stay on the island of Kassos and getting their friend Finia, a wonderful home baker, to bake some artos for me to take pictures of. Also in Kassos, Zografula Tira and Mrs. Bonaparte. Panos Manuelides and his mother, Vali. Nena Ismirnoglou for showing me how to make her greens pie. Argyrou Barbarigou; Mr. George, my driver in Rhodes; Mr. Kotsaris, who has the best bakery in Athens where he makes fabulous pittas and wholemeal bread; Albert Arouh; and Diana Farr Louis for letting me adapt recipes from her book, *Feasting and Fasting in Crete*.

In Morocco: Iman and Bbushra at Dar Liqama where I teach for showing me how to make r'ghayef and matlü'. My friend Mortada Chami, owner of the fabulous Stylia restaurant in Marrakesh, for being gracious and generous as ever and organizing a demonstration of how to make *warqa* by one of his cooks for me and my students. And finally Peter Dyer, his brother Lawrence, Aziz and his family, and Khadija and her sister, at Maison Mnabha.

In Turkey: My great friend and guru for all things Turkish, Nevin Halici, for letting me adapt recipes from her books. Engin Akin for organizing a börek day at her lovely home on the Bosphorus where her cooks, Gulnur and Nevin, showed me how to make all kinds of böreks and flatbreads. Engin also took me around to various börek makers. And Nadir Gulluoglu for showing me around his baklova factory.

In Lebanon: My mother, Laurice Helou, who for once didn't test recipes for me but was always ready to share her knowledge of Lebanese savory baking. Jamil, my driver, for taking me around to the most difficult places in his amazing 1968 Plymouth. My sister Marie Karam and her family. Reda, Reema, and Rawan Mamari. Also Jeanine, Tony, and Elias Mamari. Josette Calil, Kamal Mouzawak, and Rabih Kairouz. Rabih's family has one of the biggest bakeries in Lebanon and his sister took me around to these to show me how they bake their breads and ka'k. Chérine Yazbeck, who took me to one of the most magical bakeries up in the mountains east of Tripoli to watch tabüneh being made by Rafqa, the owner of the bakery, and her family. And last but not least, Nayla Audi, who introduced me to various breads from the south that I didn't know. Also Ali and Tlimo Haidar.

In Spain: Alicia Rios, food artist extraordinaire; Clara Maria G. De Amezúa, of Alambique in Madrid; and Maria Jose Sevilla.

As with every book, I am certain I have not mentioned all the friends who have helped me. Sadly, it's a terrible habit of mine to always forget something or someone and I would like to apologize to those I have omitted.

✤ Introduction ✤

There is a saying in Spain that goes *Sin pan, no se puede comer,* which means "Without bread, you cannot eat." The saying may belong to the Spaniards, but the sentiment is not theirs alone. All the peoples of the Mediterranean believe that no meal is complete without bread. This book is my exploration of the variety of savory breads and other baked goods one encounters at tables around the Mediterranean. It includes simple breads that serve as accompaniments to main courses and it includes more complex filled breads and pastries, such as pies and tarts, that serve as meals in themselves. In between there are lots of savory baked preparations to be eaten as meze, hors d'oeuvres, snacks, and other little bites, some traditionally made by home cooks and others by street vendors or small family-run bakeries.

The story of bread and baking began in the Fertile Crescent, which straddles the Syrian desert to the north, the Mediterranean Sea to the west, and the Tigris and Euphrates rivers to the east. It was in Mesopotamia, the eastern part of the crescent, that wheat was first domesticated. With agriculture came settlements—towns and cities—and thereby Mesopotamia became the cradle of civilization. Other outposts in the eastern Mediterranean were important in the early history

of bread. The Egyptians are said to have discovered leavening, setting in motion the evolution of bread as we know it today. Later, the Ancient Greeks elevated bread baking to an art: they developed the front-loaded bread oven and they invented sweet breads, which they often prepared in symbolic shapes to serve at ceremonies and other special occasions. Although all of the recipes in this book are thoroughly crafted for the modern kitchen, I try, in the text that introduces the recipes, to give a sense of the depth of tradition—in techniques, in ingredients, and in the origins of specific recipes—that underlies contemporary Mediterranean savory baking.

As it turns out, my own engagement with the foods in this book began at the edge of the Fertile Crescent. As a child I spent summer holidays in Syria, at my aunt's beautiful stone house, surrounded by fields where all our food was grown. The house was part of a village, Meshta el-Helou, which was owned by the family. The main part of the village was a large eighteenth-century square building, made up of a series of vaulted rooms built around a paved courtyard with a marble fountain in the middle. The complex was owned by my father, his siblings, and his extended, and often intermarried, family. It was in the Helou Mountains, above our village, that the advance of the Crusaders had been brought to a halt.

In those faraway days we had no electricity or running water, and there was no store in the village. One of my cousins kept, in one of the vaulted rooms, a few necessities that could not be grown or made at home, along with a huge pair of scales for weighing the grain and other produce of the estate. Some of that produce was sold, but most was for the use of the family.

My aunt made everything at home, including bread. She baked once a week, getting up earlier than usual to light the tannour, a kind of pit oven that is built on, not in, the ground and may be the oldest form of oven in history. Once the oven, which was situated in the field opposite the house, was lit, she returned to the house and made a large tub of dough. Sadly, I don't remember how she made her dough, nor what kind of leavening, if any, she used, nor how long she let it rise. But I still can picture how she and my mother divided the dough into pieces, rolled the pieces into balls, and flattened the balls into circles by passing them from one hand to another. My mother never performed the task of slapping the dough against the hot walls of the oven; she had the hands of a city dweller and they couldn't tolerate the heat. But my aunt's hands seemed to be made of asbestos. Repeatedly she leaned over the burning hot tannour, inserted her arm deep inside to slap a circle of dough against its walls, and, seconds later when the breads were done, reached in again to peel them off before they came loose and fell into the embers.

I watched every movement, curious about and fascinated by the whole spectacle. And I also wanted to eat the bread straight out of the oven, still crackling. This weekly ritual was one of the highlights of my year, together with the killing of chickens and the milking of cows. In Beirut, where we lived the rest of the year, my mother never baked bread at home. She made savory pastries, but she always got our bread from the baker.

In the years since, I have remained an enthusiastic student of Mediterranean baking. I've traveled throughout the region many times, always eager to learn, from commercial bakers and home cooks alike, how they go about their cooking. More recently, I spent some three years in my own kitchen translating what I encountered into recipes that will work for readers who, like me, have more modern equipment than my aunt had. I hope that in some measure I have held on to the sense of adventure I first felt during those summers in Syria, and that I have communicated that, along with a spirit of fun and confidence in the kitchen, to the readers of these pages.

"Bake your own bread, because it is the only serious way to understand and appreciate the most basic of all civilized foods," writes Raymond Sokolov in his book *The Cook's Canon*. I could not agree with him more. I hope that you will, too, and that the recipes I have included in this book will inspire you to bake. The selection I offer is by no means comprehensive; for that I would need one or more volumes for each country. Instead, I have chosen classics and personal favorites to give you a good overview of Mediterranean savory baking.

SOME HINTS FOR THE HOME BAKER

I have often heard people say that you are either a good baker or a good cook, but not both; something about cool hands was the explanation. I don't agree, but it is a fact that you need to be more precise when you are baking than when you are cooking. Ingredients have to be measured accurately, and temperatures, both ambient and those of ingredients, need to be taken into account. But this is not to say that a home baker need be as precise as a professional one. Consistency is the main reason why professional bakers insist on exact quantities and temperatures.

In fact, part of the fun of home baking is the somewhat unpredictable nature of it. One day, your bread will rise perfectly and the slashes will open up beautifully. Another day, the results will not be so perfect, though they will still be good. Many of the Mediterranean home bakers I spoke to and watched during the research for this book never measured anything. In Greece particularly, they followed their "eye" and went by feel. Admittedly, they have experience on their side and I do not suggest you go to the same extreme. Still, there is a happy medium where you can allow yourself some latitude and improvise successfully even if you do not always have exactly the right equipment or ingredients.

For instance, although I own several, I rarely bring my kitchen thermometers out of their drawer. I simply make sure that my kitchen and work surface are cool. I dip my finger in water to test it for heat; the rule is that the water should not be so hot that you cannot keep your finger in it. I use my guest bathroom to let my dough ferment and proof. It has no windows and the temperature in there is constantly warm without being too hot, which makes it the perfect environment for dough.

I never use a baking stone, either. When I was testing the recipes for this book, I assumed that many readers wouldn't have one and I wanted to make sure the breads baked well despite not being placed on a preheated surface. Of course, you get excellent results baking on a stone, but the recipes work very well baked on a nonstick baking sheet.

Sometimes, I tested at friends' houses where the conditions were not quite right. Once in Los Angeles, during an unseasonably cold spell, I stayed with a friend who never put on the heating. My breads were not rising properly, even though I allowed extra time. I hit on the idea of filling the bathtub with hot water to heat up and steam the room. It may have been a wasteful solution to create the right environment, but it worked.

If I need steam in my oven, I make my own by heating a metal baking dish on the bottom rack of the oven and throwing a tray of ice cubes into the dish just before I load the bread—a tip I learned in Jeffrey Hamelman's excellent book *Bread: A Baker's Book of Techniques and Recipes*.

Professional bakers are very good at explaining the technical aspects of baking but their recipes can be quite daunting. That said, there are many useful professional methods you can use at home. The autolytic method is one; it refers to the action of letting dough rest before kneading in the salt, yeast, and any other ingredients. Flour and water are mixed and kneaded into a rough dough. The dough is then left to sit for about 45 minutes, before the remaining ingredients are added and kneaded in. This allows the gluten to develop and, as a result, reduces the need for prolonged kneading. I have adapted the principle, although what I suggest is no longer the professional baker's notion of autolysis. Instead, I mix all the ingredients for the dough together and knead until the dough is no longer rough but not exactly smooth, either. Then I let the dough rest for 15 minutes before kneading it again. This fifteen-minute resting period does wonders for the dough. It allows the dough to become smooth and elastic without requiring you to knead until your arms fall off.

In contrast to bread doughs, short-crust pastries should be kneaded as little as possible, so as not to develop the gluten.

Knowing when and how to fold a dough is quite useful. Most people tell you to punch the dough to degas it. I did this for a long time, until Amy Scherber kindly allowed me to do a three-day apprenticeship at her bakery in New York, where I noticed her bakers folding but not punching their doughs. When I asked why, they told me that folding gives strength to the dough and evens out its temperature.

To fold dough, flour your work surface and hands well so that the dough does not stick. Then invert the bowl that contains your dough, holding one floured hand open underneath it so that the dough can drop onto it. Place the dough on the work surface and flatten the dough by hand into a circle, expelling some of the gasses. Fold one third of the circle over, flatten again, and brush off any excess flour. Then fold the opposite third over and flatten to make a rectangle. Brush off excess flour, then fold one third of the rectangle and fold the other third over.

Brush off flour and return seam side down to the bowl. Be sure to sprinkle your bowl with more flour before replacing the dough in it.

I always use unbleached all-purpose flour. It is easily available and if you use a good brand, such as King Arthur or Pillsbury, you will consistently achieve good results. Flours do differ from country to country (and even region to region) and from brand to brand. The protein content is not the same and, as a result, water absorption will differ. The higher the protein content, the more hydration you need. That is why the recipes in this book say that you should add water gradually to flour. In this way you can gauge how much hydration is needed.

When measuring flour, fluff it up first by stirring the flour, scooping it up, and letting it fall back into its bag or canister. Then use a scoop to transfer it to the measuring cup. Never shake the measuring cup or try to press the flour down. My cup of flour is 150g.

Always mix dry ingredients such as salt, sugar, or spices with the flour so as to distribute them evenly before you add any liquid or fat. Use a dough cutter to divide the dough—a plastic cutter if you are cutting on a nonstick surface and metal otherwise. Tearing the dough by hand damages it.

Remember that home ovens can be inaccurate. Their temperature is generally less than that shown by the gauge. An oven thermometer will help you make sure you are baking at the right temperature. Bake your breads and savory pastries on the second rack from the bottom, about one-third of the way up.

Once baked, breads need to cool on a wire rack with good air flow. Both flavor and texture continue to develop as the bread cools; it is usually better to reheat bread than to serve it still warm from the oven. The exceptions to the rule are flatbreads, which are best served immediately. Note that bread in the refrigerator will dry up; if you want to keep it longer than a day or two, freeze it.

❖ Shaping Breads ❖

Shaping is probably the most difficult part of baking. Much of your success will depend on how well—evenly, tightly, and so on—you shape your bread. Before the final shaping you also need to preshape the dough, which usually involves shaping the dough into somewhat tight balls and letting them rest before you give them the final shaping.

Once you have shaped your bread, you need to let it proof. During proofing, the dough should be covered with a wet but not dripping kitchen towel to keep it moist and to prevent it from forming a skin.

Here are some more detailed tips for preshaping and rolling out and for making some of the most commonly used shapes in Mediterranean baking.

PRESHAPING

Depending on the size of the piece of dough, you will need either both hands or only one. If the piece of dough is small, cup your hand over it, keeping your thumb and pinky in contact with your work surface, and roll the dough, pressing lightly on it, in a clockwise motion until it turns into an even, smooth ball. It is important that your hand remain dry so that the dough doesn't stick and tear. However, you want the opposite for the work surface: it should be slightly tacky. If it is floured, the dough will slide and not rotate and you won't be able to form the ball. If you are working with a large piece of dough, cup both hands around it, keeping your pinkies and the sides of your palms in contact with the work surface. Rotate the dough clockwise until you have an even ball.

ROLLING OUT

When you are rolling out dough to form a circle, it's easier to make an even circle if you rotate the circle a quarter turn after each rolling out. For some breads an even circle is especially important. Pita, for example, puffs up and separates properly only with a neat circle.

If you are baking a lot, consider acquiring a couche, also called a baker's linen. When a dough doesn't stretch easily and keeps springing back, you cover it with a floured couche (which can be made of linen or canvas) and let it rest awhile before continuing with the rolling out.

It is important to keep the dough lightly floured on both sides as you are rolling it out so that it does not stick to the rolling pin or the work surface. Always start rolling from the middle of the piece of dough. Roll out the top side away from you and then roll out the bottom side toward you. This will ensure even thickness.

BÂTARD

Flatten the ball of dough into an oval, gently pressing out the gases. Then fold one third of the top end of the oval toward the center, and press gently to flatten. Bring in the two square ends that were created by the first fold to form a round pointed end. Rotate the dough 180 degrees and do the same at the other end, again flattening the dough well and gently pressing the gases out. Now position the dough so that the pointed ends are on your left and right. Fold the top third of the dough over, pressing on the edge with the heel of your hand to seal. Then fold over the bottom third, aligning the edges. Press on the edge with the heel of your hand as you go along to seal the seam and form a fat roll. Turn the roll of dough seam side down. Place your palms in the middle of the log of dough and roll back and forth, fanning your hands out and pressing on the ends of the log to taper them, until the bread is the desired length and is fat in the middle with tapered ends. It is important at this stage to have an even thickness. If one side is thicker than the other, roll it back and forth until it evens out.

BAGUETTE

Flatten the ball of dough into an oval, gently pressing out the gases. Then fold over one long third of the oval, pressing gently to flatten. Rotate the dough 180 degrees and fold over the opposite third, to form a long rectangle. Gently press on the dough to flatten it and expel more gases. Fold one long third over again, pressing on the seam with the heel of your hand as you go along to seal the joint. Fold over the bottom third, so that the edges align, and press again with the heel of your hand to seal. Turn the roll of dough seam side down. Place the palm of your hand on the middle of the loaf and press, rolling back and forth, to create a dip in the center. Then place your hands palm side down in the middle of the loaf and roll back and forth, fanning out your hands, until the loaf is the desired length and has evenly tapered ends. If one side is thicker than the other, roll it back and forth until it evens out.

BOULE

Lift up the preshaped ball of dough and stand it on its side with the seam facing away from you. Start tucking in the sides toward the seam, turning the dough as you tuck, until you have shaped a smooth ball. Place the dough seam side down, cup your hands around the ball of dough, and rotate it clockwise until you have a smooth, even ball of dough. Be gentle and don't work the dough too hard or you will tear it.

STRANDS

Preshape the dough into a ball or an oval (or multiple balls and ovals, for braided breads and other recipes that call for multiple strands). With the palm of your hand, press on the middle of the ball or oval and roll back and forth until you make a noticeable dip in the top of the piece of dough. Then place your hands palm side down in the middle of the dip and roll back and forth, fanning out your hands, until the dough is the desired length and diameter and has evenly tapered ends. If the dough is not elastic enough, let the strands rest, covered with plastic wrap, for a while, then roll them back and forth.

✤ Scoring Dough ✤

Scoring dough is done to create a weak section on the surface of the dough to allow for a controlled expansion during baking. Not many Mediterranean breads are scored, but for the few that are, here is how to best do the scoring. If you don't have a baker's lame (razor), use a regular razor blade and thread it through an ice-cream stick to bend it a little. One of the bakers at Amy's Bread in New York had improvised her lame this way, and it was very effective, similar to a professional lame. Hold the razor at a 30-degree angle and cut into the dough to less than ½ inch. Do this lightly, as you don't want to compromise the risen dough and cause it to deflate. If the dough is properly risen, the cut section will open nicely to show a fermented section of the dough, and of course the cut will expand farther in the oven to make crunchy edges and a golden crinkly crust in between.

There are two basic types of breads: flat and raised. Flatbreads are found in different shapes and forms throughout the Mediterranean, whereas raised breads are mainly, though not wholly, confined to the western part. In a way, the classification "raised breads" is a misnomer, as many flatbreads are leavened as well. However, they are shaped flat and remain so after baking, whereas raised breads are shaped high and rise even higher when they bake, hence the classification.

The variety of flatbreads is astonishing, but the types remain limited to only two: breads that are one layer and those that are two layers or more. Again, there is a regional divide. Most of the one-layered flatbreads are found in the western Mediterranean, whereas the two- or multilayered ones are found in the eastern part.

Some flatbreads don't look "flat," such as ciabatta, the ubiquitous Italian sandwich bread, while others are paper-thin. The dough for some of the latter, like that for marqūq, or handkerchief bread as I call it, is flattened by slapping a disk of dough from one hand to the other. With each movement, the disk stretches thinner and thinner until its diameter is the length of the baker's arm, a feat once performed by all mountain village girls because it was an essential skill to have if they wanted to find a good husband. And for other breads, such as yufka, gözleme, and lavash that are equally large and thin, the dough is rolled out with a long, very thin rolling pin known as *oklava* in Turkish. These breads are cooked over a flat or concave saj, while the Syrian khobz tannour, a smaller and slightly thicker bread, is cooked against the walls of a tannour.

Some thin breads are baked until they become completely crisp, such as the Sardinian Pane Carasau, while the Jewish matzoh, another cracker, needs to be made by a chain of people in eighteen minutes flat so that it doesn't leaven.

Flatbreads can also be sweet. They are usually baked for religious occasions or celebrations. Only the Spanish Torta de Aceites is not associated with a feast.

Mediterranean raised breads are not easily categorized. Some have a hard crunchy crust, others a thin smooth one. Some have a dense crumb, others a fluffy one. Some are more like cake than bread, while others are like brioche. Many include herbs, olives, vegetables, or meat, while a few are baked plain. Some are sweet or spicy, and others so plain as to not even have added salt. Some are enriched with fats, milk, or egg, and others are made with just flour, water, and yeast.

They come in all kinds of shapes and forms: long loaves, round ones, individual buns or rolls, rings or crescents. Some have sexual shapes—long and phallic to make the bread masculine; slit in the middle to make it feminine—and others take the shape of human parts, such as the famous crusty white Italian bread seen in the photograph of "Picasso's hands." Some breads are white, made with white flour; others brown, made with rye, wholewheat, or barley flour; and others yellow, made with semolina flour. Some are baked hard as biscuits, while others are baked purely for decoration, made in incredibly elaborate shapes like the Cretan wedding crown, which is sculpted with birds, flowers, and jewelry. These decorative breads seem to be island specialties. The Sicilians also make them for the Day of the Dead on November 1.

Perhaps the easiest way to categorize raised breads is by their leavenings. They can be divided in two main categories: those that are leavened naturally, using sourdough, and those that are leavened artificially, using commercial yeast, fresh or dry. Often commercial yeast is combined with a portion of the bread ingredients to make pre-ferments, liquid or stiff mixtures left to ferment from 30 minutes up to 18 hours before being mixed with the bread dough. The first factory producing commercial yeast was not set up until the late nineteenth century, but sourdough has been in use for eons.

Sourdough is a culture started by letting a yeast-free dough ferment long enough for it to leaven naturally and, as a result, to act as leavening itself. The culture can be kept forever, provided it is stored in the right conditions and refreshed at proper intervals; by "refreshed" I mean fed with added water and flour to stimulate the fermentation process. In some places, as in the south of France, the fermentation process is begun by soaking fruit, usually raisins and cubed apples, in water and letting these ferment for a few days until bubbles appear on the surface. The water is then drained and mixed with flour to start the sourdough. In Greece, Turkey, Syria, and Lebanon, crushed chickpeas are used, soaked in hot water and allowed to ferment until foam appears on the surface. The latter process is far more complex and more prone to failure. The temperature at which the mixture is kept is critical, as is the timing of the different stages of feeding the culture.

This method is used by the Greeks to leaven a celebration bread called eftazymo. *Efta* means "seven," and some people say that the name of the bread means "kneaded seven times," while others say it means "fermented seven times." However, Aglaia Kremezi, author of *The Foods of the Greek Islands,* says that both theories are wrong. She explains in her book that *efta* is a "phonetic variation of the prefix auto, referring to bread that rises itself." This seems more plausible, since there is no benefit to kneading a bread or letting it ferment seven times. In Lebanon, Syria, and Turkey the culture is made slightly differently and is used to leaven hard breads called ka'k.

The use of sourdough is not so prevalent in the Mediterranean today. Instead bakers rely on yeasted pre-ferments to improve the taste of their bread and its keeping qualities. There are three main types of pre-ferments: pâte fermentée, poolish, and biga. Pâte fermentée is simply old dough, poolish a liquid mixture of equal amounts water and flour, and biga the Italian name for a yeasted starter dough that can be stiff or soft. In Lebanon, there is a tradition of starting a pâte fermentée every year on the day of Epiphany, January 6. The baker hangs a piece of dough on a tree for Christ to pass over and bless. This initial pâte fermentée is called *khamiret al-Massih* ("leavening of Christ").

Many bread doughs are also used to make savory pastries: pies, tarts, dainty (and not so dainty) parcels, salty nibbles, and so on. The variety is truly astonishing. The east-west divide here is mostly in the kinds of dough and pastry used. In the western Mediterranean, the dough or pastry casing can be thick or thin, made in one or several layers, whereas in the eastern and southern parts, the casing is almost always thin, and often made in several layers.

However, two approaches unite the region as far as savory pastries are concerned. One is the culture of not wasting food. Leftovers are always recycled, often to make savory pies or pastries. And the other is the need for portable foods, food that people can carry with them to the fields, to market, or when they are traveling from one town to the other. And what better way to make food portable than by wrapping meat, fish, vegetables, or cheese in dough or pastry and baking it all-in-one. Pies were apparently a staple of Roman centurions; theirs consisted of meat wrapped in a primitive kind of pastry, which kept the contents warm on long marches.

Greece is the bridge between east and west in the Mediterranean, certainly as far as savory pastries are concerned. Some are similar to those found in the western part, while others are much closer to those found on the eastern side. I am not a great fan of Greek cooking, but I love the Greeks' savory baking. It is varied, sophisticated, and always scrumptious, which cannot be said of many of their cooked dishes. Perhaps Nicholas Tselementes, the early-twentieth-century equivalent of Martha Stewart who introduced béchamel sauce to Greek cooking, was not interested in baking and, as a result, he was not able to spoil their breads and pies.

Focaccias and Pizzas

Cheese Focaccia

Focaccia al Formaggio

This focaccia from Naples is made in thin layers, not unlike a puff pastry. Cheese and butter are spread over successive layers of dough, which then are folded over and rolled out again. The result is a flakier, less dense focaccia.

SERVES 4 TO 6

4½ teaspoons (2 packages) active dry yeast
3 cups plus 1 tablespoon unbleached all-purpose flour, plus extra for
    kneading and shaping
7 tablespoons butter, melted
1 teaspoon fine kosher salt or sea salt
6 tablespoons finely grated Parmigiano-Reggiano
Unsalted butter, softened, for greasing the baking sheet
1½ tablespoons extra-virgin olive oil, plus extra for drizzling over the
    focaccia
Coarse sea salt

1. Dissolve the yeast in ⅔ cup warm water in a medium bowl. Stir until creamy. Add 1 cup of the flour, 1 tablespoon of the butter, and ¼ teaspoon of the fine salt. Mix until you have a rough batter. Sprinkle 1 tablespoon of the flour over the top, cover with plastic wrap, and let ferment in a warm, draft-free place for 1 hour. This will be the sponge, or biga.

2. Combine the remaining 2 cups flour and ¾ teaspoon fine salt in a large bowl. Make a well in the center and place the sponge in the well. Add ⅓ cup plus

2 tablespoons warm water. Mix the water by hand with the sponge, and then gradually work in the flour. Knead briefly to make a rough ball of dough.

3. Dust a work surface with flour and knead the dough for 2 to 3 minutes. Invert the bowl over the dough and let rest for 15 minutes. Knead for 2 to 3 minutes more, until the dough is smooth and elastic. Shape the dough into a ball, cover with a damp kitchen towel, and let rest for 20 minutes.

4. Roll out the dough to a rectangle 15 inches by 10 inches. Brush with about one-third of the remaining melted butter. Sprinkle one-third of the Parmesan over one short half of the dough. Fold the plain half over the cheese-covered half, rotate the dough 90 degrees, and roll out the dough to a rectangle the same size as the original one. Brush the dough with one-third of the butter and sprinkle a short half with one-third of the Parmesan. Fold, rotate, and roll out the dough again. Brush with the remaining butter and sprinkle with the remaining Parmesan, then fold, rotate, and roll out to a rectangle one last time.

5. Generously grease a large baking sheet with the butter. Transfer the focaccia onto it. Cover the focaccia with a wet but not dripping kitchen towel and let it rise in a warm, draft-free place for 1½ to 2 hours, until doubled in volume. Preheat the oven to 400°F.

6. Uncover the focaccia for 5 minutes to let the surface dry. Brush with the 1½ tablespoons olive oil. Bake for 25 to 30 minutes, until the focaccia is well puffed up, golden-brown all over, and rather crisp. Remove from the oven, drizzle with more olive oil, and sprinkle with a little coarse salt. Serve warm, at room temperature, or reheated.

Cheese Focaccia from Recco

Focaccia di Formaggio di Recco

In Recco, a small city on the Ligurian coast in Northern Italy, this focaccia is made with a local cheese called *formagetta* or *formaggio ligure*. But a soft cow's-milk cheese such as taleggio will work very well. Although this is an unleavened focaccia, it bubbles up beautifully when it bakes and has a light, flaky texture.

SERVES 4

1⅓ cups unbleached all-purpose flour, plus extra for kneading and shaping
¾ teaspoon fine kosher salt or sea salt
3 tablespoons extra-virgin olive oil, plus extra for brushing the pan
    and the focaccia
9 ounces taleggio, trimmed of skin, thinly sliced
Coarse sea salt

1. Combine the 1⅓ cups flour and the fine salt in a large bowl and make a well in the center. Add the 3 tablespoons oil to the well and, with fingertips, incorporate the oil into the flour completely. Gradually add ⅓ cup plus ½ tablespoon warm water. Knead briefly to make a rough ball of dough.

2. Dust the work surface with flour and knead the dough for 2 to 3 minutes. Invert the bowl over the dough and let rest for 15 minutes. Knead for 2 to 3 minutes more, until the dough is smooth and elastic. Shape the dough into a ball and place it in a lightly floured clean bowl. Cover with plastic wrap and let ferment in a warm, draft-free place for 1 hour. Fold the dough (see pages 6–7), cover again, and let ferment for 1 hour more. The dough should have doubled in volume.

3. Return the dough to the work surface, divide it in half equally, and shape each half into a ball. Cover both balls with a damp kitchen towel and let rest for 15 minutes.

4. Dust the work surface with flour. Roll out one piece of dough very thin to a diameter of at least 12 inches, sprinkling with flour every now and then so that it does not stick. Generously brush with olive oil a large nonstick baking sheet, or a baking sheet lined with parchment paper or a silicone pastry mat, and transfer the rolled-out dough to the sheet. Preheat the oven to 500°F.

5. Place the cheese slices evenly over the dough, leaving ½ inch free at the edges. Roll out the other piece of dough to the same diameter as the first and place this layer over the cheese. Press on the edges to seal. Brush liberally with olive oil and let rest while the oven is preheating.

6. Press with fingertips on the focaccia to make dimples all over. Sprinkle with coarse salt. Bake for 8 to 10 minutes, or until golden brown all over. Serve hot, while the cheese is still melted.

Potato Focaccia

Focaccia di Patate

This focaccia is a specialty of Puglia, the "heel" of Italy. The mashed potato makes for a rather moist bread, which I use to make sandwiches filled with mortadella or with pecorino cheese.

SERVES 6 TO 8

2¼ teaspoons (1 package) active dry yeast
3 cups unbleached all-purpose flour, plus extra for kneading and
    shaping
1½ teaspoons fine kosher salt or sea salt
5 ounces all-purpose potatoes, cooked and mashed
Extra-virgin olive oil

1. Dissolve the yeast in ½ cup warm water and stir until creamy.

2. Combine the flour and salt in a large bowl and make a well in the center. Add the mashed potatoes and the yeast, and, using fingertips, bring in a little of the flour. Gradually add ⅔ cup warm water and bring in the remaining flour as you go along. Knead briefly to make a rough ball of dough.

3. Dust a work surface with flour. Sprinkle the ball of dough with a little extra flour and knead for 2 to 3 minutes. Invert the bowl over the dough and let rest for 15 minutes. Knead for 2 to 3 minutes more, sprinkling with extra flour if the dough is sticky, until the dough is smooth and somewhat soft.

4. Grease a 12-inch round pie plate with olive oil. Transfer the dough to the pie plate and flatten and stretch the dough by hand to cover the bottom of the plate; the dough should be about ½ inch thick. Cover with a wet but not dripping kitchen towel and let rise in a warm, draft-free place for 1½ hours. The dough should have doubled in volume.

5. Preheat the oven to 350°F. Press with fingertips on the focaccia to make dimples all over. Brush generously with olive oil. Bake for 35 to 45 minutes, until the focaccia is well risen and golden brown all over. Serve warm, or transfer to a wire rack to let cool and serve at room temperature.

✣ Focaccia from Puglia

Puddica (*or* Puddiche)

Puglia, the "heel" of Italy, has an amazing variety of breads. Luigi Sada, author of *La Cucina Pugliese,* devotes an entire five pages just to listing all the Pugliese breads. This is a simply flavored focaccia that goes with just about anything at mealtime, and it's also delicious on its own as a snack.

SERVES 4 TO 6

2¼ teaspoons (1 package) active dry yeast
2 cups unbleached all-purpose flour, plus extra if needed
1 teaspoon fine kosher salt or sea salt
Extra-virgin olive oil
6 cherry tomatoes, quartered and seeded
3 garlic cloves, thinly sliced
1 teaspoon dried oregano
Coarse sea salt

1. Dissolve the yeast in ¼ cup warm water and stir until creamy.

2. Combine the flour and the fine salt in a large bowl and make a well in the center. Add the yeast and gradually add another ½ cup warm water, bringing in the flour as you go along. Knead briefly to make a rough dough.

3. Remove the dough to a lightly floured work surface. Knead for 2 to 3 minutes. Invert the bowl over the dough and let rest for 15 minutes. Knead for 2 to 3 minutes more, until the dough is smooth and elastic. Shape into a ball. Grease

a bowl with a little olive oil, place the dough in it, and turn the dough to coat all over with oil. Cover with plastic wrap and let rise in a warm, draft-free place for 1 hour. Fold the dough (see pages 6–7), cover again, and let rise for 1 hour more. The dough should have doubled in volume.

4. Brush a 12 by 14-inch baking sheet with olive oil. Remove the dough to the baking sheet and flatten and stretch the dough by hand to cover the sheet. Cover with a wet but not dripping kitchen towel and let rise for 45 minutes to 1 hour. Meanwhile, preheat the oven to 450°F.

5. Dip fingertips in olive oil and make dimples all over the dough, dipping for more oil every now and then. Place the pieces of tomato and garlic in the dimples. Sprinkle with the oregano and coarse salt to taste. Drizzle with more oil all over. Bake for 10 to 15 minutes, until golden all over. Slide onto a wire rack to cool slightly. Serve warm or at room temperature.

✥ Walnut Focaccia

Schiacciata con le Noci

Schiacciata, meaning "squashed flat," is the name Tuscans give to their focaccia. Here the dough is rather unusual in that it is made with a mixture of all-purpose flour and cornmeal, with walnuts folded into it for extra texture and flavor.

SERVES 4

1 heaping teaspoon (½ package) active dry yeast

1 cup unbleached all-purpose flour, plus extra for kneading and shaping

⅓ cup plus 1 tablespoon coarse cornmeal

1 teaspoon fine kosher salt or sea salt

2 tablespoons extra-virgin olive oil, plus extra for greasing the bowl and baking sheet and brushing the focaccia

⅓ cup coarsely chopped walnuts (about 1½ ounces)

½ tablespoon chopped fresh rosemary

Coarse sea salt

1. Dissolve the yeast in ¼ cup warm water and stir until creamy.

2. Combine the flour, cornmeal, and salt in a large bowl and make a well in the center. Add the olive oil to the well and, with fingertips, rub it into the flour mixture. Add the yeast and 3 to 4 tablespoons warm water, bringing in the flour as you go along. Knead briefly to make a rough dough.

3. Remove the dough to a lightly floured work surface. Knead for 2 to 3 minutes. Invert the bowl over the dough and let rest for 15 minutes. Knead for 2 to 3 minutes more, until the dough is smooth and elastic. Flatten the dough into a large rectangle and spread the walnuts over the dough. Fold a long third of the dough over the walnuts, and then fold the opposite third to form a long envelope. Fold the short ends into thirds and gently shape into a ball.

4. Grease a bowl with a little olive oil, put the dough in the bowl, and turn it to coat all over with oil. Cover with plastic wrap and let rise in a warm, draft-free place for 1 hour. Fold the dough (see pages 6–7), cover again, and let rise for 1 hour more. The dough should have doubled in volume.

5. Return the dough to the work surface. Shape the dough into a ball again, cover with plastic wrap, and let rest for 15 minutes. Grease a 12 by 10-inch baking sheet with a little olive oil.

6. Transfer the dough to the baking sheet and, pressing down with hands, flatten and stretch it until it covers the sheet evenly. Cover with a wet but not dripping kitchen towel and let rise for 45 minutes to 1 hour. Preheat the oven to 450°F.

7. Dip fingertips in olive oil and make dimples all over the dough, dipping for more oil every now and then. Sprinkle the rosemary and coarse salt into the dimples. Bake for 15 to 20 minutes, until golden brown all over. Slide onto a wire rack to cool slightly. Serve warm or at room temperature.

Sicilian Focaccia

Sfincione

The thick and spongy focaccias that most American bakeries turn out are rather more in the Sicilian style than in the style favored on Italy's mainland. And sfincione, Sicilian focaccia, is rather more like a pizza: the dough is spread with tomato sauce and a little cheese, and because Sicilians use breadcrumbs on everything, it is also sprinkled with breadcrumbs before baking. I learned how to make sfincione from the food writer Anna Tasca Lanza. Her sfincione is superior by far to most of the versions you find in Sicily, whether from street vendors or from restaurants.

SERVES 4

For the dough

2¼ teaspoons (1 package) active dry yeast

3⅓ cups unbleached all-purpose flour, plus extra if needed

Juice of 2 lemons (about 7 tablespoons)

2 tablespoons extra-virgin olive oil, plus extra for greasing the baking dish

1 cup grated Parmigiano-Reggiano (about 2 ounces)

½ teaspoon fine kosher salt or sea salt

½ teaspoon freshly ground black pepper

For the topping

3 tablespoons extra-virgin olive oil

1 small onion, finely chopped (about ⅓ cup)

1 14½-ounce can diced tomatoes

2 tablespoons finely chopped flat-leaf parsley

Fine kosher salt or sea salt

Freshly ground black pepper

8 salted anchovies, rinsed and filleted

5 ounces caciocavallo or pecorino romano cheese, thinly sliced

2 tablespoons fine breadcrumbs

1. Make the dough: Dissolve the yeast in ½ cup warm water and stir until creamy. Put the flour in a large bowl and make a well in the center. Mix the lemon juice, olive oil, Parmesan, salt, and pepper in a small bowl, add the mixture to the well, and, using fingertips, work the mixture into the flour. Add the yeast and ¼ cup warm water. Knead briefly to make a sticky, rough ball of dough.

2. Liberally sprinkle a work surface with flour. Remove the dough to it and sprinkle with more flour. Knead for 3 minutes. Invert the bowl over the dough and let rest for 15 minutes. Knead for 2 to 3 minutes more, until the dough is smooth and elastic. Transfer to a lightly floured clean bowl, cover with plastic wrap, and let rise in a warm, draft-free place for 45 minutes. Fold the dough (see pages 6–7), cover again, and let rise for 45 minutes more. The dough should have doubled in volume.

3. Meanwhile, make the topping: Put the olive oil and onion in a sauté pan over medium-high heat. Cook, stirring occasionally, until the onions are golden. Add the tomatoes and parsley and bring to a boil. Cook for about 20 minutes, or until very thick. Season with salt and pepper to taste, and set aside.

4. Preheat the oven to 400°F. Grease a deep-sided 10-inch round baking dish with a little olive oil. Return the dough to the work surface. Shape the dough into a ball, cover with a damp kitchen towel, and let rest for 15 minutes. Place the dough in the baking dish. Flatten and stretch the dough by hand until it covers

the bottom of the dish. Press the anchovy fillets into the dough at regular intervals. Scatter the caciocavallo or pecorino over the dough, and spread the tomato sauce all over. Sprinkle with the breadcrumbs.

5. Bake for 45 to 50 minutes, until well risen and golden brown all over. Let rest for 10 to 15 minutes. Serve warm or at room temperature.

Anchovy and Olive Fougasse

Fougasse aux Anchois et Olives

Known as fougasse in the south of France and fouace in the north, and as focaccia in Italy, the term comes from the ancient Roman expression *panis focacius*, which described a flatbread cooked in ashes (*focus* means hearth in Latin). Fougasses differ from region to region and baker to baker. Some are made with *pâte feuilletée* (puff pastry), and others with regular bread dough. Sometimes the baker rolls out the bread dough in layers, brushing it with lard for a flaky texture. Others, like Basile Kamir at the Moulin de la Vièrge in Paris, whose recipe I have adapted here, make fougasse using a light, fluffy dough that is closer to an Italian focaccia dough. The garnishes also vary. You can use olives or anchovies together, as here, or separately; or use sautéed lardons (cubed bacon). For a sweet version, see Fouace Aveyronnaise, page 100.

MAKES 2 MEDIUM FOUGASSES

Heaping ½ teaspoon (¼ package) active dry yeast

2⅓ cups unbleached all-purpose flour, plus extra for kneading and
    shaping

1 teaspoon fine kosher salt or sea salt

⅓ cup pitted black olives, coarsely chopped (about 1½ ounces)

6 anchovy fillets in oil, coarsely chopped

Extra-virgin olive oil

1 egg, beaten

10 to 15 ice cubes

1. Dissolve the yeast in 2 tablespoons warm water and stir until creamy.

2. Combine the flour and salt in a large bowl and make a well in the center. Add the yeast to the well and gradually add another ¾ cup warm water, bringing in the flour as you go along. Knead until you have a rough dough.

3. Remove the dough to a lightly floured work surface. Knead for 3 minutes, and shape the dough into a ball. Invert the bowl over the dough and let rest for 15 minutes. Knead for 2 to 3 minutes more, until the dough is smooth and elastic. Flatten the dough by hand to form a large rectangle. Spread the olives and anchovies all over and press them into the dough. Fold a long third of the dough over the center, then fold the opposite third to form a long envelope. Fold the short ends in thirds and gently shape the dough into a ball.

4. Grease a large bowl with a little olive oil. Place the ball of dough in the bowl seam side down, turning it to coat all over with oil. Cover with plastic wrap and let rise in a warm, draft-free place for 1 hour. Fold the dough (see pages 6–7), cover again, and let rise for 1 hour more. The dough should have doubled in volume.

5. Return the dough to the work surface. Using a dough cutter, divide the dough in half and shape each half into a ball. Cover with a damp kitchen towel and let rest for 15 minutes. Roll out each piece of dough into an oval about ¾ inch thick. Transfer to a nonstick baking sheet, or to a baking sheet lined with parchment paper or a silicone pastry mat. Using a plastic dough cutter, make 3 or 4 slits all the way through the dough, at regular intervals. Gently pull the cuts apart to make an opening. Cover with a wet but not dripping kitchen towel and let rise for 1 hour. Meanwhile, preheat the oven to 475°F and place a baking dish on the bottom rack of the oven.

6. Uncover the fougasses for about 5 minutes to let the surface dry. Brush the breads with the egg. Immediately before baking, toss the ice cubes into the baking dish on the oven bottom to create steam. Bake the breads for 20 to 25 minutes, until golden brown all over; check after 15 minutes, and if the breads are coloring too quickly, reduce the heat to 350°F. Transfer to a wire rack to cool. Serve warm or at room temperature.

Il Forno's White Pizza

Pizza Bianca dal Forno di Campo dei Fiori

This is my homemade adaptation of a recipe that was given to me by Fabrizio Roscioli, who owns the bakery Il Forno, on the old market square Campo dei Fiori in Rome. Mine turned out fine, but it was rather spongy, and it was less crisp and had fewer holes than theirs. There are several likely reasons for this. First, American all-purpose flour is different from Italian flour. Also, however good a domestic oven is, it cannot compare with Il Forno's industrial brick oven. And, finally, professional bakers seem to have a knack for working with a much wetter dough, which makes for a lighter bread. Still, it's an excellent and simple recipe that's definitely worth trying. The only drawback is that you have to wait a long time for the dough to rise. I first tested it with a 4½-hour rise, but on a subsequent visit to Il Forno, the baker told me that they let the dough rise for longer. Given the small amount of yeast, I guess it cannot do the dough any harm to let it rise longer than indicated here, perhaps even overnight to shape and bake in the morning. This pizza is eaten as a snack and it is also served, like a bread, with meals.

SERVES 6 TO 8

¼ teaspoon active dry yeast
3⅓ cups unbleached all-purpose flour, plus extra for kneading and
    shaping
1½ teaspoons fine kosher salt or sea salt
1 teaspoon sugar
Extra-virgin olive oil
Coarse sea salt

1. Dissolve the yeast in ¼ cup warm water and stir until creamy.

2. Combine the flour, salt, and sugar in a large bowl and make a well in the center. Add the yeast to the well and gradually add another 1 cup warm water, bringing in the flour as you go along. Knead briefly to make a rough ball of dough.

3. Remove the dough to a lightly floured work surface. Sprinkle with a little flour and knead for 3 minutes. Invert the bowl over it and let rest for 15 minutes. Knead for 2 to 3 minutes more, until the dough is smooth and elastic. Shape the dough into a ball and transfer it to a clean bowl brushed with a little olive oil. Turn the ball to coat all over with oil. Cover with plastic wrap and let rise in a warm, draft-free place for at least 4½ hours, folding the dough (see pages 6–7) at 1-hour intervals. The dough should have doubled in volume.

4. Preheat the oven to 500°F. Brush a 16 by 12-inch, or a little larger, baking sheet with olive oil. Place the dough in the center, and flatten and stretch it by hand

to cover the sheet; press lightly and quickly on the dough, so that the air is not pressed out. Brush the top generously with olive oil. Loosely cover with plastic wrap and let rest for about 30 minutes.

5. Lightly sprinkle the pizza with coarse salt. Bake for 10 to 12 minutes, until golden brown all over. If the dough has risen properly, it will develop a gorgeous golden crust; if not, it will remain pale or streaky. Transfer to a wire rack to cool slightly, or let cool in the pan. Serve warm.

Thyme "Pizza"

Manaqish bil-Za'tar

These pizza-like breads are a typical Lebanese breakfast, served plain or with strained yogurt—known as labneh (see page 296)—and olives, and they are a favorite of mine. Za'tar is the Arabic word for "thyme," but it also describes a mixture made with dried wild thyme, sumac, and sesame seeds, which is salted and sautéed in a dry pan to bring out the aroma of the herb and seeds and to make the mixture last longer. The mixture is available in Middle Eastern markets and from online merchants. You cannot cultivate the type of thyme needed to make za'tar. The herb grows wild in the Lebanese mountains and is picked in full bloom, dried, and then rubbed and sieved to produce the base for the za'tar mixture. The best-quality za'tar contains a lot of the thyme flower, while lesser versions will have more leaves, even stalks, and be greener. The topping here may also be served as a dip with pita bread, or you can spread it on small squares of toast and grill these for a minute or two to serve as canapés, garnished with tiny cubes of cucumber.

SERVES 8

1 recipe dough for Pita Bread (page 71) through step 3
6 tablespoons za'tar mixture
½ cup extra-virgin olive oil, plus extra for brushing the dough

1. Divide the dough into 8 pieces.

2. Combine the za'tar and olive oil in a bowl. Raise the edges of the circles of dough by pinching them, and make dimples all over the dough inside the raised edges. Spread one-eighth of the mixture over each circle of dough. Brush the

edges with oil and let rest for 15 to 20 minutes. Meanwhile, preheat the oven to 500°F.

3. Bake for 7 to 10 minutes, until golden. Serve immediately, or while still warm.

✣ Kishk "Pizza"

Manaqish bil-Kishk

Kishk is a floury mixture made by mixing bulgur wheat with yogurt and strained yogurt, letting it ferment for several days, drying it in the sun, and then rubbing it and passing it through a sieve to produce a fine powder. Kishk is used with garlic and *qawarma,* preserved lamb, to make a winter soup, or it is mixed with olive oil, onions, and tomatoes to make the topping for this pizza-like bread. Kishk is an important part of Lebanese mountain people's foodstuffs, and is prepared in the fall to use throughout the winter months. It is available at Middle Eastern markets and from online merchants.

SERVES 6

1 recipe dough for Pita Bread (page 71) through step 3

For the topping
1 cup kishk
4 tablespoons toasted white sesame seeds
⅓ cup very finely chopped onion
¾ to 1 cup extra-virgin olive oil, plus extra for brushing the dough
1 ripe medium tomato, seeded and diced (about ½ cup)
Fine kosher salt or sea salt to taste
Pinch of cayenne pepper

1. Divide the dough into 6 equal pieces. Shape each into a ball, cover with a wet but not dripping kitchen towel, and let rise for 30 to 45 minutes.

2. Mix the topping ingredients well in a bowl. Set aside.

3. Remove the dough to a lightly floured work surface. Flatten one ball of dough by hand into a circle 7 to 8 inches in diameter and transfer to a large nonstick baking sheet, or to a baking sheet lined with parchment paper or a silicone pastry mat. Raise the edges of the circle by pressing on the dough with fingertips about ½ inch inside the edge. Then, make dimples all over the inside of the raised edges. Spread one-sixth of the topping all over the dough. Brush the edges with a little olive oil. Make the remaining breads in the same way. Let rest for 15 to 20 minutes. Meanwhile, preheat the oven to 450°F.

4. Bake the breads for 12 to 14 minutes, until the topping is slightly crisp and the edges are golden brown. Serve immediately, or transfer to a wire rack to cool, and serve warm. The breads freeze well; to reheat, simply put them frozen in the oven, turn on the heat to 350°F, and heat for 10 to 15 minutes, until completely thawed and hot.

❖ Eggplant "Pizza"

Patlicanli Pide

Turkish cooks use a variety of toppings for their version of pizza, including greens, eggs, cheese, spicy sausage, and meats. I have adapted this recipe from one in Ayla Algar's *Classic Turkish Cookery*. I first made it for my friend Jeremy Lee, the wonderful chef at the Blueprint Café in London, who liked the breads so much he asked for the recipe so that he could have them on his menu. I am not normally mean-spirited, but I showed a remarkable lack of generosity by refusing to share the recipe with him. Ever since, we have had a running joke about when I would give him the recipe for the eggplant breads. I almost relented once or twice, but I decided to wait until this book was published. And now that this book is in print, he can finally have patlicanli pide on his menu.

SERVES 4

For the dough

¾ teaspoon (⅓ package) active dry yeast

1¾ cups unbleached all-purpose flour, plus extra for kneading and
    shaping

1 teaspoon fine kosher salt or sea salt

2 tablespoons extra-virgin olive oil

For the topping

3 tablespoons extra-virgin olive oil, plus extra to drizzle over the
breads

1 medium eggplant (about ½ pound), cut into small cubes

½ red bell pepper, cored, seeded, and finely chopped

Kosher salt or sea salt

Freshly ground black pepper

1 garlic clove, crushed

7 to 8 ounces canned peeled tomatoes, drained

⅛ teaspoon red pepper flakes, or to taste

¼ cup finely chopped flat-leaf parsley

¼ cup finely chopped cilantro

Fresh basil leaves, for garnish

1. Make the dough: Dissolve the yeast in ½ cup warm water and stir until creamy. Combine the flour and salt in a large bowl and make a well in the center. Add the olive oil to the well and, with fingertips, rub it into the flour until well incorporated. Add the yeast and mix until you have a rough ball of dough.

2. Remove the dough to a lightly floured work surface. Knead for 3 minutes. Invert the bowl over the dough and let rest for 15 minutes. Knead for 2 to 3 minutes more, until the dough is smooth and elastic. Cover with a wet but not dripping kitchen towel and let rise in a warm, draft-free place for 30 minutes.

3. Meanwhile, make the topping: Put the olive oil, eggplant, and bell pepper in a sauté pan over low heat. Season with salt and pepper to taste. Cook, covered, for 15 minutes, stirring frequently. Add the garlic, tomatoes, and pepper flakes and cook, covered, for 15 minutes more, stirring occasionally and breaking up the tomatoes, until the vegetables are cooked through and the sauce is very thick. Add the parsley and cilantro and cook, uncovered, for another minute. Remove from the heat, cover with a kitchen towel, and let cool.

4. Preheat the oven to 400°F. Return the dough to the work surface and divide it into 4 equal pieces. Shape each into a ball, cover with a damp kitchen towel, and let rest for 15 minutes. Flatten each ball by hand into a circle about 5 inches in diameter, then stretch the circles into ovals and flatten further. Transfer to a large nonstick baking sheet, or to a baking sheet lined with parchment paper or a silicone pastry mat. Make indentations with fingertips inside the edges of the ovals to raise them slightly. Spread one-quarter of the filling inside the raised edges of each pizza.

5. Bake for 10 to 15 minutes, until the crust is golden. Garnish with basil leaves and serve hot or warm.

Neapolitan Pizza

Pizza Napoletana

One of the best pizzas I have ever had was in Naples at Ciro's in the city center (there is a second Ciro's on the waterfront), where I had been taken by my great friend Franco Santasilia, author of *Aristocratic Neapolitan Cuisine*. The pizza I ate there was a revelation. The dough was neither particularly thin nor thick. What made it so different was its border, which was like a bread with a perfect thin, crisp crust and a lovely chewy crumb with lots of holes. This, Franco explained, was because of how they manipulate the dough to flatten it. The pizzaiolo flattens the circle of dough slightly on his work surface, then lifts up the dough on his knuckles. He then flips it in the air and turns it around, and, as it falls back on his knuckles, he stretches the dough farther, pushing the gas bubbles to the edges. Another amazing thing about the pizza at Ciro's was that not one bit of it went soggy before I finished it. The topping was simple: tomato, mozzarella, and a few basil leaves with a good drizzle of olive oil. This is how any self-respecting Neapolitan eats his or her pizza.

MAKES 2 8-INCH PIZZAS (SERVES 2 TO 4)

For the dough

1½ teaspoons (⅔ package) active dry yeast

2 cups unbleached all-purpose flour, plus extra for kneading and
     shaping

¾ teaspoon fine kosher salt or sea salt

2 tablespoons extra-virgin olive oil, plus extra for greasing the bowl
     and drizzling over the pizzas

For the tomato sauce
3 tablespoons extra-virgin olive oil, plus more for drizzling
2 tablespoons finely chopped flat-leaf parsley
1 28-ounce can whole peeled tomatoes, finely chopped
1 tablespoon dried oregano
Fine kosher salt or sea salt

Fresh basil leaves, for garnish

1. Make the dough: Dissolve the yeast in ⅔ cup warm water and stir until creamy. Combine the flour and salt in a large bowl and make a well in the center. Add the olive oil to the well and, with fingertips, rub it into the flour until well incorporated. Gradually add the yeast and mix with the flour as you go along until you have a rough ball of dough.

2. Remove the dough to a lightly floured work surface. Knead for 3 minutes. Invert the bowl over the dough and let rest for 15 minutes. Knead the dough for about 2 to 3 minutes more, flouring hands every now and then, until the dough is smooth and elastic. Shape the dough into a ball. Lightly grease a bowl with olive oil and place the ball of dough in it, turning it to coat all over with oil. Cover with plastic wrap and let rise in a warm, draft-free place for 1 hour. Fold the dough (see pages 6–7), cover again, and let rise for 1 hour more. The dough should have doubled in volume.

3. Meanwhile, make the sauce: Put the olive oil and parsley in a sauté pan over medium-high heat. Cook for 2 minutes, stirring occasionally. Add the tomatoes, oregano, and salt to taste, and cook, uncovered, for 25 to 30 minutes, stirring frequently, until the sauce is very thick. Taste and adjust the seasoning if necessary. Set aside.

4. Return the dough to the work surface. Divide it in half equally and shape each half into a ball. Cover with a damp kitchen towel and let rest for 15 minutes.

5. Preheat the oven to 500°F. Lightly flour the work surface. Take a ball of dough, dip it lightly in flour, shake off the excess, and, rotating it 90 degrees and flouring the dough and work surface every now and then, roll it out to a circle about 8 inches in diameter. Flatten the inside of the circle with the palms of your hands. Prepare the other pizza in the same manner.

6. Transfer the pizzas to a nonstick baking sheet, or to a baking sheet lined with parchment paper or a silicone pastry mat. Spread each with half the tomato sauce. Bake for 10 to 15 minutes, until crisp and golden on the edges; check after 7 or 8 minutes to see if one side is coloring more than the other, and, if so, rotate the pizza so that the other edge can brown. Remove from the oven, drizzle with a little olive oil, and garnish with basil leaves. Serve immediately.

French "Pizza"

Pissaladière à la tomate

Many French people will say that this is not a true pissaladière because it has tomatoes, an absolute no-no as far as they are concerned. Yet I have found pissaladières with tomatoes in books written by perfectly respectable French chefs, and so, while this may not be the most traditional version, I don't think it's completely without authenticity. It is a delicious twist on the traditional, and it certainly is worth trying.

SERVES 6

For the dough
1½ teaspoons (⅔ package) active dry yeast
2⅓ cups unbleached all-purpose flour, plus extra for kneading and
    shaping
1 teaspoon fine kosher salt or sea salt
2 tablespoons extra-virgin olive oil, plus extra to grease the bowl

For the topping

4 tablespoons extra-virgin olive oil

2 pounds onions, thinly sliced (about 6 cups)

2 garlic cloves, finely chopped

2 large tomatoes, peeled, seeded, and finely chopped

1 tablespoon fresh thyme leaves

1 teaspoon sugar

Kosher salt or sea salt

Freshly ground black pepper

1 large tomato, quartered and thinly sliced

12 salted anchovy fillets, rinsed and filleted

12 black olives

1. Make the dough: Dissolve the yeast in ⅓ cup water and stir until creamy. Combine the flour and salt in a large bowl and make a well in the center. Add the oil to the well and, with fingertips, rub it into the flour until well incorporated. Add the yeast and an additional ½ cup warm water and mix until you have a rough ball of dough.

2. Remove the dough to a lightly floured work surface. Knead for 3 minutes. Invert the bowl over the dough and let rest for 15 minutes. Knead for 2 to 3 minutes more, until the dough is smooth and elastic. Shape into a ball. Place in an oiled bowl and turn to coat all over with oil. Cover with plastic wrap and let rise in a warm, draft-free place for 1 hour. Fold the dough (see pages 6–7), cover again, and let rise for 1 hour more. The dough should have doubled in volume.

3. Meanwhile, make the topping: Put 3 tablespoons of the olive oil and the onions, garlic, chopped tomatoes, thyme, and sugar in a sauté pan over medium-high heat. Season with salt and pepper to taste. Cook, stirring frequently, until the onions are soft, 20 to 25 minutes. Set aside to let cool.

4. Return the dough to the work surface and flatten it with fingertips to a large rectangle about 16 by 10 inches. Transfer to a 16 by 10-inch nonstick baking sheet, or a regular baking sheet of the same size that is lined with parchment paper or a silicone pastry mat. Raise the edges by pressing on the dough with fingertips about ½ inch in from each edge. Cover with a wet but not dripping kitchen towel and let rise for 30 to 45 minutes. Meanwhile, preheat the oven to 425°F.

5. Uncover the dough and let it dry for about 5 minutes. Spread the onion and tomato mixture over the dough to about ½ inch from the edge. Arrange the sliced tomato and the anchovies and olives in a regular pattern and drizzle the remaining 1 tablespoon olive oil over all. Bake for 20 to 25 minutes, until the crust is golden. Serve hot or warm.

Other Flatbreads

Mini Turkish Flatbreads

Yufka Ekmegi

Yufka are the Turkish version of lavosh, a soft or hard, paper-thin bread. Yufka can be sprinkled with water, wrapped in a kitchen towel, and left to sit until they soften and refresh, when they can be served as is or used, much like phyllo, to make pies. (To use in pies, the dough needs to be rolled out farther and thinner than here.) Or they may be left in their harder state, to be served as crackers.

MAKES 10 INDIVIDUAL BREADS

⅓ cup unbleached all-purpose flour, plus extra for kneading and
    shaping
⅓ cup bread flour
3 tablespoons whole wheat flour
½ teaspoon fine kosher salt or sea salt

1. Combine the flours and salt in a large bowl and make a well in the center. Gradually add ⅓ cup plus 2 teaspoons warm water and knead until you have a rough ball of dough.

2. Remove the dough to a lightly floured work surface. Knead for 3 minutes. Invert the bowl over the dough and let rest for 15 minutes. Knead for 2 to 3 minutes more, until the dough is smooth and elastic.

3. Divide the dough into 10 equal pieces. Shape each into a small ball, rolling the dough in between the palms. Sprinkle a tray, or part of the work surface, with

flour, and place the balls of dough on the floured surface. Cover with a wet but not dripping kitchen towel and let rest for 30 minutes.

4. Roll out each ball of dough, sprinkling with more flour every now and then, to a circle 7 or 8 inches in diameter. (Turkish women, who have a special thin rolling pin called an *oklava,* can roll the dough larger and thinner, but this is as far as I can go.) Place the circles of dough between floured couches (baker's linens), preferably, or dry kitchen towels.

5. Place a large nonstick pan over medium heat. When the pan is very hot, cook the breads, one at a time, for about 1 minute on each side, until they are lightly golden and small lightly burned spots have bubbled up. Stack between clean kitchen towels as they are finished. Use immediately, to make wraps for example, or let harden and stack in a dry place, where they will keep for weeks. To refresh the breads, sprinkle each sheet with a little water, fold in half, and wrap in a clean kitchen towel. Let rest for 30 minutes until the bread becomes soft and pliable, as if freshly baked.

Turkish Flatbreads with Spinach and Cheese

Saç Böregi

These breads, commonly called böreks in the West, are an Anatolian specialty, but today you see them being made everywhere in Istanbul. Some restaurants on Istiklal Street, the main pedestrian shopping street in Istanbul, have hired women, dressed in traditional Anatolian garb, to make the breads all day long behind the restaurant's front window. The women work at a low wooden table on which they roll out the very thin sheets of dough using a long, thin rolling pin called an *oklava*. They fill and fold the breads and then deftly transfer them to a hot metal sheet, where they cook in seconds on each side.

SERVES 4

For the dough
1 cup unbleached all-purpose flour, plus extra for kneading and
     shaping
½ teaspoon fine kosher salt or sea salt

For the filling
¾ cup crumbled feta cheese
2 tablespoons chopped flat-leaf parsley
2½ cups finely shredded spinach (about 3½ ounces)
Freshly ground black pepper
3 tablespoons butter, melted

1. Combine the flour and salt in a large bowl and make a well in the center. Gradually add just over ⅓ cup warm water to the well, bringing in the flour as you go along. Knead to make a rough ball of dough.

2. Transfer the dough to a lightly floured work surface. Knead for 3 minutes. Invert the bowl over the dough and let rest for 15 minutes. Knead the dough for about 2 to 3 minutes more to make a smooth, firm dough.

3. Divide the dough into 4 equal pieces. Form each piece into a ball. Cover with a wet but not dripping kitchen towel and let rest for 30 minutes. Meanwhile, mix together the cheese and parsley.

4. Sprinkle a work surface and rolling pin with flour. Roll out a ball of dough to a circle about 12 inches in diameter, lightly sprinkling with flour every now and then. Sprinkle a quarter of the spinach over half the dough. Cover the spinach with a quarter of the cheese mixture. Fold the dough over the fillings to make a half circle. Prepare the remaining böreks in the same way. Heat a nonstick griddle or frying pan over medium heat. Transfer the böreks, one or two at a time, to the hot griddle or pan and cook for 1 to 2 minutes on each side, until lightly crisp and golden. Transfer to a serving plate and brush with melted butter. Serve immediately.

✣ Turkish Bread

Pide

These long, flat, oval loaves are the most common bread in Turkey. Unlike pita, pide is a one-layered, rather spongy bread that is served plain or used to serve kebabs. Sometimes the bread is spread with seasoned parsley and onion before the kebab meat is laid on it. The same dough can be used with various toppings to make the Turkish equivalent of pizza (see page 39).

SERVES 4

2¼ teaspoons (1 package) active dry yeast

3 cups unbleached all-purpose flour, plus extra for kneading and
   shaping

2 teaspoons sugar

2 teaspoons fine kosher salt or sea salt

2 tablespoons extra-virgin olive oil, plus extra for greasing the bowl
   and baking sheet

1 egg beaten with 1 teaspoon water

2 tablespoons white sesame seeds

1. Dissolve the yeast in ¼ cup warm water and stir until creamy. Combine the flour, sugar, and salt in a large bowl and make a well in the center. Add the 2 tablespoons oil and the yeast to the well. Bring in a little of the flour to mix with the oil and yeast, then gradually add ⅔ cup warm water, bringing in the remaining flour as you go along. Knead to make a rough ball of dough.

2. Remove the dough to a lightly floured work surface. Knead for 3 minutes. Invert the bowl over the dough and let rest for 15 minutes. Knead for about 2 to 3 minutes more, until the dough is smooth and elastic.

3. Grease a large clean bowl with a little oil, place the dough in it, and turn the dough to coat with oil. Cover with plastic wrap and let rise in a warm, draft-free place for 1 hour. Fold the dough (see pages 6–7) and let rise, covered, for 1 hour more. The dough should have doubled in volume.

4. Return the dough to the work surface and shape into a ball. Transfer to a non-stick baking sheet, or to a baking sheet lined with parchment paper or a silicone pastry mat. Cover with a damp kitchen towel. Let rest for 15 minutes.

5. Flatten the dough by hand into an oval loaf 14 to 16 inches long and ½ inch thick. Cover with a wet but not dripping kitchen towel and let rise for 45 minutes. Meanwhile, preheat the oven to 425°F.

6. Uncover the dough about 5 minutes before baking to let the surface dry. Brush the top with the egg mixture. With fingertips, make dimples all over the top and sprinkle with the sesame seeds. Bake for 30 minutes, until golden all over. Transfer to a wire rack to cool. Serve at room temperature, or reheated.

⚓ Moroccan Bread

K'sra

Most people in Morocco still prepare their own bread at home. If they live in town, they take their risen loaves to bake in the local baker's oven; and if they live in the country, they cook their bread in a large earthenware dish that they heat over a wood fire. On a recent visit to Morocco, I spent a day at the family farm of a friend. I watched his aunt and cousin make the bread for our lunch while his mother and sisters prepared tagines and salads. The whole meal was being prepared in an amazingly medieval kitchen with a mud floor, no running water, and only one portable gas burner on which to cook, but there was a large fireplace in which they cooked the bread over a raging olive wood fire.

The cousin kneaded and proofed the bread in a large round shallow earthenware bowl called a *g'saa,* and the aunt cooked it in a similar although flatter dish. My friend's aunt seemed impervious to the heat as she crouched very near the fire to watch over the bread. She lifted the loaf every few minutes to see if it was coloring too fast, and when it was ready, she lifted it with her hand, even though it was burning hot, and turned it over.

There aren't very many different types of bread in Morocco. One variation is to add aniseed and sesame seeds to the dough to make it festive—½ tablespoon aniseed and 1 tablespoon sesame seeds are what you need for the quantities below. This flavored bread is also served for breakfast. There are also regional versions that are made with barley or whole wheat flour and one made with meat (Berber Hamburger All-in-One, page 60).

MAKES 1 MEDIUM LOAF

2¼ teaspoons (1 package) active dry yeast
2½ cups fine semolina or semolina flour
1 teaspoon fine kosher salt or sea salt
½ tablespoon aniseed, optional
1 tablespoon white sesame seeds, optional
All-purpose flour for kneading and shaping

1. Dissolve the yeast in ¼ cup warm water and stir until creamy.

2. Combine the semolina and salt and, if using, the anise and sesame seeds in a large bowl and make a well in the center. Add the yeast to the well. Gradually add 1 cup warm water, bringing in the flour as you go along. Knead to make a rough ball of dough.

3. Remove the dough to a lightly floured work surface. Knead for 3 minutes. Invert the bowl over the dough and let rest for 15 minutes. Knead for about 2 to 3 minutes more, until the dough is smooth and elastic. Shape the dough into a ball, cover with a damp kitchen towel, and let rest for 15 minutes.

4. Flatten the dough by hand into a circle about ¾ inch thick. Transfer to a non-stick baking sheet, or to a baking sheet lined with parchment paper or a silicone pastry mat. Cover with a wet but not dripping kitchen towel and let rise in a warm, draft-free place for about 1 hour, until the dough has about doubled in volume. Meanwhile, preheat the oven to 400°F.

5. Bake for 35 to 40 minutes, until golden all over. Transfer to a wire rack to cool. Serve at room temperature, or reheated.

✵ Berber Hamburger All-in-One

Medfouna

There is some confusion regarding the name of this bread. *Medfouna,* Arabic for "buried," is also used to describe a Moroccan dish of vermicelli and stewed pigeons in which the stewed pigeons are "buried" under a mound of steamed vermicelli. That medfouna is a far grander dish than this stuffed bread, which is a southern specialty. I found a recipe for this bread on a postcard while browsing through a rack of them in Marrakech. Moroccans cook the bread either on a hot stone, in which case the bread is covered with hot ashes, or in a regular wood-fired oven. My friend Hajj N'guyr Mustafa, who makes the best *méchoui* (whole lamb roasted in a sealed pit oven) in Marrakech, says that medfouna can also be made with *khlii,* dried preserved strips of spiced beef, but simple lamb shoulder, much easier to find, works splendidly as well.

SERVES 6 TO 8

For the filling
2 pounds lamb shoulder, trimmed of skin and fat and finely diced
1 large onion, very finely chopped
½ cup finely chopped flat-leaf parsley
1 tablespoon ground coriander
½ teaspoon ground cumin
½ teaspoon ground cinnamon
1 teaspoon finely ground black pepper
1 teaspoon fine kosher salt or sea salt
¼ cup extra-virgin olive oil

For the bread

1½ teaspoons (⅔ package) active dry yeast

2 cups unbleached all-purpose flour, plus extra for kneading and
    shaping

1⅓ cups fine semolina or semolina flour

1½ teaspoons fine kosher salt or sea salt

1. Combine the filling ingredients in a large bowl. Mix well. Let marinate, stirring occasionally, as the dough is prepared.

2. Make the bread: Dissolve the yeast in ¼ cup warm water and stir until creamy. Combine the flours and salt in a large mixing bowl and make a well in the center. Add the yeast and gradually add 1 cup warm water, bringing in the flour as you go along. Knead to make a rough ball of dough.

Medfouna à la viande

3. Remove the dough to a lightly floured work surface. Knead for 3 minutes. Shape into a ball. Invert the bowl over the dough and let rest for 15 minutes. Knead for about 2 to 3 minutes more, until the dough is smooth and elastic. Shape into a ball and place in a lightly floured clean bowl. Cover with plastic wrap and let rise in a warm, draft-free place for 1 hour. Fold the dough (see pages 6–7) and let rise, covered, for 1 hour more. The dough should have doubled in volume.

4. Return the dough to the work surface. Divide into 2 pieces, one slightly larger than the other. Shape each piece into a ball, place the balls on a floured surface, and sprinkle a little flour over them. Cover with plastic wrap and let rest for 15 minutes.

5. Roll out the smaller piece of dough to a circle about 12 inches in diameter, flouring the work surface and the dough occasionally. Transfer the dough to a large nonstick baking sheet, or to a baking sheet lined with parchment paper or a silicone pastry mat. Prick the surface with a fork here and there. Spread the meat filling evenly over the dough, leaving about ¾ inch around the edges. Brush the edges with water. Roll out the other piece of dough to a slightly larger circle. Place this circle over the filling and press gently on the edges to seal. Prick the top of the dough in a few places. Cover with a wet but not dripping kitchen towel and let rise for 35 minutes. Meanwhile, preheat the oven to 375°F.

6. Bake for 45 minutes, until crisp and golden brown all over. Remove from the oven; if there is juice that has run out of the meat and is soaking the bread, carefully tip the baking sheet and drain the juice. Let the bread rest for 5 minutes, then transfer to a wire rack to cool slightly. Serve hot or warm, or let cool completely and freeze for later use. If freezing, keep the bread wrapped as it defrosts. Once it has thawed, reheat in a 400°F oven for 10 to 15 minutes and serve.

Moroccan Multilayered Breads

R'ghayef

You find r'ghayef, with slight variations, in Tunisia and Algeria as well as in Morocco. In Algeria, the breads are known as m'hajjib and in Tunisia as m'lawi. In Tunisia, plain m'lawi are used as wraps to make sandwiches. R'ghayef are also called m'semmen in Morocco. There is a recipe for a similar bread, *musammana* (which means "buttered"), in a thirteenth-century cookbook from across the sea in Andalucia.

MAKES 8 INDIVIDUAL BREADS

For the dough
½ teaspoon (scant ¼ package) active dry yeast
1 cup unbleached all-purpose flour, plus extra for kneading
1 cup semolina flour
1 teaspoon fine kosher salt or sea salt

For the filling
1 medium onion, very finely chopped
¼ cup finely chopped flat-leaf parsley
½ teaspoon ground cumin
1 teaspoon sweet paprika
⅛ teaspoon crushed red pepper flakes
Kosher salt or sea salt

Vegetable oil

1. Dissolve the yeast in ⅔ cup plus 2 tablespoons warm water and stir until creamy.

2. Combine the flours and salt in a large bowl and make a well in the center. Add the yeast and mix with the flour until you have a rough, sticky dough.

3. Remove the dough to a lightly floured work surface. Sprinkle the dough with flour and knead for about 3 minutes. Invert the bowl over the dough and let rest for 15 minutes. Knead for about 2 to 3 minutes more, until the dough is smooth and elastic. Cover with a damp kitchen towel and let rest while the filling is prepared.

4. Combine the filling ingredients in a medium bowl. Mix well.

5. Divide the dough into 8 equal pieces. Oil a work surface and your hands. Flatten a ball by hand on the work surface into a very thin circle using more oil if necessary. Spread one-eighth of the filling over the center of the circle. Fold the left third of the circle over the filling, then fold the right third over to make a rectangle. Fold the top third over the bread and the bottom third under the bread to make a square about 5 inches on each side; folding one side up and the other down encloses the filling evenly and securely. Let rest while you make 3 more squares in the same manner (the last 4 breads will be made in a second batch). Flatten with fingertips the squares of filled dough until they are quite thin.

6. Oil a large nonstick frying pan and place over medium-high heat. Place 1 or 2 squares in the hot pan. Drizzle a little additional oil over the bread. Cook for 1½ to 2 minutes on each side, until golden. Remove to parchment paper or a wire rack. Cook the remaining 2 or 3 breads from this first batch, then shape, fill, and cook the remaining 4 breads, using plenty of oil as needed for work surface, hands, and pan. Serve immediately.

Tunisian Spicy Breads

Touarits

These are a Tunisian spin on r'ghayefs. Here the dough is made entirely with semolina flour and enriched with oil and egg, and the filling is enclosed between two circles of dough. The breads are usually pan-fried, but I prefer to bake them. Although the amount of harissa and cayenne pepper in the filling may seem excessive, the heat of the spices is tempered by the bread casing. The filling, which is called *chakchouka,* may also be served on its own as a salad or a dip. Harissa, made by grinding chili peppers, garlic, and caraway seeds, is widely available in Middle Eastern markets and in some supermarkets.

MAKES 20 TO 22 SMALL BREADS

For the dough

3⅓ teaspoons (1½ packages) active dry yeast

3⅓ cups fine semolina or semolina flour

1½ teaspoons fine kosher salt or sea salt

1½ tablespoons extra-virgin olive oil, plus extra for brushing the
    breads

1 medium whole egg

All-purpose flour for kneading and shaping

For the filling

3 tablespoons extra-virgin olive oil

1 medium onion, finely chopped

2 medium tomatoes, finely chopped (about 1 heaping cup)

1 medium bell pepper, cored, seeded, and finely chopped (about
    ¾ cup)
2 small chili peppers, such as serranos, seeded and finely chopped
1 teaspoon harissa
½ teaspoon cayenne pepper
Fine kosher salt or sea salt

1. Dissolve the yeast in ¼ cup warm water and stir until creamy.

2. Combine the semolina and salt in a large bowl and make a well in the center.
   Add the 1½ tablespoons olive oil and the egg to the well. Gradually add the
   yeast and ⅔ cup plus 2 tablespoons warm water, bringing in the semolina as
   you go along. Knead until you have a rough ball of dough.

3. Remove the dough to a lightly floured work surface. Knead for 3 minutes. Invert the bowl over the dough and let rest for 15 minutes. Knead for about 2 to
   3 minutes more. Cover with a damp kitchen towel and let rest while the filling
   is prepared.

4. Make the filling: Heat the oil in a sauté pan over medium-high heat. Add the
   onion and cook until golden. Add the tomatoes, chopped peppers, harissa, and
   cayenne. Season with salt to taste and cook, stirring occasionally, until the bell
   pepper is soft and the sauce is very thick. Remove from the heat and set aside.

5. Divide the dough into two pieces and shape each piece into a ball. Place on
   a lightly floured work surface, cover with plastic wrap, and let rest for 15
   minutes.

6. Preheat the oven to 400°F. Roll out one ball of dough until it is ¼ inch thick.
   Using a 3½-inch pastry cutter, cut out as many circles of dough as possible and
   set aside. Briefly knead the extra dough together, and place under the plastic
   wrap, next to the other ball of dough. Turn the circles over and place 1 teaspoon
   of filling in the middle of half of the circles. Cover with the remaining plain

circles and press on the edges to seal. Flatten the breads slightly by hand and pinch the edges to flatten further and seal well. Brush with olive oil on both sides and transfer to a nonstick baking sheet, or to a baking sheet lined with parchment paper or a silicone pastry mat. Cover with a damp kitchen towel. Continue making the breads until the dough, including the scraps, is used up.

7. Bake for 12 to 15 minutes, until lightly crisp and golden. Transfer to a wire rack to cool. Serve warm.

Note: To pan-fry the breads, heat a little oil in a large pan over medium-high heat. When the oil is hot, place as many breads as will fit in the pan, brush the tops with olive oil, and cook for 3 to 5 minutes, until golden on the bottom, pressing on the breads if they puff up. Turn the breads over, brush the cooked bottoms with oil, and cook for 3 minutes more, or until golden all over. Serve immediately.

✛ Pita Bread

Khobz Arabi

Homemade pita bread is quite different from what is prepared in most commercial bakeries in Lebanon. Commercial pita from Middle Eastern bakeries has more texture; the flour that is used is milled from hard wheat and has a little bran left in it. And commercial bakers are able to produce two extremely thin, miraculously equal layers, thanks to the highly automated process. The process can be partially, but not entirely, replicated at home: you can knead the dough in a machine instead of by hand, and you can use a pasta machine instead of a rolling pin to roll out an evenly flattened dough. But, however good your oven is, it will never produce the fierce heat of commercial ovens, which makes the dough puff up in seconds and the layers separate equally. That said, homemade pita is good. I love taking the puffed balls of bread out of the oven and watching them deflate, a little slower than in a commercial bakery, perhaps because the layers are not so thin.

MAKES 10 INDIVIDUAL PITAS

Heaping teaspoon (½ package) active dry yeast

3⅓ cups unbleached all-purpose flour, plus extra for kneading and
   shaping

2 teaspoons fine kosher salt or sea salt

¼ cup extra-virgin olive oil, plus more for greasing the bowl

1. Dissolve the yeast in ¼ cup warm water and stir until creamy.

2. Combine the flour and salt in a large bowl and make a well in the center. Add the oil to the well and, using fingertips, rub the oil into the flour until well

incorporated. Add the yeast and gradually add another ¾ cup warm water, bringing in the flour as you go along. Knead until you have a rough, rather sticky ball of dough.

3. Remove the dough to a lightly floured work surface. Sprinkle the dough with flour. Knead for 3 minutes, sprinkling with more flour if the dough sticks. Invert the bowl over the dough and let rest for 15 minutes. Knead for about 2 to 3 minutes more, until the dough is smooth, elastic, and rather soft. Shape the dough into a ball and place in an oiled clean bowl, turning the dough to coat with oil. Cover with plastic wrap and let rise in a warm, draft-free place for 1 hour. Fold the dough (see pages 6–7), cover again, and let rise for 1 hour more. The dough should have doubled in volume.

4. Remove the dough to a work surface and divide it into 10 equal pieces. Roll each piece into a ball. Place on a floured surface. Cover with a wet but not dripping kitchen towel and let rise for 45 minutes.

5. Preheat the oven to 500°F. Roll out each ball of dough to a circle 6 or 7 inches in diameter, adding flour to the work surface and dough as needed. Try to form perfectly rounded circles; a good way to achieve this is to give the circle a quarter turn between each rolling out. (A pasta machine also may be used to roll out the circles.) Transfer the circles of dough to a nonstick baking sheet. Cover the circles of dough with a floured couche (baker's linen), preferably, or a dry kitchen towel. Let rest for 15 to 20 minutes.

6. Bake the pitas for 6 to 8 minutes, until well puffed and very lightly golden. The baking time will vary depending on how hot the oven is; it is a good idea to start checking the breads after 5 minutes. Bake in separate batches if the oven

is not large enough. These are best served immediately or still warm. Or let them cool on a wire rack and freeze them in a plastic freezer bag. Simply defrost them in the bag, then remove them from the bag and reheat in a warm oven.

Lebanese Morning Bread

Khobz al-Sabah

Jawad Yussef Daher, the baker who gave me the recipe for mishtah (page 79), also told me about this Lebanese variation on the pita theme. I never asked him why he calls it morning bread, but presumably it is because it is eaten mostly for breakfast. The two different flours and the cornmeal give the bread more texture and make it more interesting than pita.

MAKES 12 INDIVIDUAL BREADS

2¼ teaspoons (1 package) active dry yeast
3⅓ cups unbleached all-purpose flour, plus extra for kneading and for
     the bowl
⅔ cup whole wheat flour
⅔ cup cornmeal
4 teaspoons fine kosher salt or sea salt

1. Dissolve the yeast in ⅓ cup warm water and stir until creamy.

2. Combine the flours, cornmeal, and salt in a large bowl and make a well in the center. Add the yeast, then gradually add 1¼ cups warm water, bringing in the flour as you go along. Knead until you have a rough ball of dough.

3. Remove the dough to a lightly floured work surface. Knead for 3 minutes. Invert the bowl over the dough and let rest for 15 minutes. Knead for about 2 to 3 minutes more, until the dough is smooth and elastic. Roll into a ball and place in a lightly floured clean bowl. Cover with plastic wrap and let rise in a warm,

لائحة الأسعار

ربطة الخبز	١٤٢٥
كيلو عجين سفيحة	٢٠٠
كيس كعك	٢١٠٠٠
كيس مشاليح	
منقوشة جبنة	٥٠٠
منقوشة زعتر	٢٥٠
عجينة منقوشة	

من
دون
T.V.A

مع تحيات
فرن اللوز

draft-free place for 1 hour. Fold the dough (see pages 6–7), cover again, and let rise for 1 hour more. The dough should have doubled in volume.

4. Return the dough to the work surface and divide it into 12 equal pieces. Shape each into a ball and place on a lightly floured tray or baking sheet. Cover with a wet but not dripping kitchen towel and let rise for 45 minutes.

5. Preheat the oven to 500°F. Return the dough to the work surface and roll out each ball to a circle about 6 or 7 inches in diameter. Transfer to a nonstick baking sheet, or to a baking sheet lined with parchment paper or a silicone pastry mat. Cover with a floured couche (baker's linen), preferably, or a dry kitchen towel. Let rest for 15 minutes.

6. Bake for 6 to 8 minutes, until puffed up and very lightly golden. The baking time will vary depending on how hot the oven is; it is a good idea to start checking the breads after 5 minutes. These are best served immediately or still warm. Or let them cool on a wire rack and freeze them in a plastic freezer bag. Simply defrost them in the bag, then remove them from the bag and reheat in a warm oven.

Lebanese Bread from the South

Mishtah

I learned how to make this bread from a wonderful, old-fashioned baker, Jawad Yussef Daher, whose bakery is in Kfar Rumman in south Lebanon. My friend Nayla Audi, who was born in Kfar Rumman, first told me about mishtah, a bread unique to the south (Lebanon, though a tiny country, has distinct regional culinary variations). Nayla invited me to her home—a large nineteenth-century stone house with the family graveyard on one side of the leafy courtyard—for a typical southern lunch preceded by a visit to Jawad's bakery, to see how mishtah was made. As we were telling Nayla's father about my quest for regional breads, he suggested we take some za'atar (see page 35) with us to have Jawad make us manaqish with the dough for mishtah, which they call manaqish jreesh. Jreesh is the name given to the cracked wheat used in the dough in this recipe. If you want to make manaqish with this dough, follow the instructions for manaqish on page 35, but use the recipe below for the dough.

Mahlep is the tiny dried nut found in the kernel of the sour cherry. It is sold whole for cooks to grind at home or you can buy it already ground. Its fragrant flavor adds an exotic touch to many Mediterranean breads. Anise is a flowering plant that is native to the eastern Mediterranean and the seeds are used to flavor both sweet and savory preparations. As for dakkat el-ka'k, it is a fragrant mixture of spices that is generally used in rusks (*dakkat* means "the ground," and *ka'k* means "biscuits" or "rusks").

MAKES 6 INDIVIDUAL BREADS

2¼ teaspoons (1 package) active dry yeast

3⅓ cups whole wheat flour

1 teaspoon fine kosher salt or sea salt

3 tablespoons whole aniseed

3 tablespoons white sesame seeds

½ teaspoon ground mahlep

½ teaspoon ground aniseed

½ teaspoon dakkat el-ka'k spice mixture, optional

¾ cup jreesh or similar cracked wheat, such as King Arthur's organic
    cracked wheat, soaked in cold water for 1 hour and drained

All-purpose flour for kneading and shaping the dough

Extra-virgin olive oil to grease the bowl

1. Dissolve the yeast in ⅓ cup warm water and stir until creamy.

2. Combine the whole wheat flour, salt, seeds, and spices in a large bowl. Mix well so that the ingredients are distributed evenly.

3. Stir in the cracked wheat and make a well in the center. Add the yeast and gradually add another ⅔ cup plus 1 tablespoon warm water, bringing in the flour as you go along. Knead until you have a rough ball of dough.

4. Remove the dough to a lightly floured work surface. Knead for 3 minutes. Invert the bowl over the dough and let rest for 15 minutes. Knead for about 2 to 3 minutes more, until the dough is smooth and elastic. Grease a large bowl with olive oil. Shape the dough into a ball and place it in the bowl, turning the dough to coat with oil. Cover with plastic wrap and let rise in a warm, draft-free place for 1 hour. Fold the dough (see pages 6–7), cover again, and let rise for 1 hour more. The dough should have doubled in volume.

5. Return the dough to the work surface and divide it into 6 equal pieces. Shape each piece into a ball. Cover with a wet but not dripping kitchen towel and let rise for 45 minutes.

6. Preheat the oven to 500°F. Flatten each ball by hand into a circle about 7 or 8 inches in diameter. Transfer to a nonstick baking sheet, or to a baking sheet lined with parchment paper or a silicone pastry mat. Cover with a floured couche (baker's linen), preferably, or a dry kitchen towel, and let rest for 10 to 15 minutes.

7. Bake the breads for 10 to 12 minutes, until lightly golden. Serve warm or let cool on a wire rack to serve at room temperature.

⸓ Yemeni Bread

M'lawwah

Although Yemen does not lie on the Mediterranean, this bread has become a staple in Israel, where it was introduced by Jewish immigrants from Yemen. It is very simple to make and makes a wonderful starter when served with hami-nado eggs (eggs simmered for about 6 hours with onion skins to make them brown inside and out) and z'houg, a Yemeni relish made with cilantro, garlic, chili peppers, and olive oil. You can also simply serve it for breakfast, spread with butter, jam, or honey, or as a lunch or dinner bread.

MAKES 6 INDIVIDUAL BREADS

3⅓ cups unbleached all-purpose flour, plus extra for kneading and
    shaping
1 teaspoon sugar
2 teaspoons fine kosher salt or sea salt
1 tablespoon white wine vinegar
1 tablespoon extra-virgin olive oil, plus extra for pan-frying the breads
½ cup (1 stick) unsalted butter, softened slightly

1. Combine the flour, sugar, and salt in a large bowl and make a well in the center. Add the vinegar and 1 tablespoon of the oil to the well and gradually add 1 cup warm water, bringing in the flour as you go along. Knead until you have a rough ball of dough.

2. Remove the dough to a lightly floured work surface. Knead for 3 minutes. Invert the bowl over the dough and let rest for 15 minutes. Knead for about 2 to

3 minutes more, until the dough is smooth and elastic but slightly firm. Shape into a ball, cover with a wet but not dripping kitchen towel, and let rest for 30 minutes.

3. Divide the dough into 6 equal pieces. Shape each piece into a ball, cover again with a wet but not dripping towel, and let rest for 30 minutes more.

4. Divide the butter into 6 equal portions. Roll out a ball of dough to a circle about ¼ inch thick. Spread with 1 portion of the butter. Fold over one-third of the circle and then the opposite third to make a narrow rectangle, wrap in plastic wrap, and set aside. Roll out, butter, fold, and wrap the remaining dough in the same way. Refrigerate the dough for at least 2 hours.

5. Fold the rectangle in thirds to make a square. Roll out each square of dough into a larger square that is very thin—not paper-thin but thin enough for the dough to cook through quickly in a frying pan without becoming too brown. Heat a little olive oil in a large pan over medium heat. When the oil is hot, place one bread in the pan and cook, covered, for 2 to 3 minutes on each side, until lightly golden. Remove onto parchment paper or a dry kitchen towel and keep warm. Cook the remaining breads, using more oil if necessary and placing parchment paper between the breads when they are done. Serve immediately.

Flatbread from Emilia Romagna

Piadina Romagnola

Piadina is traditionally cooked over a *testo* or a *teglia*. A testo is a flat earthenware disk while a teglia is a cast-iron griddle like the one pictured on page 86. Either of these are usually placed over an open fire to cook the piadina and, as a result, the bread has a slightly smoky taste. You can just as easily use a cast-iron skillet, a smooth griddle, or even a nonstick pan on a gas or electric stove for good results, but without the smoky flavor.

MAKES 6 INDIVIDUAL BREADS

3⅓ cups unbleached all-purpose flour, plus extra for kneading and
   shaping
1½ teaspoons fine kosher salt or sea salt
1 teaspoon baking soda
2 tablespoons lard or extra-virgin olive oil
1 cup whole milk

1. Combine the flour, salt, and baking soda in a large bowl and make a well in the center. Add the lard or olive oil to the well and, with fingertips, rub it into the flour until well incorporated. Add the milk gradually, mixing with the flour to make a rough ball of dough.

2. Remove the dough to a lightly floured work surface. Knead for 3 minutes but not more; overworking the gluten in the dough will prevent the bread from being crumbly. Divide the dough into 6 equal pieces. Shape each piece into a ball, and cover the balls of dough with a wet but not dripping kitchen towel.

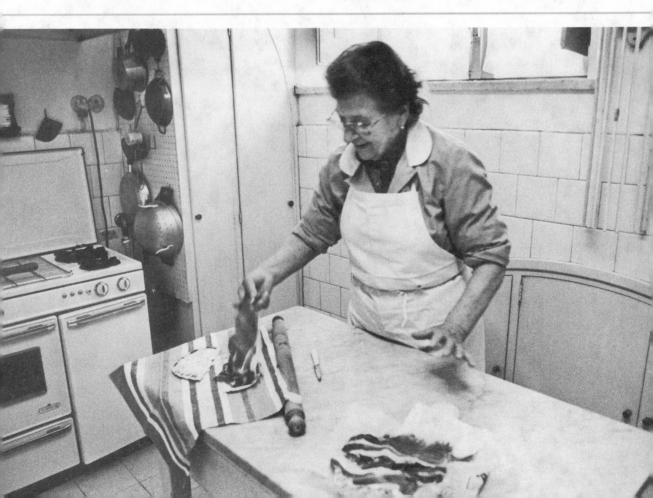

3. Heat a large cast-iron pan over medium-high heat. Roll out a ball of dough into a circle 8 inches in diameter. When the pan is quite hot, place the circle in it and prick the dough in several places with a fork. Cook for about 2 minutes, until there are golden spots on the bottom, then turn over and cook for 2 minutes more. Remove and cover with a clean kitchen towel. Make the remaining breads in the same manner, stacking them in layers of cloth as they finish.

4. Serve hot or warm, perhaps folded over or filled with Italian meats such as prosciutto or salami.

Olive and Anchovy "Mille-Feuille"

Sfogliata con Olive e Acciughe

Sfogliata is the Italian name for either a multilayered pastry or a French mille-feuille. In this sfogliata, the dough is rolled out very thin and spread with a mixture of chopped olives and anchovies. Then the dough is rolled around the filling and flattened to create the multilayered effect. This specialty from Puglia is quite fun to make, even though it is time-consuming.

SERVES 6 TO 8

For the dough
2¼ teaspoons (1 package) active dry yeast
2⅓ cups unbleached all-purpose flour, plus extra for kneading and shaping
2 tablespoons extra-virgin olive oil, plus extra to grease the pan and to
     brush the mille-feuille

For the filling
10 large green olives, pitted and finely chopped
5 salt-cured anchovies, rinsed, filleted, and finely chopped
3 tablespoons extra-virgin olive oil
Freshly ground black pepper

1. Dissolve the yeast in ¼ cup warm water and stir until creamy.

2. Put the flour in a large bowl and make a well in the center. Add the oil to the well and, with fingertips, rub into the flour until well incorporated. Add the

yeast and gradually add another ½ cup plus 1 tablespoon warm water, bringing in the flour as you go along. Knead until you have a rough dough.

3. Remove the dough to a lightly floured work surface and knead for 3 minutes. Invert the bowl over the dough and let rest for 15 minutes. Knead for about 2 to 3 minutes more, until the dough is smooth and elastic. Divide into 10 equal pieces and form each piece into a ball. Place on a floured surface, cover with a damp kitchen towel, and let rest for 15 minutes.

4. Roll out the balls of dough into circles 8 inches in diameter. Stack the circles between floured couches (baker's linens), preferably, or dry kitchen towels. Let rest for 30 minutes. Grease a 12-inch round tart pan or pie plate with olive oil.

5. Mix the olives, anchovies, and olive oil in a bowl. Season with pepper to taste. Spread about 1 tablespoon of the olive mixture over one circle of dough. Roll the garnished circle into a fairly tight cylinder shape and coil the cylinder backward to make a rosette-shaped coiled pastry. Flatten slightly with the palm of your hand. Place in the center of the tart pan. Roll out and prepare the remaining circles of dough in the same way, coiling each concentrically around the first coiled pastry; most of the tart pan will be covered. Flatten the coiled pastries with the palm of your hand until the sfogliata covers the bottom completely. Brush with olive oil and let rest for 20 minutes. Meanwhile, preheat the oven to 425°F.

6. Bake the sfogliata for 30 to 40 minutes, until golden all over. Serve hot or warm.

✥ Sicilian Flatbread with Mozzarella and Prosciutto

Schiacciata con Mozzarella e Prosciutto

This simple filled bread is great for picnics, and it makes an easy and fun alternative to sandwiches for children's parties. It's made with the same dough as that used to make Sicilian Sausage Rolls (page 140). If you like, you can fill this bread with prosciutto only, or cooked ham; or you can use lightly salted sliced tomatoes instead of the prosciutto or cooked ham, with or without mozzarella.

SERVES 6 TO 8

1 recipe dough for Sicilian Sausage Rolls (page 140), prepared to step 3
9 ounces fresh mozzarella, drained well and sliced thin
4 thin slices of prosciutto
3 tablespoons white sesame seeds

1. Prepare the dough. Divide the dough in two and shape each piece into a ball. Cover with a damp kitchen towel and let rest for 15 minutes.

2. Roll out one piece of dough to a circle large enough to line the bottom of a nonstick 12-inch round pie plate or tart pan (or a regular pie plate or tart pan brushed with a little olive oil). Place the dough over the bottom of the dish and, if necessary, gently flatten further by hand so that it covers the bottom completely.

3. Place the mozzarella slices over the dough, leaving about ½ inch free around the edge. Cover with the prosciutto slices. Roll out the other piece of dough to the same size and place over the filling. Gently press along the edges to seal. Cover with a wet but not dripping kitchen towel and let rise for 30 minutes. Meanwhile, preheat the oven to 450°F.

4. Brush the bread with a little water and sprinkle the sesame seeds over the top. Bake for 15 minutes, or until golden brown. Remove from the oven, let sit for 5 minutes, then carefully slide onto a wire rack and let cool for 10 minutes. Serve warm or at room temperature.

✣ Sicilian Eggplant Bread Rolls

Focaccia di Modica

Also known as scaccie or focaccia di Ragusa, this rolled and stuffed flatbread is a speciality of Modica, a gorgeous town south of Ragusa in southeastern Sicily. In the commercial bakeries of Modica, the roll is made very long, with two people helping to make it, and then it is cut into individual portions and baked. Filling combinations include ricotta and scallions (with or without parsley) and tomatoes and eggplants (with or without basil). Sicilians often have these for a snack; they also make wholesome picnic or school lunches for children.

SERVES 6

1 recipe dough for Sicilian Bread (page 126)
Semolina flour for baking sheet

For the filling
Vegetable oil for frying
2 medium eggplants, peeled and sliced thin lengthwise, to yield 18
    slices
3 ripe medium tomatoes, peeled, seeded, and finely chopped
Handful of fresh basil leaves, finely chopped
½ cup grated Parmigiano-Reggiano
Fine kosher salt or sea salt
Freshly ground black pepper
2 tablespoons extra-virgin olive oil, plus extra for brushing the breads

1. Prepare the dough through step 3 (see pages 126–27).

2. Pour vegetable oil to a depth of 1½ inches in a large frying pan. Over medium-high heat, bring the oil to a temperature of 375°F. Fry the eggplant slices, in batches, 2 to 3 minutes on each side, until golden. Remove with a slotted spoon onto several layers of paper towels to drain.

3. Combine the tomatoes, basil, and Parmesan in a medium bowl. Season with salt and pepper to taste. Cover and set aside.

4. Place the dough on a work surface. Divide into 6 equal pieces and shape each piece into a ball. Place the balls on a floured surface, sprinkle with a little more flour, cover with plastic wrap, and let rest for 15 minutes.

5. Lightly flour the work surface. Roll out one ball of dough into a rectangle 12 or 13 inches long and 7 or 8 inches wide. Place 3 eggplant slices across the rectangle, leaving about 2½ inches free at both ends. Spread one-sixth of the tomato mixture over the eggplant, and sprinkle with a little more salt and pepper to taste. Fold 1 end of plain dough over the first slice of eggplant and continue folding along the length of the rectangle until the filling is completely enclosed. Sprinkle a large baking sheet with semolina flour and transfer the roll onto it. Brush the top of the bread with olive oil and loosely cover with plastic wrap. Make the remaining rolls in the same way. Let the rolls rest for 20 minutes. Meanwhile, preheat the oven to 450°F.

6. Uncover the breads and bake them for 10 minutes. Reduce the heat to 350°F and bake for 5 to 7 minutes more, until golden all over. Remove to a wire rack. Serve warm or at room temperature.

Sardinian Crackers

Pane Carasau

Pane Carasau is sold at many markets in Sardinia. The classic version is plain, but nowadays bakers make it with all kinds of garnishes. You can add sesame, anise, or nigella seeds to the dough; or you can brush the circles of dough with oil and top with salt, herbs, garlic, or onions before baking. Although the good commercial crackers are not easy to replicate at home, there is still a real thrill to making your own—to see how thin you can roll out the dough and how creatively you can choose flavorings or garnishes. The crackers may be eaten on their own as a snack or they can be served with other breads as part of a bread basket.

The crackers featured in the photograph (opposite) are my own version of the traditional pane carasau. Traditionally, the breads are made much larger, and once they puff up in the oven, they are taken out, and the two layers are separated to have two extremely thin sheets, which are placed back in the oven and baked until they harden and become crackers. My crackers puffed up unevenly. I liked the way they looked and I decided to carry on baking them as they were until they became crackers.

MAKES 12 LARGE CRACKERS

1 cup unbleached all-purpose flour, plus extra for kneading and
     shaping
1 cup fine semolina or semolina flour
1 teaspoon fine kosher salt or sea salt

1. Combine the flours and salt in a large bowl and make a well in the center. Gradually add ¾ cup warm water, bringing in the flour as you go along. Knead until you have a rough ball of dough.

2. Remove the dough to a lightly floured work surface. Knead for 3 minutes. Invert the bowl over the dough and let rest for 15 minutes. Knead for about 2 to 3 minutes more, until the dough is smooth and elastic. Shape into a ball, invert the bowl over the dough again, and let rest for 30 minutes.

3. Divide the dough into 12 equal pieces and shape each piece into a ball. Place the balls on a floured work surface and sprinkle them with a little flour. Cover with plastic wrap and let rest for 15 minutes. Meanwhile, preheat the oven to 450°F.

4. Flatten one ball of dough slightly, dip it in flour on both sides, and shake off the excess flour. Roll it out to as thin a circle as you can, sprinkling with a little flour as needed so that it doesn't stick.

5. Transfer the circle of dough to a large nonstick baking sheet or to a baking sheet lined with parchment paper or a silicone pastry mat. Roll out 1 or 2 more balls of dough (depending on how many will fit on the baking sheet) and transfer to the sheet.

6. Bake the crackers for 3 minutes, until lightly golden on top, then turn them with tongs and bake for 3 minutes more, until completely crisp. Transfer to a wire rack to cool. Roll out and bake the remaining crackers in the same manner. The crackers will keep, sealed in an airtight container, for up to 2 weeks.

✣ Holy Bread

Qurban

Also known as prosphoro or artos in Greece, this is the holy bread of communion in the Eastern Orthodox Church. It is stamped with the sign of the
cross, and inside the cross are Greek characters spelling out the words "Jesus
Christ Saves." I have bought the wooden stamps in the central market in Athens,
but you can also find them online. There is a fairly comprehensive description of
the communion ritual in Helen Corey's *The Art of Syrian Cookery:* how the priest
divides the bread and what each part means. But my main memory of these religious occasions is not so much of the ritual as of the sweet, slightly exotic taste of
the bread cube that the priest gave me to eat, followed by the delicious sip of
sweet wine. More recently I had my "madeleine moment" with this bread, when
I stopped at a church in the Coptic quarter in Cairo where they had quite large
qurban on sale, to raise money for a charitable cause. I bought one and ate my fill,
to make up for all those measly bites of communions past. The bread is delicious
on its own and it is also good for making sweet-savory sandwiches. I like it filled
with mortadella or kashkaval, a hard, mild sheep's-milk cheese also made in the
Balkans. Not a very holy suggestion, I know; but qurban is also sold in regular
bakeries for home consumption, so I am not the only one who's eating it outside
the church.

MAKES 6 INDIVIDUAL BREADS

2¼ teaspoons (1 package) active dry yeast

3⅓ cups unbleached all-purpose flour, plus extra for kneading and
    shaping

2 teaspoons fine kosher salt or sea salt

¼ cup sugar

¼ teaspoon mahlep (see page 79), optional

2 tablespoons unsalted butter, softened

1 tablespoon orange blossom water

1. Dissolve the yeast in ⅓ cup warm water and stir until creamy.

2. Combine the flour, salt, sugar, and, if using, mahlep in a large bowl and make a well in the center. Add the butter to the well and with fingertips rub it into the flour until well incorporated. Add the yeast and orange blossom water and gradually add ½ cup warm water, bringing in the flour as you go along. Knead until you have a rough ball of dough.

3. Remove the dough to a lightly floured work surface. Knead for 3 minutes. Shape the dough into a ball, invert the bowl over it, and let rest for 15 minutes. Knead for about 2 to 3 minutes more, until the dough is smooth and elastic. Shape into a ball again and transfer to a lightly floured clean bowl. Cover with

plastic wrap and let rise in a warm, draft-free place for 1 hour. Fold the dough (see pages 6–7), cover again, and let rise for 1 hour more. The dough should be about doubled in volume.

4. Return the dough to the work surface, divide into 6 equal pieces, and shape each piece into a ball. Cover with plastic wrap and let rest for 15 minutes.

5. Roll out the balls of dough to circles about 6 inches in diameter. Transfer to a nonstick baking sheet, or to a baking sheet lined with parchment paper or a silicone pastry mat. Cover with a wet but not dripping kitchen towel and let rise for 1 hour, uncovering the breads after about 50 minutes to allow the surface to dry. Preheat the oven to 400°F.

6. Sift a thin film of flour over each bread. Stamp the surface with the special stamp that is used for holy bread, or score the surface lightly with the tip of a

knife to create geometric designs. With a chopstick or other thin stick, make 5 holes at regular intervals around the outer rim of the stamp; this keeps the bread from puffing during baking. Bake for 15 to 20 minutes, until golden. Transfer to a wire rack to cool. Serve at room temperature, perhaps with a very good unsalted butter.

Sweet Fougasse from the Aveyron

Fouace Aveyronnaise

Fouace Aveyronnaise is a specialty of Albi, Toulouse-Lautrec's birthplace, and is one of the most ancient celebration breads in the southwest of France. It is prepared to celebrate the arrival of the Magi on the day of Epiphany, January 6, or the arrival of the first days of spring at Easter. It's served piping hot with good salted butter, goat cheese, or pork rillettes. I like to have mine for breakfast, either plain or with a little unsalted butter. There is a wonderful passage in the first book of Rabelais's *Gargantua* in which he recounts the Picrocholine War, in which Picrochole fights Gargantua and Grangousier. The conflict starts because Grangousier's shepherds appropriate a couple of baskets of fouaces after the fouace maker (*fouacier*) refuses to sell them the breads. Sometimes fouace Aveyronnaise is made more like a brioche. However, the traditional version, as in this recipe, is denser.

SERVES 6

2 ounces levain (see page 111)

Heaping ½ teaspoon (¼ package) active dry yeast

1 tablespoon orange blossom water

1⅔ cups unbleached all-purpose flour, plus extra for kneading and
    shaping

3 medium eggs

⅓ cup confectioners' sugar

1 teaspoon fine kosher salt or sea salt

5 tablespoons unsalted butter, softened

1. On the day before: Make the levain. On the day of cooking: Refresh the levain and let ferment; see page 111.

2. Dissolve the yeast in the orange blossom water and stir until creamy.

3. Place the flour in a large bowl and make a well in the center. Break 2 of the eggs into the well. Add the sugar and salt and yeast mixture, mix these in with the eggs, and then mix all with the flour.

4. Add the levain to the flour mixture. Knead until the dough comes away neatly from the sides and bottom of the bowl. The dough will be quite sticky.

5. Remove the dough to a lightly floured work surface. Sprinkle the dough with more flour. Knead for 3 minutes. Invert the bowl over the dough and let rest for 15 minutes. Flatten the dough slightly by hand and distribute the butter over it. With fists, press the butter into the dough, then fold and knead until the butter is well incorporated. Shape the dough into a ball, place in a lightly floured clean bowl, cover with plastic wrap, and let rise in a warm, draft-free place for 3 hours, folding the dough (see pages 6–7) after 1 hour and again after the second hour. The dough should have doubled in volume.

6. Return the dough to the work surface and divide it into 6 equal pieces. Working quickly and delicately so that the dough is not overworked, shape each piece into a ball. Cover with plastic wrap and let rest for 15 minutes. Flatten the balls by hand into circles about ¾ inch thick. Transfer to a large nonstick baking sheet, or to a baking sheet lined with parchment paper or a silicone pastry mat. Cover with a wet but not dripping kitchen towel and let rise for 1 hour. Meanwhile, preheat the oven to 425°F and beat the remaining egg with a small pinch of salt.

7. Brush the tops of the fouaces with the beaten egg. Bake for 15 to 20 minutes, until golden brown all over. Serve hot or warm, or let cool on a wire rack and freeze.

❖ Ramadan Breads with Dates

Khobz Ramadan

Y ou will find these breads all over the souks of Tripoli, Damascus, and Aleppo
during Ramadan, the Muslim month of fasting. They are sold on vendors' carts
and in bakeries, and they are also made at home. Some are made small and others
very large; the big ones are pricked or scored decoratively on top. The breads freeze
very well, and I usually freeze a batch to have for breakfast every now and then.

SERVES 6

¾ teaspoon (⅓ package) active dry yeast

3⅓ cups unbleached all-purpose flour, plus extra for kneading and shaping

½ teaspoon powdered milk

¾ teaspoon baking powder

¼ cup sugar

⅛ teaspoon fine kosher salt or sea salt

½ tablespoon unsalted butter, softened

4 teaspoons extra-virgin olive oil

8 ounces pitted dates, preferably Medjool dates (about 10 Medjool dates)

4 tablespoons unsalted butter

½ cup toasted white sesame seeds

1 egg yolk beaten with 1 teaspoon water

1. Dissolve the yeast in 2 tablespoons warm water and stir until creamy.

2. Combine the flour, powdered milk, baking powder, sugar, and salt in a large
bowl and make a well in the center. Add the ½ tablespoon butter and the oil to

the well and, with fingertips, rub them into the flour until well incorporated. Add the yeast and gradually add 1 cup warm water, bringing in the flour as you go along. Knead until you have a rough ball of dough.

3. Remove the dough to a lightly floured work surface. Knead for 3 minutes. Invert the bowl over the dough and let rest for 15 minutes. Knead for about 2 to 3 minutes more, until the dough is smooth and elastic. Shape into a ball and place in a lightly floured clean bowl. Cover with plastic wrap and let rise in a warm, draft-free place for 1 hour. Fold the dough (see pages 6–7), cover again, and let rise for 1 hour more. The dough should have doubled in volume.

4. Meanwhile, coarsely chop the dates in a food processor. Add the 4 tablespoons butter and process to a fine paste. Shape the paste by hand into a ball, wrap in plastic wrap, and set aside in the refrigerator.

5. Return the dough to the work surface. Divide it into 6 equal pieces, and shape each piece into a ball. Cover with plastic wrap and let rest for 15 minutes.

6. Shape the date paste into a cylinder and divide the cylinder into 6 equal pieces. Roll each piece into a ball. Roll out 1 ball of dough to a circle about 6 inches in diameter. Flatten a ball of date paste to a circle about 4½ inches in diameter, and place the date circle in the middle of the dough. Fold the edges of the dough over to completely cover the filling. Pinch the edges to seal, and flatten the bread a little more by hand to make an even circle.

7. Scatter half the sesame seeds over a large nonstick baking sheet or a baking sheet lined with parchment paper or a silicone pastry mat. Transfer the filled bread seam side down to the baking sheet. Cover with plastic wrap. Make the remaining breads in the same way. Cover with a wet but not dripping kitchen towel and let rise for 45 minutes. Meanwhile, preheat the oven to 450°F.

8. Brush the breads with the beaten egg yolk and sprinkle the remaining sesame seeds over the tops. Bake for 12 to 15 minutes, until golden brown all over. Transfer to a wire rack to cool. Serve at room temperature.

✛ Spanish Sweet Oil Bread

Tortas de Aceites

Tortas de Aceites are a favorite breakfast in Seville, where the little breads are dipped in hot chocolate—not perhaps the most slimming start for the day but scrumptious all the same. Some Spanish cooks bake these tortas for a long time at a low temperature, yielding up something more like a sweet cracker than a bread. One advantage of this method is that the tortas will keep longer. I prefer to bake mine more quickly, just until golden but still soft.

MAKES 22 SMALL BREADS

1½ teaspoons (⅔ package) active dry yeast

4 tablespoons plus ¼ teaspoon sugar, plus extra for sprinkling over the breads

3⅔ cups unbleached all-purpose flour, plus extra if needed

1⅓ teaspoons fine kosher salt or sea salt

⅓ cup extra-virgin olive oil, plus extra for greasing the bowl

1 thin strip unwaxed orange zest

1 teaspoon aniseed

⅓ teaspoon baking soda

⅓ teaspoon ground cinnamon

⅛ cup toasted white sesame seeds

1. On the day before: Dissolve the yeast and ¼ teaspoon of the sugar in ⅓ cup warm water and stir until creamy. Add ⅔ cup of the flour and mix until you have a rough, sticky dough. Cover with plastic wrap and let ferment in a warm, draft-free place overnight. This will be the sponge.

2. On the day of cooking: Combine 2⅔ cups of the flour and the salt in a large bowl and make a well in the center. Add the sponge to the well and gradually add ¾ cup plus 2 tablespoons warm water, bringing in the flour as you go along. Knead until you have a rough dough.

3. Remove the dough to a lightly floured work surface and knead for 3 minutes. Invert the bowl over the dough and let rest for 15 minutes. Knead for about 2 to 3 minutes more, until the dough is smooth and elastic. Roll into a ball and place in a lightly oiled clean bowl, turning the dough to coat all over. Cover with plastic wrap and let rise in a warm, draft-free place for 1 hour. Fold the dough (see pages 6–7), cover again, and let rise for 1 hour more. The dough should have doubled in volume.

4. Heat the olive oil in a small saucepan over medium heat. Add the orange zest and cook it until it browns. Remove from the heat, add the aniseed, and set aside to let cool. Once the oil is completely cool, discard the zest. Stir in 4 tablespoons of the sugar and the baking soda and cinnamon.

5. With hands, smear the work surface with a quarter of the oil mixture from the pan. Remove the dough to the work surface and flatten it into a large rectangle. Smear the remaining oil mixture over the dough and, with knuckles, knead it into the dough. Pick up the corners and fold the dough to the center repeatedly, adding a little flour at each fold, until the remaining ⅓ cup flour is incorporated.

6. Knead for 3 minutes. Invert the bowl over the dough and let rest for 15 minutes. Knead for about 2 to 3 minutes more, until the dough is somewhat smooth and elastic. Roll the dough into a ball and place in a lightly oiled clean bowl. Cover with plastic wrap and let rise for 45 minutes. Meanwhile, preheat the oven to 350°F.

7. Divide the dough into 22 equal pieces. Roll the pieces into balls, cover them with plastic wrap, and let rest for 15 minutes. Flatten each ball by hand into a circle about 4 inches in diameter. Transfer to a nonstick baking sheet, or to a

baking sheet lined with parchment paper or a silicone pastry mat, covering the breads with plastic wrap after they go on the baking sheet.

8. When ready to bake, remove the plastic wrap and sprinkle the breads lightly with sugar and then with the sesame seeds. Bake for 20 to 25 minutes, until lightly crisp and golden. Transfer to a wire rack to cool. Serve at room temperature or store, tightly sealed, for up to 1 week.

Catalan Sweet "Pizza"

Coca

This is my adaptation of a recipe that appears in Colman Andrews's *Catalan Cuisine*. *Coques* (the plural of *coca*) are much like pizzas, except that they are shaped oval instead of round and can be sweet or savory. Savory versions are made variously with sausages, anchovies, olives, onions, peppers, and spinach, among other ingredients. This recipe is for a sweet version, topped with pine nuts and sugar. In Catalonia, cooks add candied fruits, such as orange peel, cherries, and pineapple, to the pine nuts to celebrate the feast of Saint John.

MAKES 2 INDIVIDUAL COQUES

2¼ teaspoons (1 package) active dry yeast
3⅔ cups unbleached all-purpose flour, plus extra for kneading
2 teaspoons fine kosher salt or sea salt
3 tablespoons extra-virgin olive oil, plus extra for greasing the baking
    sheet and brushing the coques
Sugar
⅓ cup pine nuts
Anisette or other sweet anise-flavored liqueur, to drizzle over the
    coques

1. Dissolve the yeast in 2 tablespoons warm water and stir until creamy.

2. Combine the flour and salt in a large bowl and make a well in the center. Add the oil to the well and, with fingertips, rub the oil into the flour until well

incorporated. Add the yeast and gradually add 1 cup warm water, mixing with the flour as you go along. Knead until you have a rough dough.

3. Remove the dough to a lightly floured work surface. Knead for 3 minutes. Invert the bowl over the dough and let rest for 15 minutes. Knead for about 2 to 3 minutes more, until the dough is smooth and elastic. Shape the dough into a ball and transfer to a clean bowl greased with a little olive oil. Turn the dough to coat with oil. Cover with plastic wrap and let rise in a warm, draft-free place for 1 hour. Fold the dough (see pages 6–7), cover again, and let rise for 1 hour more.

4. Preheat the oven to 450°F. Return the dough to the work surface, divide in half, and shape each half into a ball. Cover with plastic wrap and let rest for 15 minutes. Flatten each ball of dough into an oval about ½ inch thick.

5. Grease a large nonstick baking sheet with a little olive oil. Dust the sheet with sugar and transfer the coques to the baking sheet. Brush the coques with a little oil. Score the top of each coca with a sharp knife to make several medium diamonds. Press on the edges of the breads to form a low rim. Sprinkle the coques with a little sugar. Sprinkle the pine nuts evenly over the breads, then drizzle with a little anisette. Bake for 15 minutes, or until golden brown all over. Transfer to a wire rack to cool. Serve warm or at room temperature.

Plain Raised Breads

✢ Basic Levain

Levain

Not very many Mediterranean bread recipes begin with *levain,* which is a traditional sourdough starter. To make it, one starts with a *levain chef,* which in old bakeries was simply a leftover piece of dough from the previous day. There are many ways to make a levain. Basile Kamir, a Parisian baker who is the author of *La Journée du Pain* (*The Day of Bread*), makes his in a manner that I find much easier and less time-consuming than other methods. This is my adaptation of his levain. The recipe yields about 12 ounces, enough for about a half dozen loaves of bread. If you are making fewer than that, store the extra levain by dividing it into small pieces, each weighing about 2 ounces. Cover each piece in plastic wrap and freeze. To use, let thaw and reach room temperature. Refresh it by treating it as if it is a levain chef, and follow step 2.

MAKES ABOUT 12 OUNCES

For the levain chef
⅓ cup medium rye flour
1 teaspoon honey

For the levain
½ cup unbleached all-purpose flour, plus extra for kneading
½ cup medium rye flour

1. On the day before, make the levain chef: Put the rye flour and honey in a mixing bowl. Add 5 teaspoons warm water and knead briefly to make a rather wet dough. Cover with plastic wrap. Let ferment in a warm, draft-free place for at least 12 hours and up to 24 hours. The longer the levain chef ferments, the more flavorful it becomes.

2. Make the levain: Transfer the levain chef to a medium bowl. Add the flours and a scant ⅓ cup warm water. Knead briefly to make a rough ball of dough. Remove the dough to a lightly floured work surface and knead for about 5 minutes, until it is smooth and elastic. Place in a lightly floured clean bowl, cover with plastic wrap, and let ferment in a warm, draft-free place for 4 hours. Use to make a bread, or store for future use.

✣ Provençal Bread from Aix

Pain d'Aix

This is a great bread for sandwiches; it's slightly crusty on the outside and has a tasty, soft crumb that is not too sour despite being made with sourdough. What is interesting here, I think, is the way the bread is shaped in layers as it's made. Although much of the layering is lost in the baking, some remains and gives the bread an interesting texture.

MAKES 4 INDIVIDUAL BREADS

Heaping ½ teaspoon (¼ package) active dry yeast
1⅔ cups unbleached all-purpose flour, plus extra for kneading and
    shaping
1 teaspoon fine kosher salt or sea salt
2 ounces levain (see page 111)
10 to 15 ice cubes

1. Dissolve the yeast in 2 tablespoons warm water and stir until creamy.

2. Combine the flour and salt in a large bowl and make a well in the center. Add the yeast and gradually add another ½ cup warm water, bringing in the flour as you go along. Knead briefly to make a rough, sticky ball of dough.

3. Remove the dough to a lightly floured work surface. Sprinkle the dough with a little more flour. Knead for 3 minutes. Invert the bowl over the dough and let rest for 15 minutes. Knead the levain into the dough, sprinkling with a little flour if the dough is too sticky, until the dough is smooth and elastic and the

levain is well incorporated, about 5 minutes. Shape into a ball and place in a lightly floured clean bowl. Cover with plastic wrap. Let rise in a warm, draft-free place for 1 hour. Fold the dough (see pages 6–7), cover again, let rise for 1 hour more, fold again, and let rise for 30 minutes more. The dough should have doubled in volume.

4. Return the dough to the work surface. Shape the dough into a ball, cover with plastic wrap, and let rest for 15 minutes. With a rolling pin, roll out the dough to a rectangle 18 to 20 inches long and 6 to 8 inches wide, sprinkling the dough and the work surface with flour every now and then. Brush the dough with a little cold water, fold one long third of the rectangle over the center, and then fold the opposite third over that. Rotate 90 degrees and roll out again to a rectangle about the same size as the first one. Brush with water and fold again in thirds. With a dough cutter, cut the dough perpendicular to the folds into 4 equal pieces. Transfer the pieces fold side up to a nonstick baking sheet, or to a baking sheet lined with parchment paper or a silicone pastry mat. Cover with a wet but not dripping kitchen towel and let rise for 1¼ hours more. Meanwhile, preheat the oven to 450°F. Place a medium baking dish on the bottom of the oven.

5. Immediately before baking, toss the ice cubes into the baking dish on the oven bottom to create steam. Place the breads in the oven and bake for 15 minutes. Reduce the heat to 350°F and bake for 15 to 20 minutes more, until the breads are well puffed up and golden brown all over. Transfer to a wire rack to cool. Serve at room temperature or reheated.

✣ French Rye Bread

Pain au Seigle

Although some people find rye breads too heavy for their taste, the combination of all-purpose and rye flours makes this a relatively light, and very slightly sweet, bread.

MAKES 1 MEDIUM BAGUETTE

Heaping ½ teaspoon (¼ package) active dry yeast
⅔ cup unbleached all-purpose flour, plus extra for kneading and
    shaping
1⅓ cups medium rye flour
1 teaspoon fine kosher salt or sea salt
4½ ounces levain (see page 111)
10 to 15 ice cubes

1. Dissolve the yeast in 2 tablespoons warm water and stir until creamy.

2. Combine the flours and the salt in a large bowl and make a well in the center. Place the levain in the well. Add the yeast and gradually add another ½ cup warm water, bringing in the flour and mixing with the levain. Knead briefly to make a rough ball of dough.

3. Remove the dough to a work surface. Knead for 3 minutes. Invert the bowl over the dough and let rest for 15 minutes. Knead for about 2 to 3 minutes more, until the dough is smooth and elastic. Shape into a ball and place in a lightly floured clean bowl. Cover with plastic wrap and let rise in a warm, draft-

free place for 1 hour. Fold the dough (see pages 6–7), cover again, and let rise for 1 hour more. The dough should have doubled in volume.

4. Return the dough to the work surface. Shape again into a ball, cover with a damp kitchen towel, and let rest for 15 minutes.

5. Shape the dough into a baguette (see page 9) about 16 to 18 inches long. Place the baguette on a nonstick baking sheet, or on a baking sheet lined with parchment paper or a silicone pastry mat. Cover with a wet but not dripping kitchen towel and let rise for 1 hour. Meanwhile, preheat the oven to 450°F. Place a medium baking dish on the bottom of the oven.

6. Slash the top of the bread with a lame, preferably, or a razor blade or very sharp knife (see page 10), making the same cuts as on a baguette. Immediately before baking, toss the ice cubes into the baking dish on the oven bottom to create steam. Bake the baguette for 35 to 45 minutes, until golden brown. Check after 15 minutes to make sure it is not coloring too fast; if it is, reduce the heat to 350°F. Transfer to a wire rack to cool. Serve warm or at room temperature or reheated.

✸ French Country Bread

Pain de Campagne

This traditional bread starts out with what may seem like an unmanageably wet dough. But there is nothing to fear: Simply be generous with flour on the work surface and knead lightly. Here the bread is shaped round, as a boule, but it may be formed into a bâtard as well; see page 9.

MAKES 1 MEDIUM LOAF

1½ teaspoons (⅔ package) active dry yeast
2⅔ cups unbleached all-purpose flour, plus extra for kneading and
    shaping
1½ teaspoons fine kosher salt or sea salt
10 to 15 ice cubes

1. Dissolve the yeast in ½ cup warm water in a medium bowl. Add 1 cup of the flour. Mix with a spoon to make a very wet dough. Cover with plastic wrap and let rise in a warm, draft-free place for 3 hours. This is the poolish.

2. Combine the remaining 1⅔ cups flour and the salt in a large bowl and make a well in the center. Add the poolish to the well and gradually add ½ cup warm water, bringing in the flour as you go along. Knead briefly to make a rough, quite wet ball of dough.

3. Remove the dough to a floured work surface and sprinkle the dough with more flour. Knead for 3 minutes, sprinkling with more flour if necessary. Invert the bowl over the dough and let rest for 15 minutes. Knead the dough for

about 2 to 3 minutes more, until it is smooth and elastic. Shape the dough into a ball, place in a lightly floured clean bowl, and cover with plastic wrap. Let rise in a warm, draft-free place for 1 hour. Fold the dough (see pages 6–7), cover again, and let rise for 1 hour more. The dough should have doubled in volume.

4. Return the dough to the work surface. Shape gently into a tight ball, taking care to deflate as few air bubbles as possible. Place on a large nonstick baking sheet, or on a baking sheet lined with parchment paper or a silicone pastry mat. Cover with a wet but not dripping kitchen towel and let rise for 1 hour, until doubled in volume. Meanwhile, preheat the oven to 450°F. Place a medium baking dish on the bottom of the oven.

5. Sift a little flour over the bread. With a lame, preferably, or with a razor blade or very sharp knife, carefully cut a square pattern over the top (see page 10). Immediately before baking, toss the ice cubes into the baking dish on the oven bottom to create steam. Bake for 15 minutes, reduce the heat to 350°F, and bake for 35 to 40 minutes more, until golden brown. Transfer to a wire rack to cool. Serve warm or at room temperature, or reheated.

❖ Regular Italian Bread

Pane Commune

Bread is ever-present at the Italian table. In the cities, it's usually in the shape of a rosette, which is impossible to replicate without the particular machine that bakers use to stamp the dough in the rosette form. In the country there is a variety, by region, of loaves and shapes. This versatile bread has a thin crust and a soft, fluffy crumb that can be shaped in many ways—as rolls, mini baguettes, banana shapes, and more. This same dough may be used for calzones, and for pizza if you like a thick and spongy crust.

MAKES 6 SMALL BREADS

Heaping teaspoon (½ package) active dry yeast
2⅓ cups unbleached all-purpose flour, plus extra for kneading and
    shaping
1½ teaspoons fine kosher salt or sea salt
10 to 15 ice cubes

1. Dissolve the yeast in 2 tablespoons warm water in a medium bowl. Stir until creamy. Add ⅓ cup of the flour and mix to make a small ball of dough. This is the sponge, or biga, as it is called in Italian.

2. Put 1 cup of the flour in a large bowl. Place the biga in the middle of the flour. Cover with the remaining 1 cup flour, and cover the bowl with plastic wrap. Let rise in a warm, draft-free place for at least 6 hours or overnight.

3. Dissolve the salt in ⅔ cup warm water. Push aside the flour that covers the biga, making sure the biga remains in the middle of the flour. Gradually add the salted water, bringing in the flour as you go along. Knead to make a rough ball of dough.

4. Remove the dough to a lightly floured work surface. Knead for 3 minutes. Invert the bowl over the dough and let rest for 15 minutes. Knead for about 2 to 3 minutes more, until the dough is smooth and elastic. Shape the dough into a ball and place in a lightly floured clean bowl. Cover with plastic wrap and let rise in a warm, draft-free place for 1 hour. Fold the dough (see pages 6–7), cover again, and let rise for 1 hour more. The dough should have doubled in volume.

5. Return the dough to the work surface. Divide it into 6 equal pieces and shape each piece into a ball. Cover with a damp kitchen towel and let rest for 15 minutes. Shape the balls as small buns, or banana-shaped loaves, or mini baguettes (see pages 9–10), or make all three shapes to have an assortment. Place on a nonstick baking sheet, or on a baking sheet lined with parchment paper or a silicone pastry mat. Cover with a wet but not dripping kitchen towel and let rise for 45 minutes. Meanwhile, preheat the oven to 450°F. Place a medium baking dish on the bottom of the oven.

6. Immediately before baking, toss the ice cubes into the baking dish on the oven bottom to create steam. Bake for 15 to 20 minutes, until golden all over. Transfer to a wire rack to cool. Serve at room temperature, or reheated.

Pugliese Bread

Pane Pugliese

There are several versions of Pugliese bread, including one from Altamura, made with *semola* (semolina flour), and one from the southern part of the heel, made with *farina di grano duro* (durum wheat flour). This leads to some confusion, as both flours are from the same durum wheat, the hardest of all wheats. Carol Field explains the differences in her book *The Italian Baker*. According to her, semola is made "from the amber-colored granular grain that comes from grinding the heart of the durum wheat berry," whereas *farina di grano duro,* or durum flour, is "a creamy, silky fine golden flour milled from durum wheat." The texture of the bread made with semola is slightly coarser and yellow in color. Ideally, the following recipe should be made with durum flour, but if it is unavailable, use unbleached all-purpose flour. The texture of the bread will be a little less interesting but still very good. You can also make it with semolina flour to approximate the Altamura loaf. If you use semolina flour, use a little more water. The flour is coarser and has a higher protein content, and as a result needs more hydration.

MAKES 1 ROUND LOAF

Heaping teaspoon (½ package) active dry yeast
2⅔ cups durum flour, semolina flour, or unbleached all-purpose flour,
    plus extra for kneading and shaping
1½ teaspoons fine kosher salt or sea salt
2 tablespoons extra-virgin olive oil, plus extra for greasing the bowl

1. Dissolve the yeast in ¼ cup warm water and stir until creamy.

2. Combine the flour and salt in a large bowl and make a well in the center. Add the 2 tablespoons oil to the well and, with fingertips, rub it into the flour until well incorporated. Add the yeast and gradually add ½ cup warm water, bringing in the flour as you go along. Knead briefly to make a rough ball of dough.

3. Remove the dough to a lightly floured work surface. Knead for 3 minutes. Invert the bowl over the dough and let rest for 15 minutes. Knead for about 2 to 3 minutes more, until the dough is smooth and elastic. Grease a clean bowl with a little olive oil. Shape the dough into a ball and place it in the bowl, turning to coat it all over. Cover with plastic wrap and let rise in a warm, draft-free place for 1 hour. Fold the dough (see pages 6–7), cover again, and let rise for 1 hour more. The dough should have doubled in volume.

4. Return the dough to the work surface. Shape into a round loaf, or boule (see page 9). Place on a nonstick baking sheet, or on a baking sheet lined with parch-

ment paper or a silicone pastry mat. Cover with a wet but not dripping kitchen towel and let rise for 1 to 1½ hours, until doubled in volume. Meanwhile, preheat the oven to 450°F. Place a medium baking dish on the bottom of the oven.

5. Immediately before baking, toss the ice cubes into the baking dish on the oven bottom to create steam. Bake for 10 minutes, reduce the heat to 400°F, and bake for 35 to 45 minutes more, until golden brown all over. Transfer to a wire rack to cool. Serve at room temperature or reheated.

✛ Tuscan Bread

Pane Toscano

Tuscan bread is one of those rare unsalted breads that is actually good. That Tuscans don't use salt in their bread may have something to do with a prohibitive tax imposed on salt centuries ago. The absence of salt and other flavorings does give the bread a somewhat plain character, but that just makes it all the better for dipping in sauces or, even better, for making bruschette or crostini.

MAKES 1 ROUND OR OVAL LOAF

2¼ teaspoons (1 package) active dry yeast

3 cups unbleached all-purpose flour, plus extra for kneading and shaping

Semolina flour, preferably, or additional all-purpose flour, for sprinkling over the baking sheet

10 to 15 ice cubes

1. Dissolve the yeast in ¼ cup warm water in a medium bowl and stir until creamy. Add ½ cup of the flour and mix briefly to make a fairly wet ball of dough. Cover with plastic wrap and let rise in a warm, draft-free place for about 1 hour, until doubled in size. This is the sponge, or biga.

2. Put the remaining 2½ cups of flour in a large bowl and make a well in the center. Add the sponge to the well. Knead as much of the flour into the sponge as the sponge will take, then gradually add ¾ cup plus 1 to 2 tablespoons warm water (depending on how much the dough will take), bringing in the remaining flour until it is incorporated. Knead briefly to make a rough ball of dough.

3. Remove the dough to a lightly floured work surface. Knead for 3 minutes. Invert the bowl over the dough and let rest for 15 minutes. Knead for about 2 to 3 minutes more, until the dough is smooth and elastic.

4. Sprinkle enough semolina flour over a baking sheet to cover it lightly. Shape the dough into an oval or round loaf; see pages 9–10. Transfer the loaf to the baking sheet. Cover with a wet but not dripping kitchen towel and let rise for about 1 hour, until doubled in volume. Meanwhile, preheat the oven to 400°F. Place a medium baking dish on the bottom of the oven.

5. Immediately before baking, make a slash down the middle of the top of the loaf with a lame, preferably, or with a razor blade or very sharp knife (see page 10). Toss the ice cubes in the baking dish on the oven bottom to create steam. Bake for 40 to 50 minutes, until the loaf is golden brown all over. Transfer to a wire rack to cool. Serve at room temperature, or reheated.

Sicilian Bread

Pane Casereccio

Sicilian bread is quite different from other Italian breads. It is generally called *pane giallo,* yellow bread, because it is made with semolina flour and therefore has a yellow crumb. It is made in different shapes, too, the most popular being *esse casereccio,* a plain S-shaped bread that can be made large or small. Other shapes include thin baguette-like breads, called *filoni;* star-shaped ones; and attractive snake-like breads. Most of the time Sicilian bakers sprinkle the breads with sesame seeds, which adds a nutty flavor.

I learned how to make pane casereccio from the family that owns and runs the charming Panificio Bianca in Siracusa, where I spent a fascinating morning talking to Signora Bianca and her family and watching her son, Giuseppe Bottaro, make different breads and biscotti.

MAKES 6 INDIVIDUAL BREADS

Heaping teaspoon (½ package) active dry yeast
3 cups fine semolina or semolina flour
2 teaspoons fine kosher salt or sea salt
Unbleached all-purpose flour, for kneading and shaping
4 to 6 tablespoons white sesame seeds
10 to 15 ice cubes

1. Dissolve the yeast in ¼ cup warm water and stir until creamy.

2. Combine the semolina and salt in a large bowl and make a well in the center. Add the yeast and gradually add 1 cup plus 2 tablespoons warm water, bring-

ing in the flour as you go along. Knead briefly to make a rough ball of dough.

3. Remove the dough to a lightly floured work surface. Knead for 3 minutes. Invert the bowl over the dough and let rest for 15 minutes. Knead the dough, adding all-purpose flour to hands and work surface as needed (it is a soft and sticky dough), for about 2 to 3 minutes more, until it is smooth and elastic. Shape the dough into a ball and place in a lightly floured clean bowl. Cover with plastic wrap and let rise in a warm, draft-free place for 1 hour. Fold the dough (see pages 6–7), cover again, and let rise for 1 hour more. The dough should have doubled in volume.

4. Return the dough to the work surface. Divide the dough into 6 equal pieces. Shape each piece into a ball, cover with a damp kitchen towel, and let rest for

15 minutes. Shape each ball into a strand (see page 10) about 20 inches long and make S shapes with the strands. Sprinkle a large nonstick baking sheet, or a baking sheet lined with parchment paper or a silicone pastry mat, with a thin layer of sesame seeds. Transfer the breads to the baking sheet, leaving at least 2 inches between them to allow for expansion. Cover with a wet but not dripping kitchen towel and let rise for about 45 minutes. Meanwhile, preheat the oven to 450°F. Place a medium baking dish on the bottom of the oven.

5. Brush the tops of the breads with a little water and sprinkle with sesame seeds. Immediately before baking, toss the ice cubes into the baking dish on the oven bottom to create steam. Bake for 20 to 25 minutes, until well puffed up and golden brown all over. Transfer to a wire rack to cool. Serve at room temperature, or reheated.

Spanish Country Bread

Pan Campesino

This country bread varies in shape from one region of Spain to another, but the dough remains essentially the same, producing a plain, crusty white bread.

MAKES 1 ROUND LOAF

2¼ teaspoons (1 package) active dry yeast
¼ teaspoon sugar
3⅓ cups unbleached all-purpose flour, plus extra for kneading and shaping
2 teaspoons fine kosher salt or sea salt
Extra-virgin olive oil, for greasing the bowl
10 to 15 ice cubes

1. Dissolve the yeast in ⅓ cup warm water in a medium bowl and stir until creamy. Add the sugar and ⅔ cup of the flour and mix, using a spoon, to make a rough and very wet ball of dough. This will be the sponge. Cover with plastic wrap and let ferment at room temperature at least 6 hours or overnight.

2. Combine the remaining 2⅔ cups flour and the salt in a large bowl and make a well in the center. Add the sponge to the well. Gradually add ¾ cup plus 2 table-spoons warm water, bringing in the flour as you go along. Knead briefly to make a rough ball of dough.

3. Remove the dough to a lightly floured work surface. Knead for 3 minutes. Invert the bowl over the dough and let rest for 15 minutes. Knead for about 2 to

3 minutes more, until the dough is smooth and elastic. Shape into a ball. Lightly grease a large bowl with olive oil. Place the dough in the bowl, turning to coat it all over. Cover with plastic wrap and let rise in a warm, draft-free place for 1 hour. Fold the dough (see pages 6–7), cover again, and let rise for 1 hour more. The dough should have doubled in volume.

4. Return the dough to the work surface. Shape into a ball, cover with a damp kitchen towel, and let rest for 15 minutes.

5. Flatten the dough by hand into a circle about 8 inches in diameter. Transfer to a nonstick baking sheet, or to a baking sheet lined with parchment paper or a silicone pastry mat. Cover with a wet but not dripping kitchen towel and let rise for 45 minutes, until not quite doubled in size. Meanwhile, preheat the oven to 450°F. Place a medium baking dish on the bottom of the oven.

6. Immediately before baking, toss the ice cubes into the baking dish on the oven bottom to create steam. Bake for 15 minutes. Then check on the bread: If it is coloring too fast, lower the temperature to 350°F. Bake for 20 to 35 minutes more, until golden brown all over. Transfer to a wire rack to cool. Serve at room temperature, or reheated.

Flavored Raised Breads

Cheese and Salami Ring

Tortano Ripieno

One version of the origins of *tortano* says that it means "a pie, not really"—from *torta,* meaning "pie," and *no,* meaning "no." It is aptly named. I think it's closer to a bread than a pie. Tortano makes a nice accompaniment for antipasti, or you can serve slices on their own as a snack.

SERVES 6 TO 8

For the dough

4½ teaspoons (2 packages) active dry yeast

2 cups unbleached all-purpose flour, plus extra for kneading and
    shaping

½ teaspoon fine kosher salt or sea salt

1 teaspoon freshly ground black pepper

3 ounces lard, preferably, or unsalted butter, plus extra for greasing a
    ring mold or a baking sheet

1 cup grated Parmigiano-Reggiano (about 2 ounces)

For the filling

½ cup finely diced Gruyère (about 2 ounces)

½ cup finely diced provolone (about 2 ounces)

¾ cup finely diced smoked provola or smoked mozzarella (about
    3 ounces)

½ cup finely diced fresh mozzarella (about 2 ounces)

¾ cup finely diced Italian-style salami (about 3 ounces)

2 hard-boiled eggs, each sliced into 6 wedges

1. Dissolve the yeast in ¼ cup warm water in a medium bowl and stir until creamy. Add ⅔ cup of the flour and knead until you have a firm dough. Shape the dough into a ball and place in a lightly floured clean bowl. Cover with plastic wrap and let rise for 1 hour in a warm, draft-free place. This will be the sponge, or biga.

2. Combine the remaining 1⅓ cups flour and the salt and pepper in a large bowl and make a well in the center. Add the lard to the well and, with fingertips, rub the lard into the flour until completely incorporated. Add the sponge and Parmesan and ¼ cup plus 1 tablespoon warm water. Knead briefly to make a rough ball of dough.

3. Remove the dough to a lightly floured work surface and knead for about 3 minutes. Invert the bowl over the dough and let rest for 15 minutes. Knead for 2 to 3 minutes more, until the dough is smooth and elastic. Shape into a ball and place in a lightly floured clean bowl. Cover with plastic wrap and let rise in a warm, draft-free place for 30 minutes. Fold the dough (see pages 6–7), and return it to the bowl, folded side down. Cover again and let rise for 30 to 45 minutes more, until doubled in volume. Meanwhile, combine the Gruyère, provolone, provola, mozzarella, and salami in a bowl. Cover and set aside.

4. Return the dough to the work surface. Shape it into a ball, cover with a damp kitchen towel, and let rest for 15 minutes. Lightly flour the work surface and place the ball of dough on it. Flatten the dough slightly by hand, sprinkle it lightly with flour, and roll it out to a large rectangle about ¼ inch thick, sprinkling with flour every now and then. If the dough won't roll out, let it rest for a few minutes before rolling out again.

5. Spread the filling over the dough, leaving about ½ inch free around the edges, and arrange the egg wedges in two rows parallel to a long side of the rectangle. Roll up the dough over the filling to form a large sausage. Press to seal the ends and join them to make a ring. Press to seal the joint.

6. Preheat the oven to 350°F. If you have a ring mold in which the tortano will fit comfortably, grease it with a little lard and place the tortano in it. If not, transfer the tortano to a nonstick baking sheet, or to a baking sheet lined with parch-

ment paper or a silicone pastry mat. Invert a heat-resistant bowl or cake mold and place it in the middle of the ring so that the tortano retains its shape as it rises and then bakes. Cover with plastic wrap smeared lightly with softened lard. Let rise for 30 minutes.

7. Remove the plastic wrap. Bake the tortano for 50 minutes to 1 hour, until golden all over. Let cool for 10 minutes, then gently transfer to a wire rack. Serve at room temperature, or reheated.

Rosemary and Raisin Bread

Pan di Ramerino

This bread is a specialty of the island of Giglio, off the coast of Tuscany. Italians sometimes call rosemary *rugiada del mare*, meaning "dew of the sea," because it grows abundant along the Mediterranean seashore. It is widely used in Tuscany, in breads and also in all kinds of meat dishes. This fragrant bread, with a cross cut on its top, is made throughout Tuscany during Easter week. Street vendors sell the breads from baskets on the evening of Maundy Thursday. The faithful buy it on their way to or from the sepulchre, to eat but also as a sign of devotion. In ancient Greece and later in the Roman Empire, rosemary was used as a remedy for coughs and liver aches, whereas in medieval times, it was used to repel evil spirits.

MAKES 6 INDIVIDUAL BREADS

2¼ teaspoons (1 package) active dry yeast

2 cups all-purpose unbleached flour, plus extra for kneading and shaping

¼ cup extra-virgin olive oil, plus extra for oiling the baking sheet

1 tablespoon fresh whole rosemary leaves

½ teaspoon fine kosher salt or sea salt

⅓ cup seedless raisins, soaked in hot water (about 2 ounces)

10 to 15 ice cubes

1. Dissolve the yeast in ¼ cup warm water in a medium bowl and stir until creamy. Add ½ cup of the flour and mix briefly to make a rough dough. Cover the bowl

with plastic wrap and let rise in a warm, draft-free place for about 1 hour, until well puffed up. This will be the sponge, or biga.

2. Put the oil and rosemary in a small frying pan over medium heat. Keep on the heat until the aroma of the rosemary rises. Set aside and let cool.

3. Combine the remaining 1½ cups flour and the salt in a large bowl and make a well in the center. Add the sponge to the well. Add the rosemary and its oil and gradually add ⅓ cup warm water, bringing in the flour as you go along. Knead briefly to make a rough ball of dough.

4. Remove the dough to a lightly floured work surface and knead for about 3 minutes. Invert the bowl over the dough and let rest for 15 minutes. Knead for 2 to 3 minutes more, until the dough is smooth and elastic. Flatten the dough into a large rectangle. Drain the raisins and spread them all over the dough. Fold one long third of the rectangle over the raisins, then fold the opposite long third to form a long envelope. Press down on the dough to embed the raisins in it. Divide the dough into 6 equal pieces. Gently shape each piece of dough into a ball. Flatten the balls lightly.

5. Transfer the small breads to a nonstick baking sheet, or to a baking sheet lined with parchment paper or a silicone pastry mat. Leave at least 2 inches between the breads to allow for expansion as they rise and bake. Cover with a wet but not dripping kitchen towel and let rise in a warm, draft-free place for about 30 minutes to 1 hour, until doubled in size. Meanwhile, preheat the oven to 400°F. Place a medium baking dish on the bottom rack of the oven.

6. Immediately before baking, toss the ice cubes into the baking dish on the oven bottom to create steam. Uncover the breads and bake them for 20 minutes, until golden brown all over. Transfer to a wire rack to cool. Serve at room temperature, or reheated.

Italian Sausage Bread

Pane alla Salsiccia

Y ou can make a vegetarian version of this bread by replacing the sausage with ¼ pound pitted green or black olives and using 2 tablespoons fresh thyme leaves instead of the sage.

MAKES 1 LARGE LOAF

Heaping tablespoon (1½ packages) active dry yeast

3⅓ cups all-purpose unbleached flour, plus extra for kneading and shaping

2 tablespoons extra-virgin olive oil, plus extra for greasing the bowl

¼ pound good-quality Italian sweet sausage (about 2 medium), cut into ½-inch pieces

3 or 4 fresh sage leaves, coarsely chopped

½ teaspoon fine kosher salt or sea salt

10 to 15 ice cubes

1. Dissolve the yeast in 3 tablespoons warm water in a medium bowl and stir until creamy. Add ⅓ cup of the flour and mix briefly to make a rough ball of dough, adding a little flour if the dough becomes sticky. Cover the bowl with plastic wrap and let rise in a warm, draft-free place for about 1 hour. This will be the sponge, or biga.

2. Heat 1 tablespoon of the oil in a frying pan over medium heat. Add the sausage slices and sage and sauté for 3 to 4 minutes, until the meat is barely cooked and the sage is slightly crisp. Set aside; do not discard the cooking oil.

3. Combine the remaining 3 cups flour and the salt in a large bowl and make a well in the center. Add the remaining tablespoon olive oil to the well and, with fingertips, rub the oil into the flour until well incorporated. Add the sponge and gradually add 1 cup warm water, bringing in the flour as you go along. Mix briefly to make a rough ball of dough.

4. Remove the dough to a lightly floured work surface and knead for about 3 minutes. Invert the bowl over the dough and let rest for 15 minutes. Knead for 2 to 3 minutes more, until the dough is smooth and elastic. Shape the dough into a tight ball and place in a lightly oiled clean bowl, turning the dough in the bowl to coat all over with oil. Cover with plastic wrap and let rise for 30 minutes.

5. Return the dough to the work surface and, with fingertips, lightly flatten it into a large rectangle, trying not to deflate too many air bubbles.

6. Remove the sausage pieces to a chopping board. Discard the skins and coarsely chop the meat. Spread the sausage meat, the sage, and the oil they cooked in all over the dough, leaving about ½ inch free around the edges. Fold one long third of the dough over the filling and press down with the heel of a hand to seal. Fold over, aligning the edges and pressing again to seal. Tuck the ends in and roll back and forth to form a 12-inch log.

7. Preheat the oven to 450°F and place a medium baking dish on the bottom rack of the oven. Transfer the bread, seam side down, to a nonstick baking sheet, or to a baking sheet lined with parchment paper or a silicone pastry mat. Lightly brush with oil. Cover loosely with plastic wrap and let rise for about 15 to 20 minutes, until well risen.

8. Immediately before baking, toss the ice cubes into the baking dish on the oven bottom to create steam. Uncover the bread and bake for 35 to 45 minutes, until golden brown all over; check after 15 minutes, and if the bread is coloring too fast, reduce the heat to 375°F. Transfer to a wire rack to cool. Serve at room temperature, or reheated.

Sicilian Sausage Rolls

Pane alla Salsiccia Siciliano

I first saw sausage rolls like these in a charming family-run bakery in Castelvetrano, a small city on the western coast of Sicily. Castelvetrano is famous for its biscotti picanti (see page 184) and also for its black bread, *pane nero* (for which I do not include a recipe in this book because it requires a durum whole wheat flour available only in that part of Sicily). Francesco Licari, a fine baker in Castelvetrano, gave me a recipe for these sausage rolls that inspired my own version here. Licari makes his dough with lard, but I make mine with olive oil; the rolls are a little less flaky but are equally good. Use the best-quality frankfurters you can find for these rolls.

MAKES 10 INDIVIDUAL ROLLS

2¼ teaspoons (1 package) active dry yeast
3⅓ cups unbleached all-purpose flour, plus extra for kneading and shaping
4 tablespoons sugar
1 teaspoon fine kosher salt or sea salt
3½ tablespoons extra-virgin olive oil or lard, plus extra for greasing the bowl
10 good-quality medium frankfurters
10 to 15 ice cubes

1. Dissolve the yeast in ¼ cup warm water and stir until creamy.

2. Combine the flour, sugar, and salt in a large bowl and make a well in the center. Add the olive oil or lard to the well and, with fingertips, rub the fat into the

flour until well incorporated. Add the yeast and gradually add another ¾ cup plus 2 tablespoons warm water, mixing it with the flour as you go along. Knead briefly to make a rough ball of dough.

3. Remove the dough to a lightly floured work surface. Knead for about 3 minutes. Invert the bowl over the dough and let rest for 15 minutes. Knead for 2 to 3 minutes more, until the dough is smooth and elastic. Place the dough in a lightly oiled clean bowl, turning it to coat all over with oil. Cover with plastic wrap and let rise in a warm, draft-free place for 1 hour. Fold the dough (see pages 6–7), cover again, and let rise for 1 hour more. The dough should have doubled in volume.

4. Return the dough to the work surface. Divide it into 10 equal pieces. Shape each piece into a ball. Cover with a damp kitchen towel and let rest for 15 minutes.

5. Shape one piece of dough into a thin strand (see page 10) that is long enough to coil around a frankfurter leaving a little sticking out at each end. Wrap the

strand around a frankfurter starting at one end, in such a way that the two ends of the strand end up on the same side of the frankfurter. Place, loose side down, on a nonstick baking sheet, or on a baking sheet lined with parchment paper or a silicone pastry mat. Make the remaining rolls in the same manner, leaving at least 2 inches between them on the baking sheet to allow for expansion as they rise and bake. Cover with a wet but not dripping kitchen towel and let rise for 30 to 35 minutes. Meanwhile, preheat the oven to 450°F. Place a medium baking dish on the bottom rack of the oven.

6. Immediately before baking, toss the ice cubes into the baking dish on the oven bottom to create steam. Uncover the rolls and bake them for 15 to 20 minutes, until golden brown all over. Transfer to a wire rack to cool. Serve at room temperature, or reheated.

Greek Olive Bread

Eliopsomo

In Greece, where this bread is made either as a loaf or as individual rolls, most cooks knead the greens and olives into the dough. But this method often tears the dough. Instead I use a method I learned from Amy Scherber, of Amy's Bread in New York City. I flatten the dough into a large rectangle, spread the filling over the dough, and then fold the dough in thirds to form a long envelope. After that I gently work the dough to make whatever shape I want. I prefer to make this bread in one long loaf—the coiled filling looks very attractive when the loaf is sliced, and the flavors come through in a more concentrated way.

MAKES 1 LARGE LOAF

2¼ teaspoons (1 package) active dry yeast

3⅓ cups unbleached all-purpose flour, plus extra for kneading and shaping

1 teaspoon fine kosher salt or sea salt

5 tablespoons extra-virgin olive oil, plus extra for oiling hands and the bowl

½ pound fresh spinach, finely chopped, rubbed (using fingertips) with a little salt, and squeezed very dry

2 tablespoons finely chopped flat-leaf parsley

2 tablespoons finely chopped mint leaves, or 1 tablespoon dried mint

1 tablespoon finely chopped cilantro

8 scallions, trimmed and thinly sliced

½ pound oil-packed olives, pitted and halved

10 to 15 ice cubes

1. Dissolve the yeast in ¼ cup warm water and stir until creamy.

2. Combine the flour and salt in a large bowl and make a well in the center. Add the olive oil to the well and, with fingertips, rub it into the flour until well incorporated. Add the yeast and gradually add ½ cup plus 2 tablespoons warm water, mixing it with the flour as you go along. Knead briefly to make a rough ball of dough.

3. Remove the dough to a work surface and knead for about 3 minutes. Invert the bowl over the dough and let rest for 15 minutes. Knead for 2 to 3 minutes more, until the dough is smooth and elastic. Shape the dough into a ball. Grease a bowl with a little olive oil and place the dough in the bowl, rolling it to coat all over with oil. Cover with plastic wrap and let rise in a warm, draft-free place for 45 minutes.

4. With a fist, gently punch down the dough in the middle. Fold one half over the other and return the dough to the work surface. Oil your hands and press on the dough to flatten it into a rectangle about 14 inches by 7 inches.

5. Combine the spinach, parsley, mint, cilantro, scallions, and olives in a bowl. Spread the mixture over the dough, leaving ½ inch free around the edges. Press the filling into the dough. Fold one long third of the dough over the filling, pressing with the heel of a hand to seal. Then fold over, aligning the edges and pressing to seal them. Tuck the ends in and roll back and forth to shape into a long loaf.

6. Preheat the oven to 450°F. Place a medium baking dish on the bottom rack of the oven. Transfer the loaf seam side down to a nonstick baking sheet, or to a baking sheet lined with parchment paper or a silicone pastry mat. Liberally brush with olive oil. Cover with plastic wrap and let rise for 20 to 25 minutes.

7. Immediately before baking, toss the ice cubes into the baking dish on the oven bottom to create steam. Remove the plastic wrap. Bake the bread for 40 minutes, until golden brown all over; check after 20 minutes, and if the bread is coloring too fast, reduce the heat to 350°F. Transfer to a wire rack to cool. Serve at room temperature, or reheated.

French Bacon Bread

Pain aux Lardons

The dough for this bread is like that for a good hamburger bun. In fact, if you want to make homemade hamburger buns, simply omit the bacon and shape the dough into 4 flattened balls. Diastatic malt powder helps yeast grow more completely and enhances the texture and flavor of the bread. It's available in health-food stores and from the King Arthur Baker's Catalogue and other specialty sources for bakers.

MAKES 4 INDIVIDUAL BREADS

3½ ounces smoked bacon, diced (heaping ½ cup)

1½ teaspoons (⅔ package) active dry yeast

2⅓ cups unbleached all-purpose flour, plus extra for kneading and shaping

1 teaspoon fine kosher salt or sea salt

2 teaspoons powdered milk

¾ teaspoon diastatic malt powder

1½ tablespoons unsalted butter, softened

10 to 15 ice cubes

1. Put the bacon in a sauté pan over medium heat. Cook until crisp and golden. Transfer with a slotted spoon to a bowl and set aside.

2. Dissolve the yeast in 2 tablespoons warm water and stir until creamy. Combine the flour, salt, powdered milk, and malt powder in a large bowl and make a well in the center. Add the yeast to the well and gradually add ⅔ cup warm

water, bringing in the flour as you go along. Knead briefly to make a rough dough, then knead in the butter.

3. Remove the dough to a lightly floured work surface. Sprinkle the dough with a little more flour and knead for about 3 minutes. Invert the bowl over the dough and let rest for 15 minutes. Knead for 2 to 3 minutes more, until the dough is smooth and elastic. Flatten the dough by hand into a large rectangle. Scatter the bacon all over it. Fold one long third over the bacon, and then fold over to make a long envelope. Fold the short sides over in thirds, and gently roll the dough into a ball. Place in a lightly floured clean bowl. Cover with plastic wrap and let rise in a warm, draft-free place for 1 hour. Fold the dough (see pages 6–7), cover again, and let rise for 1 hour more. The dough should have doubled in volume.

4. Return the dough to the work surface. Divide into 4 equal pieces. Shape each piece into a ball. Cover with a damp kitchen towel and let rest for 15 minutes.

5. Shape each ball into a small bâtard (see page 9). Transfer to a nonstick baking sheet, or to a baking sheet lined with parchment paper or a silicone pastry mat. Shape the remaining balls of dough in the same way, leaving at least 2 inches between them on the baking sheet to allow for expansion as they rise and bake. Cover with a wet but not dripping kitchen towel and let rise for 1 hour. Meanwhile, preheat the oven to 475°F. Place a medium baking dish on the bottom rack of the oven.

6. Immediately before baking, toss the ice cubes into the baking dish on the oven bottom to create steam. Uncover the breads and bake them for 20 to 25 minutes, until golden brown all over; check after 10 minutes, and if the breads are coloring too fast, reduce the heat to 350°F. Transfer to a wire rack to cool. Serve at room temperature, or reheated.

Neapolitan Easter Bread

Casatiello

Casatiello is an Easter bread from Naples. The eggs, which are set, uncooked and in their shells, into the dough before the bread is baked, are safe to eat but become rather hard after so long in the oven. Neapolitans treat them more as decorations than as something to eat.

SERVES 8

4½ teaspoons (2 packages) active dry yeast
4 cups unbleached all-purpose flour, plus extra for kneading and
    shaping
2½ teaspoons fine kosher salt or sea salt
1 tablespoon finely ground black pepper
2 tablespoons lard or unsalted butter
4 medium eggs

1. Dissolve the yeast in ⅓ cup warm water and stir until creamy.

2. Combine the flour, salt, and pepper in a large bowl and make a well in the center. Add the lard to the well and, with fingertips, rub into the flour until well incorporated. Add the yeast and another 1 cup plus 2 tablespoons warm water, mixing in with the flour as you go along. Knead briefly to make a rough ball of dough.

3. Remove the dough to a lightly floured work surface. Knead for about 3 minutes. Shape the dough into a ball. Invert the bowl over the dough and let rest for 15 minutes. Knead for 2 to 3 minutes more, until the dough is smooth and

elastic. Shape the dough into a ball. Place in a lightly floured clean bowl and cover with plastic wrap. Let ferment in a warm, draft-free place for 1 hour. Fold the dough (see pages 6–7), cover again, let rise for another hour, fold again, cover, and let rise for 1 hour more. The dough should have doubled in volume.

4. Return the dough to the work surface. Shape the dough into a ball, cover with plastic wrap, and let rest for 15 minutes. Then shape the ball into a strand (see page 10) 16 to 18 inches long. Join the ends to make a ring shape and press to seal them together. Transfer to a nonstick baking sheet, or to a baking sheet lined with parchment paper or a silicone pastry mat. Place an inverted small heat-proof round custard cup or pie dish in the middle of the ring so that the dough does not close in as it rises and bakes. Press the 4 eggs into the dough, one at the seam and the others at regular intervals. Cover with a wet but not dripping kitchen towel and let rise for 30 minutes. Meanwhile, preheat the oven to 350°F.

5. Uncover the bread and bake for 45 to 55 minutes, until golden all over. Transfer to a wire rack to cool. Serve at room temperature, or reheated.

Cheese "Cake"

Pizza al Formaggio

Unlike the flatter Neapolitan standard-bearer, pizza al formaggio is thicker and more substantial, closer to a savory "cake" than a pizza. In fact, pizza al formaggio predates Neapolitan pizza by centuries. It's common still in Umbria and Le Marche, where it is eaten at Easter with that season's freshly made *salami*. Serve with antipasti on a picnic or for a light lunch.

SERVES 6

Heaping tablespoon (1½ packages) active dry yeast
3 cups all-purpose unbleached flour, plus extra for kneading and
   shaping
2 large eggs
3 tablespoons freshly grated Parmigiano-Reggiano
3 tablespoons freshly grated pecorino romano
1 teaspoon fine kosher salt or sea salt
2 tablespoons extra-virgin olive oil, plus extra for brushing the cake
   pan and cake
2 ounces provolone, cut into ½-inch cubes (about 1 cup)
1½ ounces Gruyère, cut into ½-inch cubes (about ¾ cup)

1. Dissolve the yeast in ½ cup warm water in a medium bowl and stir until creamy. Add 1 cup of the flour and mix briefly to make a rough dough. Cover with plastic wrap and let ferment in a warm, draft-free place for about 1 hour, until well risen. This will be the sponge, or biga.

2. Break the eggs into a bowl. Add the grated cheeses and mix well.

3. Combine the remaining 2 cups flour and the salt in a large bowl and make a well in the center. Add the olive oil to the well and, with fingertips, rub the oil into the flour until well incorporated. Add the sponge, the egg mixture, and ½ cup warm water to the flour. Knead briefly to make a sticky dough.

4. Remove the dough to a lightly floured work surface and knead for about 3 minutes, adding a little flour every now and then, until the dough is no longer sticky but still is very soft. Invert the bowl over the dough and let rest for 15 minutes. Knead for 2 to 3 minutes more, until the dough is smooth and elastic. Flatten the dough by hand into a large rectangle. Spread the cubed cheeses all over. Fold one long third of the dough over the cheeses, then fold over to form a long envelope. Fold the short ends over in thirds, and gently shape into a ball.

5. Brush a 7-inch round cake pan with olive oil, or line it with parchment paper. Place the ball of dough in the pan. Lightly press on it until it covers the bottom of the pan. Brush the top with oil. Cover with a wet but not dripping kitchen towel and let rise in a warm, draft-free place for about 1½ hours, until it has more than doubled in volume and has risen slightly above the top edge of the pan. Meanwhile, preheat the oven to 400°F.

6. Bake for 20 minutes. Reduce the heat to 350°F and bake for 20 minutes more, until golden brown. Remove from the oven, let sit for a minute or two, then unmold onto a wire rack. Let cool. Serve at room temperature, or reheated.

Cheese and Ham Brioche Ring

La Ciambella di Brioscia

This is an impressive creation, which in Italy often is served hot with sliced red and yellow peppers sautéed in olive oil, garnished with chopped parsley and capers and seasoned with a little vinegar. The peppers are piled inside the ring of bread and the whole thing is served as a starter. It's also good at room temperature with a simple green salad and a selection of salami and cheeses. The ciambella keeps well for several days and makes a great snack, sliced and toasted.

SERVES 6 TO 8

4½ teaspoons (2 packages) active dry yeast

3 cups plus 1 tablespoon unbleached all-purpose flour

¾ teaspoon fine kosher salt or sea salt

4 tablespoons (½ stick) unsalted butter, melted, plus extra butter for
        greasing the ring mold and plastic wrap

3 large eggs

½ cup lukewarm milk

½ teaspoon freshly ground black pepper

1½ cups freshly grated Parmigiano-Reggiano (about 3 ounces)

1 cup coarsely grated provolone (about 2 ounces)

3 ounces ham, cut into short, thin strips

I. Dissolve the yeast in ¾ cup warm water in a medium bowl and stir until creamy. Add 1 cup of the flour and ¼ teaspoon of the salt and mix with a rubber spatula to make a thick, rough batter. Sprinkle 1 tablespoon flour over the top. Cover with plastic wrap and let rise in a warm, draft-free place for 1 hour. This will be the sponge, or biga.

2. Put the melted butter in a large bowl. Stir in the eggs, one at a time. Add the sponge and mix, using a whisk, until all the ingredients are well blended.

3. Gradually add the remaining 2 cups flour, adding the milk between additions and mixing with a rubber spatula to make a smooth, thick batter. Cover with plastic wrap and let rise in a warm, draft-free place for 1 hour, until doubled in volume.

4. Use about 2 tablespoons of the extra unsalted butter to generously butter a large ring mold. Add the remaining salt and the pepper to the batter together with the grated cheeses and the ham. Mix with a spatula until all the ingredients are evenly incorporated.

5. Pour the mixture into the ring mold, lightly pressing on it with the back of a spoon to distribute it evenly and to break up air pockets. Cover with a buttered piece of plastic wrap and then with a heavy kitchen towel. Let rise for about 1 hour. The batter should have doubled in volume. Meanwhile, preheat the oven to 375°F.

6. Uncover the bread and bake for 25 to 30 minutes, until well risen and golden all over. Remove the mold to a wire rack. Let sit for about 15 minutes, then unmold the bread onto the rack to cool. Serve at room temperature.

⁑ Pugliese Brioche

La Brioscia alla Pugliese

Serve this luscious and substantial bread for lunch with a green salad, cherry tomatoes, and a variety of olives. Once the bread is baked, let it rest for at least fifteen minutes before cutting it so that it doesn't crumble.

SERVES 8

4½ teaspoons (2 packages) active dry yeast

¾ cup milk, slightly warm

3 cups unbleached all-purpose flour, plus extra for kneading and shaping

½ teaspoon fine kosher salt or sea salt

⅓ cup unsalted butter, melted, plus extra for greasing the cake pan
   and plastic wrap

½ cup sugar, plus extra for sprinkling the cake pan

4 medium eggs, beaten

3 ounces prosciutto, thinly sliced

4 ounces fresh mozzarella, thinly sliced

1. Dissolve the yeast in half the milk and stir until creamy. Combine the flour and salt in a large bowl and make a well in the center. Add the yeast, the remaining milk, the melted butter, and the sugar and eggs to the well. Mix, first with a fork and then with a rubber spatula, until the pastry is smooth and comes away from the sides of the bowl.

2. Grease a 10-inch round cake pan with a little butter and sprinkle the bottom and sides with a little sugar. With a rubber spatula, spread half the pastry over

the bottom of the cake pan. Arrange a layer of prosciutto over the pastry and then arrange the cheese over the ham, leaving about ¾ inch clear around the edges. Cover the cheese with the remaining ham, then top with the remaining pastry, pressing down to break up air pockets. Cover with a buttered piece of plastic wrap, and then with a heavy kitchen towel. Let rise in a warm, draft-free place for 1½ hours. Meanwhile, preheat the oven to 350°F.

3. Bake the bread, uncovered, for 20 minutes. Then cover loosely with aluminum foil and bake for 15 minutes more, until well risen and golden and a skewer inserted in the middle (just until it hits the ham) comes out dry. Remove from the oven and let sit for 5 minutes, then unmold onto a wire rack and let cool. Serve warm, at room temperature, or reheated.

Campofranco Brioche

Pizza Campofranco

Although the natives of Campofranco, a village just outside of Naples, call this a pizza, it's really closer to a brioche. It is similar to the Pugliese Brioche (page 153), except that in this case the bread is baked first, then cut open and filled. The top is then garnished like a pizza and the bread is baked again. Vary the fillings by using fresh tomatoes, garlic, and basil leaves. Thinly slice the tomatoes and sauté them in a bit of olive oil for a minute or two on both sides and use to fill the pizza, garnishing with basil leaves.

SERVES 6 TO 8

Heaping tablespoon (1½ packages) active dry yeast

3⅔ cups unbleached all-purpose flour, plus extra for kneading and shaping

½ teaspoon fine kosher salt or sea salt

4 medium eggs, slightly beaten

¾ cup plus 1 tablespoon unsalted butter, softened, plus extra for greasing the plastic wrap

8 ounces fresh mozzarella, thinly sliced

2 ounces Parmigiano-Reggiano, grated (about 1 cup)

1 recipe tomato sauce for Neopolitan Pizza, page 42

1. Dissolve the yeast in ⅓ cup plus 1 tablespoon warm water in a medium bowl. Stir until creamy. Add 1 cup of the flour and mix briefly to make a rough, rather wet dough. Cover with plastic wrap and let ferment in a warm, draft-free place for 1 hour. This will be the sponge, or biga.

2. Combine the remaining 2⅔ cups flour and the salt in a large bowl and make a well in the center. Add the eggs and butter and knead briefly to make a rough, sticky dough. Remove the dough to a floured work surface.

3. Add the biga to the dough. Sprinkle with more flour and knead for about 5 minutes, until the biga is well incorporated and the dough is very soft and rather smooth. Shape loosely into a ball.

4. Place the dough in a nonstick 10- or 12-inch round cake pan and press to spread it evenly all over the bottom. Lightly butter a large piece of plastic wrap and cover the dough. Let rise in a warm, draft-free place for 2 hours. Meanwhile, preheat the oven to 325°F.

5. Uncover the bread and bake for 50 minutes, until golden all over. Remove from the oven and let cool in the cake pan for 10 minutes. Then remove the bread to a wire rack and let cool completely.

6. Preheat the oven to 500°F. Cut the brioche in half horizontally. Place the bottom half on a baking sheet, cut side up. Spread half the mozzarella all over the bottom half. Sprinkle half the Parmesan over the mozzarella and cover with half the tomato sauce. Place the top half of the bread, cut side down, over the filling. Spread the remaining mozzarella all over the top. Cover with the remaining Parmesan and then the remaining tomato sauce.

7. Bake for 10 to 15 minutes, until the cheese is melted, the top and bottom are lightly crisp, and the brioche is heated through completely. Serve immediately.

Saint Claire's Bread

Gatto Santa Chiara

H ere is another savory bread that makes a perfect informal meal, served along
with salume (Italian charcuterie, such as prosciutto, salami, and mortadella)
and a green salad. The monks of the various monasteries in Naples were known
for their culinary skills, and there are several Santa Chiara preparations such as
the one below and also broscine Santa Chiara (Saint Claire's small buns), made
with cheese, salami, and ham. Presumably both are named after the magnificent
cloisters of Saint Claire.

SERVES 6 TO 8

2¼ teaspoons (1 package) active dry yeast

1⅔ cups unbleached all-purpose flour, plus extra for kneading and
    shaping

½ teaspoon fine kosher salt or sea salt

1 medium all-purpose potato, boiled, peeled, and mashed

3 tablespoons lard or unsalted butter, plus extra for greasing the cake
    pan and plastic wrap

2 medium eggs, beaten

¾ cup fresh mozzarella, diced (about 3 ounces)

¾ cup diced cooked Italian ham (about 3 ounces)

1. Dissolve the yeast in 2 tablespoons warm water in a medium bowl. Stir until
   creamy. Add ¼ cup of the flour and knead briefly to make a rather firm ball of
   dough. Cover with a wet but not dripping kitchen towel and let rise in a warm,

draft-free place for 30 minutes, until doubled in volume. This will be the sponge, or biga.

2. Combine the remaining flour and the salt in a large bowl and make a well in the center. Add the potato to the well. Add the lard, eggs, and sponge and mix together to make a rough ball of dough.

3. Remove the dough to a lightly floured work surface. Knead for about 3 minutes, sprinkling with a little flour if the dough is too sticky. Invert the bowl over the dough and let rest for 15 minutes. Knead for about 2 to 3 minutes more, until the dough is smooth and elastic. Flatten the dough into a large rectangle. Spread the mozzarella and ham all over. Fold one long third of the dough over the filling and then over to form a long envelope. Fold in thirds the other way and gently shape into a ball.

4. Grease a 9-inch round cake pan with a little lard. Sprinkle the bottom and sides with flour and shake out the excess. Place the dough in the pan and gently flatten to cover the bottom. Lightly grease a piece of plastic wrap with lard and cover the dough. Let rise in a warm, draft-free place for 1½ hours, until doubled in volume. Meanwhile, preheat the oven to 375°F.

5. Bake the bread for 45 to 50 minutes, until well risen and golden brown; if the bread browns too fast, loosely cover with foil for the last 10 to 15 minutes. Let cool in the cake pan for 5 to 10 minutes, then remove to a wire rack to continue cooling. Serve warm, at room temperature, or reheated.

Greek Easter Bread

Tsoureki

Tsoureki is a traditional Easter bread, redolent of spices. Sometimes the breads are decorated with eggs that have been dyed red. Among the spices that Greek cooks use in tsoureki are mahlep, the bitter nut found inside the kernel of the wild cherry, and mastic, the dried resin that seeps through the bark of the Mediterranean evergreen tree *Pistacia lentiscus*. Mahlep is available widely in Middle Eastern markets; mastic is less widely sold, but it can be found from some online merchants. If you have trouble finding these spices, the bread may be made without them.

MAKES 1 LARGE LOAF

1¾ teaspoons (¾ package) active dry yeast

3 tablespoons warmed (but not scalded) milk

2 cups unbleached all-purpose flour, plus extra for kneading and
    shaping

⅓ cup sugar

⅛ teaspoon salt

1 teaspoon extra-virgin olive oil

Scant ½ teaspoon ground mahlep or ¼ teaspoon ground mastic,
    optional

⅛ teaspoon ground cardamom

1 large egg

3 tablespoons unsalted butter, melted, plus extra for greasing the bowl

1 egg yolk mixed with 1 teaspoon water, for brushing the dough

1. Dissolve the yeast in ⅓ cup warm water in a medium bowl. Stir until creamy. Add the milk and 1 cup of the flour and mix briefly to make a rough ball of dough. Cover with plastic wrap and let rise in a warm, draft-free place for about 30 minutes, until the dough has doubled in volume. This will be the sponge.

2. Combine the sugar, salt, oil, and spices in a large bowl. Stir in the egg. Add the sponge. Add the remaining 1 cup flour in 2 batches, mixing it in after each addition. Knead briefly to make a soft, slightly sticky dough; add 1 to 2 tablespoons water if the dough is too firm.

3. Remove the dough to a lightly floured work surface. Gradually work the butter into the dough, taking care not to overwork the dough. Grease a large bowl with a little butter and place the dough in it. Cover with plastic wrap and let rise in a warm, draft-free place for 1 hour. Fold the dough (see pages 6–7), cover again, and let rise for 1 hour more, until the dough has at least doubled in volume.

4. Return the dough to the work surface, divide it into 3 equal pieces, and roll each piece into a ball. Cover with plastic wrap and let rest for 15 minutes. Shape each piece into a 12- to 14-inch-long strand (see page 10). Transfer the strands to a nonstick baking sheet, or to a baking sheet lined with parchment paper or a silicone pastry mat. Twist the strands together to form a long braided loaf. Cover with a wet but not dripping kitchen towel. Let rise for 30 to 45 minutes, until doubled in volume. Meanwhile, preheat the oven to 400°F.

5. Uncover the loaf and let the surface dry for about 5 minutes. Brush the loaf with about half of the egg yolk, taking care not to let the egg pool in the crevices. Let rest for 15 minutes. Brush with the remaining yolk. Bake for 20 to 25 minutes, until golden brown all over. Transfer to a wire rack to cool.

✤ Greek Saints' Day Bread

Artos

While visiting the island of Kassos, I told my lovely hosts, Alexandros and Marilena Kedros, about my research for this book. We happened to be there on Saint Dimitri's Day, when all the locals cook for a festive dinner to celebrate the saint's name day. All the women bake artos, a bread made on various saints' days, and then take the loaves to church to be blessed by the priest before being cut and distributed to the congregation at the end of mass.

I was able to watch Finia, a great lady who cooks for private households on Kassos, prepare her bread and then bake the loaves in her outdoor wood-fired oven, as seen in the photographs. With its subtle sweet and spicy flavors, artos is a perfect breakfast or teatime bread to be enjoyed with thick Greek-style yogurt and honey, or with very good butter.

MAKES 1 MEDIUM LOAF

4½ teaspoons (2 packages) active dry yeast

3⅓ cups unbleached all-purpose flour, plus extra for kneading and
    shaping

1½ teaspoons fine kosher salt or sea salt

⅔ cup sugar

1 tablespoon ground cinnamon

1 teaspoon ground cloves

2 tablespoons aniseed

2 tablespoons extra-virgin olive oil, plus extra for greasing the baking dish

2 tablespoons red wine

1½ tablespoons white sesame seeds

1½ tablespoons nigella seeds, optional

1. Dissolve the yeast in ½ cup warm water and stir until creamy.

2. Combine the flour, salt, sugar, cinnamon, cloves, and aniseed in a large bowl and make a well in the center. Add the olive oil and, with fingertips, rub the oil into the flour until well incorporated. Add the wine, yeast, and ¾ cup additional warm water and mix to make a very wet and sticky dough. With your hand, spread 2 tablespoons water over the surface of the dough. Cover with plastic wrap and let rise for 1 hour.

3. Grease a deep 9-inch round baking dish with olive oil. Sprinkle half the sesame seeds (or, if using, half of a mixture of the sesame and nigella seeds) over the bottom of the dish.

4. Sprinkle a thick layer of flour over a work surface. With wet hands, scoop out the dough and transfer it to the work surface. Pick up the top edges of the dough and

fold them toward the middle, then pick up the bottom edges and fold them toward the middle to make a circular loaf. Quickly rinse hands clean, and dry and flour them, and then pick up the dough quickly and invert it seam side down into the baking dish. Gently pat it to spread it evenly into the dish. Wet hands again and spread more water over the top of the dough. Sprinkle the remaining sesame seeds (or seed mixture) all over the top. Cover with plastic wrap and let rise for 1 hour, until doubled in volume. Meanwhile, preheat the oven to 400°F.

5. Uncover the bread and bake for 20 minutes, then reduce the heat to 350°F and bake for 30 minutes more, or until golden brown all over. Turn out onto a wire rack to let cool. Serve at room temperature, or wrap in a kitchen towel and keep for up to 2 days. The bread is delicious sliced and toasted.

✛ Italian Nut Bread

Pane dei Santi

Also known as *pan dei morti,* "bread of the dead," and *pane co' Santi,* "bread of the saints," this bread is a specialty of the provinces of Grosseto and Siena in Tuscany. It has a light, fluffy texture and an intriguing sweet-savory taste. Like artos, this bread is ideal for breakfast or teatime, served on its own or with good unsalted butter.

MAKES 1 MEDIUM LOAF

4½ teaspoons (2 packages) active dried yeast

3⅔ cups unbleached all-purpose flour, plus extra for kneading and
　　　shaping

½ cup extra-virgin olive oil, plus extra for greasing the plastic wrap

1 tablespoon lard or unsalted butter

½ cup coarsely chopped walnuts (about 2 ounces)

½ cup coarsely chopped blanched almonds (about 2 ounces)

⅓ cup raisins (about 2 ounces), soaked in warm water for 30 minutes
　　　and drained

¼ cup sugar

¼ teaspoon kosher salt or sea salt

Grated zest of ½ lemon

Grated zest of ½ orange

½ teaspoon ground aniseed

½ teaspoon freshly ground black pepper

1. Dissolve the yeast in ½ cup warm water in a large bowl. Stir until creamy. Add ⅔ cup of the flour and mix briefly to make a rough, sticky dough. Cover the bowl with plastic wrap and let the dough rise for about 1 hour, until more than doubled in volume. This will be the sponge, or biga.

2. Heat the olive oil and lard together in a sauté pan over medium heat. Add the walnuts and almonds and sauté until aromatic. Remove from the heat, stir in the raisins, and set aside to let cool.

3. Add the nuts and raisins with their cooking oil to the sponge and mix. Add the sugar, salt, citrus zests, aniseed, and pepper. Mix well.

4. Put the remaining 3 cups flour in a large bowl and make a well in the center. Add the sponge mixture to the well. Gradually add ⅓ cup warm water, bringing in the flour as you go along. Mix briefly to make a rough ball of dough.

5. Remove the dough to a lightly floured work surface. Knead for about 3 minutes. Invert the bowl over the dough and let rest for 15 minutes. Knead for about 2 to 3 minutes more, until the dough is smooth and elastic. Shape the dough into a long loaf (see page 9) and transfer to a nonstick baking sheet, or to a baking sheet lined with parchment paper or a silicone pastry mat. Brush a large piece of plastic wrap with oil and cover the loaf. Let rise in a warm, draft-free place for about 1 hour, until doubled in size. Meanwhile, preheat the oven to 400°F.

6. Uncover the bread and bake for 35 to 45 minutes, until golden brown all over. Transfer to a wire rack to cool. Serve at room temperature, or reheated.

Greek Christmas Bread

Christopsomo

This Christmas loaf is a variation on Greek Easter bread, Tsoureki (page 159), but this dough has more butter along with flaked almonds and raisins. In some regions, chopped mixed candied fruit is added. If you like this variation, use ½ cup chopped candied fruit for the measurements given below. The candied fruit variation brings christopsomo even closer to panettone, which it resembles, although the texture of christopsomo is a lot denser.

MAKES 1 LARGE LOAF

Heaping tablespoon (1½ packages) active dry yeast

¾ cup sugar

5 cups unbleached all-purpose flour, plus extra for kneading and
    shaping

Heaping ½ teaspoon fine kosher salt or sea salt

2 medium eggs

¾ cup whole milk, brought to a boil and then removed from the heat
    to cool to room temperature

½ teaspoon ground mastic (see page 159), optional

½ cup (1 stick) unsalted butter, melted

½ cup slivered almonds (about 2 ounces)

¼ cup raisins soaked in warm water for 30 minutes and drained (about
    1½ ounces)

½ teaspoon grated lemon zest

1 egg beaten with 1 teaspoon water

1. Dissolve the yeast in ¼ cup warm water in a medium bowl. Stir until creamy. Add ½ teaspoon of the sugar, 2 tablespoons of the flour, and half the salt. Mix briefly to make a rough batter. Cover with plastic wrap and let ferment in a warm, draft-free place for 30 minutes.

2. Mix the 2 eggs and the milk with the remaining sugar and salt in a medium bowl. Add the yeast mixture and mix well.

3. Combine the remaining flour and, if using, the mastic in a large bowl and make a well in the center. Add the butter to the well and, with fingertips, rub the butter into the flour until well incorporated. Add the almonds, raisins, lemon zest, and yeast mixture. Knead briefly to make a rather sticky rough ball of dough.

4. Liberally sprinkle a work surface with flour. Remove the dough to it, sprinkle with more flour, and knead for about 3 minutes. Invert the bowl over the dough and let rest for 15 minutes. Knead for about 2 to 3 minutes more, until the dough is smooth and elastic. Shape into a ball and transfer to a lightly floured clean bowl. Cover with plastic wrap and let rise in a warm, draft-free place for 1 hour. Fold the dough (see pages 6–7), cover again, and let rise for 1 hour more. The dough should have doubled in volume.

5. Return the dough to the work surface and divide into 3 equal pieces. Shape each piece into a ball. Cover with a damp kitchen towel and let rest for about 15 minutes. Roll each piece into a strand about 18 inches in length (see page 10). Transfer the strands to a nonstick baking sheet, or to a baking sheet lined with parchment paper or a silicone pastry mat. Braid the strands to make a loaf about 15 inches in length. Cover with a wet but not dripping kitchen towel and let rise for 1 hour. Meanwhile, preheat the oven to 375°F.

6. Uncover the loaf and let the surface dry for about 5 minutes. Brush the loaf with the beaten egg, taking care not to let the egg pool in the crevices. Bake for 30 to 40 minutes, until golden brown all over. Transfer to a wire rack to cool. Serve at room temperature, or reheated.

Little Milk Breads

Petits Pains au Lait

Pains au lait, like baguettes, are made all over France. But while it's hard to make a good baguette in a home kitchen, homemade pains au lait are just as good as commercial ones—or even better, if made with the best flour, butter, and milk. In France they are used primarily for sandwiches, but they are also served plain with meals.

MAKES 6 INDIVIDUAL BREADS

1¼ teaspoons (just over ½ package) active dry yeast
¾ cup plus 2 tablespoons whole milk, at room temperature
2⅓ cups unbleached all-purpose flour, plus extra for kneading and
    shaping
2 tablespoons confectioners' sugar
1½ teaspoons fine kosher salt or sea salt
2 tablespoons unsalted butter, softened
1 egg yolk beaten with 1 teaspoon water

1. Dissolve the yeast in the milk and stir until creamy.

2. Combine the flour, sugar, and salt in a large bowl and make a well in the center. Add the yeast and butter to the well and, with fingertips, gently and gradually mix with the flour until well incorporated. Knead briefly to make a rough ball of dough.

3. Remove the dough to a lightly floured work surface. Knead for about 3 minutes. Invert the bowl over the dough and let rest for 15 minutes. Knead for about 2 to 3 minutes more, until the dough is smooth and elastic. Shape the dough into a ball and place in a lightly floured clean bowl. Cover with plastic wrap and let rise in a warm, draft-free place for 1 hour. Fold the dough (see pages 6–7), cover again, and let rise for 1 hour more. The dough should have doubled in volume.

4. Return the dough to the work surface and divide it into 6 equal pieces. Gently shape each piece into a ball. Cover with a damp kitchen towel and let rest for 15 minutes. Shape the pieces into bâtards about 8 inches long (see page 9). Press down on the ends to flatten them slightly and transfer seam side down to a nonstick baking sheet, or to a baking sheet lined with parchment paper or a silicone pastry mat, leaving at least 2 inches between the pieces to allow them to expand as they rise and bake. Cover with a wet but not dripping kitchen towel and let rise for 1 hour. Meanwhile, preheat the oven to 450°F.

5. Uncover the breads and let their surfaces dry for about 5 minutes. Brush with the egg yolk mixture. Bake for 15 to 20 minutes, until golden all over; check after 10 minutes, and if the breads are coloring too fast, reduce the heat to 350°F. Transfer to a wire rack to cool. Serve at room temperature, or reheated.

Breadsticks, Rings, and Rusks

Sicilian Sesame Grissini

Grissini al Sesamo

Sicilian grissini are different from the ones made in Turin, where the breads originated. They are shorter and fatter, and they are coated with sesame seeds. They also seem harder to crunch on. The Lebanese and Syrians have similar sesame breadsticks, called ka'k, which are sold in most bakeries. I once thought that the practice of sprinkling sesame seeds on breads in Sicily was a remnant of the Arab occupation, but I discovered that it is mentioned in the writings of the Greek physician Dioscorides, in the first century AD, and therefore predates the Arab invasion by a few centuries.

Diastatic malt powder, an ingredient here, is readily available in catalogs and specialty stores that cater to bakers, and also in natural-foods stores. It is an "improver," made from sprouted grains that have been dried and ground, and it is full of enzymes and vitamins that feed the yeast and brown the crust. It helps both flavor and appearance. In Lebanon, all of the professional bakers I met included *mühassan,* or "improver," in whatever recipes they were giving me. None of them could explain what mühassan is, but I now suspect it is diastatic malt powder.

MAKES 16 LONG OR 32 SHORT BREADSTICKS

2¼ teaspoons (1 package) active dry yeast

3⅓ cups unbleached all-purpose flour, plus extra for kneading and shaping

2 teaspoons fine kosher salt or sea salt

1 tablespoon diastatic malt powder

1 tablespoon lard or unsalted butter

⅓ cup white sesame seeds

1. Dissolve the yeast in ¼ cup warm water and stir until creamy.

2. Combine the flour, salt, and malt in a large bowl and make a well in the center. Add the lard to the well and, with fingertips, rub the lard into the flour until well incorporated. Add the yeast and gradually add ¾ cup plus 1 tablespoon warm water, bringing in the flour as you go along. Knead briefly to make a rough ball of dough.

3. Transfer the dough to a lightly floured work surface. Knead for about 3 minutes. Invert the bowl over the dough and let rest for 15 minutes. Knead for about 2 to 3 minutes more, until the dough is smooth and elastic. Shape the dough into a ball and place in a lightly floured clean bowl. Cover with plastic wrap and let rise in a warm, draft-free place for 45 minutes to 1 hour.

4. With a fist, gently punch the dough down the middle. Fold one half over the other and remove to the work surface. Divide into 16 equal pieces for long

breadsticks or 32 equal pieces for short ones. Shape each piece of dough into a ball. Cover with a damp kitchen towel and let rest for 15 minutes. Shape the pieces of dough into thin strands (see page 10), about 12 to 14 inches long for long breadsticks, and 6 to 7 inches long for short ones.

5. Preheat the oven to 400°F. Sprinkle a large nonstick baking sheet, or a baking sheet lined with parchment paper or a silicone pastry mat, with some of the sesame seeds. Gently roll the grissini back and forth on the sesame seeds to coat, sprinkling more seeds on the sheet as they get used up. Leave at least ½ inch between the coated grissini to allow for expansion as they bake.

6. Bake for 12 to 15 minutes, until golden brown all over. Reduce the heat to 175°F, and bake for 30 minutes more, until the grissini are completely hard. Let cool and serve at room temperature, or store in an airtight container for up to 1 week.

Spanish Breadsticks

Piquitos

Spaniards use a decent amount of olive oil in their breadstick dough, and as a result the sticks are more crumbly than elsewhere in the Mediterranean. White whole wheat flour (available from King Arthur) isn't the traditional flour for these breadsticks, but I have found that it works quite well and makes for lighter-colored breadsticks with a somewhat sweeter flavor.

MAKES 30 BREADSTICKS

2¼ teaspoons (1 package) active dry yeast

1 teaspoon sugar

2⅔ cups white whole wheat flour

1 teaspoon fine kosher salt or sea salt

¼ cup extra-virgin olive oil, plus extra for greasing the bowl

1. Dissolve the yeast and sugar in ¼ cup warm water and stir until creamy.

2. Combine the flour and salt in a large bowl and make a well in the center. Add the oil to the well and, with fingertips, rub the oil into the flour until well incorporated. Add the yeast and gradually add ½ cup plus 2 tablespoons warm water, bringing in the flour as you go along. Knead briefly to make a rough ball of dough.

3. Remove the dough to a lightly floured work surface. Knead for about 3 minutes. Invert the bowl over the dough and let rest for 15 minutes. Knead for about 2 to 3 minutes more, until the dough is smooth and elastic. Shape the

dough into a ball, place it in a lightly oiled bowl, and roll it to coat all over with oil. Let rise in a warm, draft-free place for 1 hour, until doubled in volume.

4. With a fist, gently punch the dough down the middle. Fold one half over the other and remove to the work surface. Divide into 30 equal pieces. Shape each piece into a ball. Loosely cover with plastic wrap and let rest for 15 minutes.

5. Roll each ball of dough into a strand (see page 10) about 12 to 14 inches long. Transfer the strands to a large nonstick baking sheet, or to a baking sheet lined with parchment paper or a silicone pastry mat, leaving at least ½ inch between them to allow for expansion as they bake. Loosely cover with plastic wrap and let rise for 30 minutes. Meanwhile, preheat the oven to 400°F.

6. Uncover and bake for 15 to 20 minutes. Reduce the heat to 175°F and bake for 30 minutes more, until golden all over and completely crisp. Transfer to a wire rack to cool. Serve at room temperature or store in an airtight container for up to 2 weeks.

✢ Rusks from Puglia

Frise *or* Friselle

Frise are like hard bagels that are cut in half crosswise. In the old days, people took them on picnics by the seaside. They dipped the hard bread in sea water to soften it and make it salty and then topped it with seasoned chopped tomatoes. Italians still dip their frise in cold water, and then salt and garnish them. I prefer to drizzle mine with olive oil and then top with tomatoes. This way they soften but without losing their crunch. They make a wonderful starter and they are terrific as snacks—or *merenda,* as the Italians say. Italians also break up their frise into bite-size pieces for use in salads.

MAKES 20 INDIVIDUAL BREADS

> 3¾ teaspoons (1⅔ packages) active dry yeast
> 2⅓ cups unbleached all-purpose flour, plus extra for kneading and
>   shaping
> 1 cup whole wheat flour
> 2 teaspoons fine kosher salt or sea salt

1. Dissolve the yeast in ½ cup warm water and stir until creamy.

2. Combine the flours and the salt in a large bowl and make a well in the center. Add the yeast to the well and gradually add ¾ cup warm water, bringing in the flour as you go along. Mix briefly to make a rough ball of dough.

3. Remove the dough to a lightly floured work surface. Knead for about 3 minutes. Invert the bowl over the dough and let rest for 15 minutes. Knead for about 2 to 3 minutes more, until the dough is smooth and elastic. Shape into a ball and place in a lightly floured clean bowl. Cover with plastic wrap. Let rise in a warm, draft-free place for 1 hour. Fold the dough (see pages 6–7), cover again, and let rise for 1 hour more. The dough should have doubled in volume.

4. Return the dough to the work surface. Divide it into 20 equal pieces. Roll each piece into a strand 8 to 10 inches in length (see page 10). Pinch or press the ends of each strand together to make a ring shape. Place one ring on top of another to make 10 two-tiered rings.

5. Transfer the rings to a large nonstick baking sheet, or to a baking sheet lined with parchment paper or a silicone pastry mat, leaving at least 1 inch between them to allow for expansion as they rise and bake. Cover with a wet but not dripping kitchen towel and let rise for about 1 hour, until doubled in size. Meanwhile, preheat the oven to 350°F.

6. Uncover the breads and bake for 20 minutes. Remove from the oven. Reduce the heat to 175°F. Cut the frise horizontally through the seams to separate the rings. Bake the separated rings, cut side up, for 1¼ to 1½ hours more, until golden and completely hard. Transfer to a wire rack to cool. Serve at room temperature or store in an airtight container for 3 weeks or longer.

❖ Neapolitan Pepper Rings

Taralli col Peppe

You find taralli throughout Italy but they are a specialty of Naples. Some of the best I have had come from the Moccia bakery in Naples. The bakery enriches their taralli with extra fat and ground toasted almonds. In most other places, they are plain and quite dry. I like to take homemade taralli along as a present when I am invited to dine with friends; I think it's more fun than taking a bottle of wine.

MAKES 32 SMALL BREAD RINGS

2¼ teaspoons (1 package) active dry yeast

2¾ cups unbleached all-purpose flour, plus extra for kneading and shaping

¾ teaspoon fine kosher salt or sea salt

2 teaspoons coarsely ground black pepper

¼ cup coarsely ground toasted almonds

6 tablespoons softened lard or unsalted butter, plus extra melted for brushing the taralli

1. Dissolve the yeast in ½ cup warm water and stir until creamy. Add ¾ cup of the flour and ¼ teaspoon of the salt and mix to make a rough, wet dough. Cover with plastic wrap and let rise in a warm, draft-free place for 1 hour. This will be the sponge, or biga.

2. Combine the remaining 2 cups flour and ½ teaspoon salt in a large bowl and make a well in the center. Add the sponge to the well. Add ⅓ cup plus 1 table-

spoon warm water and the pepper, almonds, and softened lard. Knead briefly to make a rough ball of dough.

3. Remove the dough to a lightly floured work surface. Knead for about 3 minutes. Invert the bowl over the dough and let rest for 15 minutes. Knead for about 2 to 3 minutes more, sprinkling with a little flour if the dough is too sticky. Shape into a ball and place in a lightly floured clean bowl. Let rise in a warm, draft-free place for 1 hour. Fold the dough (see pages 6–7), cover again, and let rise for 1 hour more.

4. Return the dough to the work surface. Divide it into 8 equal pieces. Shape each piece into a ball. Cover with plastic wrap and let rest for 15 minutes. Roll each piece into a long strand (see page 10) and use a dough cutter to cut each strand into 8 equal pieces.

5. Roll out each of the 64 strands into a long, thin strand. Twist or braid the strands together in pairs, to make 32 in all. Make rings by bringing the ends of each braided piece together; press on the joints to seal them securely. Transfer the taralli to a nonstick baking sheet, or to a baking sheet lined with parchment paper or a silicone pastry mat, leaving at least 1 inch between them to allow for expansion as they rise and bake. Brush the tops with melted lard. Cover with plastic wrap and let rise for 1 hour, until doubled in size. Meanwhile, preheat the oven to 325°F.

6. Brush the tops of the taralli again with melted lard. Bake for 70 minutes, or until golden and completely hard. Transfer to a wire rack to cool. Serve at room temperature, or store in an airtight container for up to 3 weeks.

Neapolitan Rings with Fennel Seeds

Taralli con i Finocchietti

These taralli are dropped, like bagels, in boiling water before being baked.

MAKES 14 LARGE BREAD RINGS

2¼ teaspoons (1 package) active dry yeast

3⅓ cups unbleached all-purpose flour, plus extra for kneading and shaping

2 teaspoons fine kosher salt or sea salt

1½ tablespoons fennel seeds

1 tablespoon unsalted butter, softened

1. Dissolve the yeast in ¼ cup warm water and stir until creamy. Add ⅔ cup of the flour and mix to make a rough dough. Shape into a ball and sprinkle with 1 tablespoon flour. Cover with plastic wrap and let ferment in a warm, draft-free place for 1 hour. This will be the sponge, or biga.

2. Combine the remaining 2⅔ cups flour and the salt and fennel seeds in a large bowl and make a well in the center. Add the sponge and butter to the well and gradually add a scant 1 cup warm water, bringing in the flour as you go along. Mix to make a rough ball of dough.

3. Remove the dough to a lightly floured work surface. Knead for about 3 minutes. Invert the bowl over the dough and let rest for 15 minutes. Knead for

about 2 to 3 minutes more, until the dough is smooth and elastic. Shape into a ball and place in a lightly floured clean bowl. Cover with plastic wrap and let rise in a warm, draft-free place for 1 hour. Fold the dough (see pages 6–7), cover again, and let rise for 1 hour more. The dough should have doubled in volume.

4. Return the dough to the work surface. Divide into 14 equal pieces and shape each piece into a ball. Cover with a damp kitchen towel and let rest for 15 minutes.

5. Shape a ball of dough into a strand about 10 inches long (see page 10). Bring the ends together to form a ring and press to seal. Transfer to a tray lined with parchment paper and cover with a damp kitchen towel. Make and cover the remaining taralli in the same manner, keeping track of which ones were made first.

6. Preheat the oven to 375°F. Bring to a boil a large pot of water. Turn off the heat under the water and, using a skimmer, immediately drop a few taralli in the water, starting with those that were shaped first. Let rest in the water for a few seconds, then remove to a nonstick baking sheet, or to a baking sheet lined with parchment paper or a silicone pastry mat.

7. Bake for 1¼ to 1½ hours, until golden and completely hard. Transfer to a wire rack to cool. Serve at room temperature, or store in an airtight container for up to 2 weeks.

❖ Sicilian Spicy Rusks

Biscotti Picanti

On a recent visit to Sicily, I had lunch with Mary Taylor Simeti, author of the masterly *Pomp and Sustenance*. When I asked Mary about Sicilian breads, she told me about biscotti picanti, a specialty of Castelvetrano where, as luck would have it, we were heading. When we got to Castelvetrano, I asked Gabriella Becchina, at whose bed-and-breakfast we were staying, where I could see these being made, and she, very kindly, took me to various bakers, including Il Forno di Licari and Giovanni e Figli, where one of the sons gave me the perfect recipe for them as well as a whole bag to sample.

I had similar ones, although not spicy, in Kassos in Greece, where they are known as kouloures (see page 189). The local baker went on his rounds in the morning, selling bread and other baked goodies, including these rusks from his van. He had worked as a baker in the U.S. for years until one day he decided he no longer wished to lead a hectic life. He returned to the island of his ancestors where he opened a bakery to the delight of all the inhabitants. He, too, gave us a bag full of kouloures when we went to visit his bakery. To make the Greek version, simply omit the pepper and replace the white wine with water.

MAKES ABOUT 36 RUSKS

2¼ teaspoons (1 package) active dry yeast

1⅔ cups unbleached all-purpose flour, plus extra for kneading and shaping

1⅔ cups semolina flour

Heaping ¼ cup aniseed

3 tablespoons white sesame seed

1 teaspoon fine kosher salt or sea salt

1 teaspoon freshly ground black pepper

½ cup plus 2 tablespoons extra-virgin olive oil, plus extra for greasing
   the bowl

¼ cup dry white wine

1. Dissolve the yeast in ¼ cup warm water and stir until creamy.

2. Combine the flours, aniseed, sesame seeds, salt, and pepper in a large bowl and make a well in the center. Add the olive oil to the well and, with fingertips, rub it into the flour until well incorporated. Add the yeast, wine, and ½ cup warm water and knead briefly to make a rough ball of dough.

3. Remove the dough to a lightly floured work surface. Knead for about 3 minutes. Invert the bowl over the dough and let rest for 15 minutes. Knead for about 2 to 3 minutes more, until the dough is smooth and elastic. Shape the dough into a ball. Grease a clean bowl with a little olive oil and place the dough in it, turning it to coat all over. Cover with plastic wrap and let rise in a warm, draft-free place for 1 hour. Fold the dough (see pages 6–7), cover again, and let rise for 1 hour more. The dough should have doubled in volume.

4. Return the dough to the work surface. Divide the dough into 3 equal pieces. Shape each piece of dough into a loaf about 12 inches long (see page 10). Transfer the loaves to a large nonstick baking sheet, or to a baking sheet lined with parchment paper or a silicone pastry mat, leaving at least 2 inches between them to allow for expansion as they rise and bake. Using a dough cutter, cut the loaves into pieces about 1 inch thick. Cover with a wet but not dripping kitchen towel and let rise for about 45 minutes. Meanwhile, preheat the oven to 500°F.

5. Uncover the sliced loaves and bake for about 15 minutes, until golden. Remove from the oven and reduce the heat to 175°F. Separate the slices and turn them so that they lie flat on the baking sheet. Return to the oven and bake for about 1 hour more, or until golden brown and completely hardened. Transfer to a wire rack to cool. If they have not hardened completely, return them to the turned-off oven to let them dry more. Serve at room temperature, or store in an airtight container for up to 3 weeks.

Cretan Rusks

Paximadi

These rusks are a specialty of Crete, where some cooks soak a cinnamon stick in the water used to make the dough to give the rusks a cinnamon flavor. Mastic and mahlep (see page 159) are available at Greek and Middle Eastern markets and from online sources. Most of the mastic sold in Greece, and also exported, comes from the Aegean island of Chios, which is five miles from the Turkish coast and the birthplace of Homer. In Roman times, women used the stiff stems of *Pistacia lentiscus,* the tree from which mastic is taken, to freshen their breath and whiten their teeth. When Christopher Columbus visited the island in February 1493, he wrote a letter to the treasurer of Aragon to announce his discovery of mastic, which he believed might be a cure for cholera.

MAKES 20 TO 24 INDIVIDUAL RUSKS

4½ teaspoons (2 packages) active dry yeast

2 cups barley flour or whole wheat flour

4 cups unbleached all-purpose flour, plus extra for shaping and kneading

2 teaspoons fine kosher salt or sea salt

Heaping ¼ teaspoon ground mastic (see page 159)

Heaping ¼ teaspoon ground mahlep (see page 159)

Extra-virgin olive oil, for greasing the bowl

1. Dissolve the yeast in ½ cup warm water and stir until creamy.

2. Combine the flours, salt, mastic, and mahlep in a large bowl and make a well in the center. Add the yeast to the well. With fingertips, work a little of the

yeast water into the flour, then gradually add 1½ cups warm water, bringing in the flour as you go along. Knead briefly to make a rough ball of dough.

3. Remove the dough to a lightly floured work surface, sprinkle with a little flour, and knead for about 3 minutes. Invert the bowl over the dough and let rest for 15 minutes. Knead for about 2 to 3 minutes more, until the dough is smooth and elastic.

4. Grease a large bowl with a little olive oil. Shape the dough into a ball and place it in the bowl, turning it to coat all over with oil. Cover with plastic wrap and let rise in a warm, draft-free place for 1 hour. Fold the dough (see pages 6–7), cover again, and let rise for 1 hour more. The dough should have doubled in volume.

5. Return the dough to the work surface. Divide it into equal halves and shape each half into a cylinder or fat strand 12 to 14 inches in length (see page 10). Place on a nonstick baking sheet, or a baking sheet lined with parchment paper or a silicone pastry mat, leaving at least 2 inches between the cylinders so that they will rise without touching. Using a dough cutter, preferably, or a sharp knife, cut halfway into the dough at about 1-inch intervals. Cover with a wet but not dripping kitchen towel and let rise for 30 to 45 minutes, until doubled in volume. Meanwhile, preheat the oven to 350°F.

6. Bake for 25 to 30 minutes. Remove from the oven and transfer to a wire rack to cool for 10 to 15 minutes. Reduce the heat to 175°F. Cut all the way through at the slashes that were made in the dough, to divide up the cylinders. Turn the pieces to lie flat on the baking sheet, and bake for 45 minutes more. Turn the pieces over and bake for 45 minutes more, or until lightly colored and completely hard. Transfer to a wire rack to cool. Serve at room temperature or store in an airtight container for up to several weeks.

✛ Bread Rings from Sfakia

Ladokoulouria

These rings are commonly known as kouloures, and there are many variations. The ones I had during a stay on the island of Kassos had cumin seeds and ground cloves in them. Most island women bake them at home on a regular basis to serve with coffee, to give to guests to take away with them, or to send to family members who live on the mainland.

MAKES 20 INDIVIDUAL RINGS

1 cinnamon stick

5 whole cloves

1½ teaspoons (about ⅔ package) active dry yeast

2⅔ cups unbleached all-purpose flour, plus extra for kneading and
    shaping

1½ teaspoons fine kosher salt or sea salt

¾ teaspoon ground aniseed

¾ teaspoon ground mastic (see page 159), optional

⅓ cup extra-virgin olive oil

¼ cup white sesame seeds or nigella seeds, or a combination

1. Put the cinnamon and cloves in a heat-proof medium bowl. Add ¾ cup boiling water and let infuse for 30 minutes. Discard the spices, reserving the infused water. Add the yeast and stir until creamy.

2. Combine the flour, salt, aniseed, and, if using, mastic in a large bowl and make a well in the center. Add the oil to the well and, with fingertips, rub the oil into

the flour until well incorporated. Add the yeast and mix to make a rough ball of dough.

3. Remove the dough to a lightly floured work surface. Knead for about 3 minutes. Invert the bowl over the dough and let rest for 15 minutes. Knead for about 2 to 3 minutes more, until the dough is smooth and elastic. Shape into a ball and place in a lightly floured clean bowl. Cover with plastic wrap and let rise in a warm, draft-free place for 1 hour. Fold the dough (see pages 6–7), cover again, and let rise for 1 hour more. The dough should have doubled in volume.

4. Return the dough to the work surface. Divide into 20 equal pieces. Shape each piece into a ball, cover with a damp kitchen towel, and let rest for 15 minutes.

5. Spread the sesame and/or nigella seeds on a baking sheet. Line another large baking sheet with parchment paper or a silicone pastry mat, or have ready a large nonstick baking sheet. Roll each ball of dough into a strand about 9 inches long (see page 10).

6. Roll a strand back and forth in the seeds to coat, then bring the ends of the strand together to make a ring. Press the joint to seal the ring. Transfer to the prepared baking sheet, and make the remaining rings in the same manner. Cover loosely with a wet but not dripping kitchen towel and let rise for 30 to 45 minutes, until nearly doubled in size. Meanwhile, preheat the oven to 375°F.

7. Bake for 15 minutes, or until golden. Reduce the heat to 175°F, and bake for 1½ to 2 hours more, until the breads have become completely hard. Transfer to a wire rack to cool. Serve at room temperature, or store in an airtight container for up to 3 months.

Pies and Tarts

Swiss Chard Pie

Erbazzone all'Emiliana

The filling for this classic pie from Emiglia-Romagna, in northern Italy, may be made with spinach, Swiss chard, or a combination of the two. The pie makes a perfect light summer lunch for two, served with a tomato salad. It freezes well; simply reheat it for 15 to 20 minutes in a 350°F oven.

MAKES 1 8- TO 9-INCH PIE

For the dough

1 cup unbleached all-purpose flour, plus extra for kneading and
      shaping
½ teaspoon kosher salt or sea salt
1 tablespoon extra-virgin olive oil

For the filling

1½ pounds Swiss chard leaves or spinach leaves, or a mixture,
      shredded
Kosher salt or sea salt
¼ pound sliced pancetta, cut into narrow 1-inch-long strips
1 garlic clove, finely chopped
Several sprigs of flat-leaf parsley, finely chopped
½ tablespoon extra-virgin olive oil, plus extra to grease the pie plate
3 to 4 scallions, white and light green parts, thinly sliced
¾ cup grated Parmigiano-Reggiano (about 1½ ounces)
Freshly ground black pepper

1. Combine the flour and salt in a large bowl and make a well in the center. Add the oil and, with fingertips, work it into the flour until well incorporated. Gradually pour in ½ cup plus 1 tablespoon warm water, bringing in the flour as you go along to make a rough ball of dough.

2. Remove the dough to a work surface and knead for about 3 minutes. Invert the bowl over the dough and let the dough rest for 15 minutes. Knead for 2 to 3 minutes more, until the dough is smooth and elastic. Cover with a wet but not dripping kitchen towel and set aside while the filling is made.

3. Pour ½ inch water into the bottom of a stockpot or a large sauté pan. Bring the water to a simmer over medium-high heat, and add the greens and a little salt. Cook, stirring frequently, until the greens are completely wilted. Drain the greens in a colander. When they are cool enough to handle, squeeze them as dry as possible by hand and transfer them to a bowl. Separate the shredded leaves. Cover the bowl and set it aside.

4. Combine the pancetta, garlic, and parsley in a bowl. Reserve 1 tablespoon of the mixture for a garnish. Heat the ½ tablespoon oil in a sauté pan over medium-high heat, and add the rest of the pancetta mixture and the scallions. Cook, stirring occasionally, until the garlic is lightly golden.

5. Preheat the oven to 400°F. Add the pancetta mixture and Parmesan to the greens. Mix well. Season with salt and pepper to taste. Grease an 8- or 9-inch pie plate with a little olive oil, or use a nonstick one.

6. Divide the dough in half. Roll out one half to a circle 10 to 11 inches in diameter. Place the circle over the pie plate to cover the bottom and sides, with a little overhang. Spread the filling evenly over the dough.

7. Roll out the other piece of dough to a circle about 10 inches in diameter. Lightly flour a rolling pin, roll the piece of dough onto it, and gently push in from two sides of the dough to create a pleated effect. Slowly unroll to cover the filling,

making sure the dough does not overlap the edges. Fold the overhang from the bottom piece of dough up and over the edges of the top piece. Scatter the reserved pancetta mixture over the top.

8. Bake for 40 to 50 minutes, until the top crust is lightly golden. Serve hot or warm.

✛ Zucchini and Rice Pie

Torta di Zucca e Riso

This pie is a specialty of the Parmensi hills, around Parma. It's made there with an Italian variety of zucchini that has a tough, hairy skin that needs to be scraped off, but has the virtue of being less watery than regular zucchini. It will be hard to find this Italian-style zucchini, so choose fresh and firm zucchini.

MAKES 1 10½-INCH PIE

2 recipes dough for Swiss Chard Pie, page 193, through step 2

2 cups whole milk

Kosher salt or sea salt

1 cup Arborio rice, rinsed under cold water

2 pounds zucchini, peeled, halved lengthwise, seeded, and very thinly sliced

⅔ cup ricotta

1 medium egg

2 tablespoons unsalted butter, softened

2 tablespoons extra-virgin olive oil, plus extra for greasing the pie plate and brushing the crust

Freshly ground black pepper

1. Make the dough and let it rest, covered with a damp kitchen towel, while the filling is prepared.

2. Pour the milk and 2 cups of water into a saucepan. Add a little salt and bring to a boil over medium heat. Add the rice and return to a boil. Boil for 3 minutes,

remove from the heat, and drain in a colander. Transfer the rice to a mixing bowl.

3. Add the zucchini, ricotta, egg, butter, and 2 tablespoons oil to the rice. Mix well. Season with salt and pepper to taste.

4. Grease a 10½-inch pie plate with olive oil. Divide the dough in two, one piece slightly larger than the other. Roll out the larger piece into a circle large enough to cover the bottom and sides of the pie plate, with a little overhang. Place the sheet of dough in the pie plate and spread the filling evenly over the dough. Roll out the remaining piece of dough to a circle large enough to cover the filling. Place over the filling. Fold the overhang from the bottom piece of dough up and over the edges of the top piece, but leave it loose enough for the rice to have room to expand. Generously brush the dough with olive oil. Cover with plastic wrap and let rest for 20 minutes. Preheat the oven to 425°F.

5. Brush the pie with more olive oil and prick the top with a fork in several places. Bake for 40 to 50 minutes, until the top crust is golden. Let the pie rest for 10 minutes. Carefully unmold to a serving plate and serve immediately, or place on a wire rack to serve later warm.

Neapolitan Macaroni Pie

Timballo di Maccheroni Napoletano

In Naples cooks use a dedicated timballo mold, not unlike a Christmas-pudding mold, to make this regal dish. It isn't easy to find such a mold outside of Italy, so I use a cake pan instead. Although the pie is time-consuming, you can prepare many of the components—the sauce and the meatballs and sausage—the day before. This is an adaptation of a recipe given to me by my great friend Franco Santasilia, author of the fascinating *La Cucina Aristocratica Napoletana,* who makes the timballo this way and also in *bianco,* with a milk-based rather than tomato-based sauce.

SERVES 8

For the dough
4 cups unbleached all-purpose flour, plus extra for rolling the dough
½ cup sugar
½ teaspoon fine kosher salt or sea salt
½ pound (2 sticks) unsalted butter, cut into ½-inch cubes
Zest of 1 lemon
Yolks of 6 medium eggs, beaten with ⅓ cup water

For the sauce
1 tablespoon lard or unsalted butter
⅓ cup extra-virgin olive oil
1 medium onion, finely chopped
1 garlic clove, finely chopped
6 ounces lean beef, from any cut, cut into 2 or 3 chunks

6 ounces lean pork, from any cut, cut into 2 or 3 chunks

⅓ cup red wine

1 14½-ounce can peeled tomatoes, drained and coarsely chopped

⅓ cup tomato paste

Fine kosher salt or sea salt

For the filling

10 ounces frozen peas

10 ounces sweet Italian sausages

⅔ cup dry white wine

10 ounces lean ground beef

1 medium egg

¼ cup fresh breadcrumbs, soaked in a little water and squeezed dry

3½ cups grated Parmigiano-Reggiano (about 7 ounces), plus extra for
    sprinkling between the layers of filling

Kosher salt or sea salt

Vegetable oil, for sautéing

1 pound small smooth penne pasta

10 ounces fresh mozzarella, cut into ¼-inch cubes

1. Make the dough: Combine the flour, sugar, and salt in a large bowl and make a well in the center. Add the butter and lemon zest to the well and, with fingertips, work them into the flour until well incorporated. Add the beaten egg yolks and, working quickly by hand, combine with the flour until you have a manageable dough; do not overwork the pastry.

2. Divide the dough into two pieces, with one about two-thirds the size of the other, and shape each piece into a ball. With the palm of a hand, flatten each ball into a thick disk. Wrap in plastic wrap and refrigerate them while the sauce and filling are prepared.

3. Make the sauce: Melt the lard in a saucepan over medium heat. Add the oil, onion, and garlic and cook, stirring occasionally, until the onion is soft and translucent. Add the beef and pork and cook them on all sides until browned and slightly caramelized. Add the red wine little by little and continue cooking, stirring occasionally, until the alcohol is evaporated.

4. Add the tomatoes and tomato paste and 1 cup water. Reduce the heat to low and simmer, stirring frequently, until the sauce is quite thick. Remove the sauce from the heat. With a slotted spoon, remove the meats; they may be discarded or saved for another purpose.

5. Make the filling: Place the peas in a heat-proof bowl and pour boiling water over them. Drain immediately and set aside. Place the sausages in one layer in a small saucepan. Add the white wine and place over medium heat. Bring the wine to a simmer and cook the sausages for 3 minutes, or until just done. Cut the sausages into thin slices and set aside.

6. Make the meatballs: Combine the ground beef, egg, breadcrumbs, half the Parmesan, and a little salt in a bowl. Shape the mixture into very small meatballs, about ½ inch in diameter. Cover the meatballs with plastic wrap and refrigerate them for at least 30 minutes, or until they stiffen slightly.

7. Heat vegetable oil in a nonstick pan over medium heat. Add the meatballs and sauté them, shaking the pan so that they cook on all sides, until lightly browned, about 3 to 4 minutes. Remove with a slotted spoon to a plate and set aside.

8. Cook the pasta in plenty of boiling salted water for a couple of minutes less than the package directions indicate. The pasta should be very al dente; it will finish cooking when the timballo bakes. Drain the pasta well and stir it into the tomato sauce. Add the remaining Parmesan and mix well. Set aside.

9. To assemble the timballo: Preheat the oven to 350°F. Dust a work surface with a little flour. Place the larger disk of dough on the surface, sprinkle it with flour, and roll it out to a circle ¼ inch thick and about 15 or 16 inches in diameter. Sprinkle with additional flour if necessary to keep the dough from sticking to the work surface and rolling pin.

10. Carefully roll the dough onto the rolling pin, then very slowly unroll it across the top of a 9-inch round nonstick springform cake pan at least 2¾ inches deep. Make sure that some of the pastry is overlapping the edges of the pan. The pastry will fall into the cake pan and line it, with some overhang; take care to work slowly enough to keep the dough from tearing or from falling unevenly into the pan. Gently press with fingertips in the corners to tuck in the pastry.

11. Spread one-third of the pasta mixture over the dough in the cake pan. Cover with half of the mozzarella, then half of the meatballs, half of the peas, and half of the sausages. Sprinkle with a little more Parmesan. Cover with half the remaining pasta, and then with the remaining mozzarella, meatballs, peas, and sausages. Top all with the remaining pasta.

12. Dust the work surface with flour again and roll out the smaller disk of dough to a circle 9 inches in diameter. Carefully roll the dough onto the rolling pin, then slowly unroll it over the filling. Fold the top ½ inch or so of the overhang from the bottom pastry up over the top piece, pressing gently to seal. Use a toothpick to prick the top pastry in several places to allow steam to escape.

13. Bake for 40 to 50 minutes, until the top crust is golden. Remove from the oven and let sit for about 10 minutes. Release the pan and transfer the timballo to a serving platter. Serve immediately.

❖ Tagliatelle Pie

Torta di Tagliatelle

This tagliatelle pie, a casual weekday version of a timballo (see page 198), is much simpler to make and, though plainer in taste, is still a wonderful informal meal. I serve it with a plain tomato sauce on the side for drizzling or pouring over each slice.

SERVES 8

For the pastry
4 cups unbleached all-purpose flour, plus extra for working the dough
½ teaspoon fine kosher salt or sea salt
½ teaspoon sugar
½ cup (1 stick) plus 2 tablespoons unsalted butter, cut into ¼-inch
    cubes
2 medium eggs

For the béchamel sauce
2 tablespoons unsalted butter
2 tablespoons unbleached all-purpose flour
1¼ cups whole milk
1 cup crème fraîche
½ teaspoon ground nutmeg
½ teaspoon crushed red pepper flakes

For the filling
1 pound tagliatelle pasta
2 tablespoons unsalted butter
½ cup grated Parmigiano-Reggiano (about 1 ounce)
¾ cup diced or shredded Fontina (about 3 ounces)
8 ounces fresh mozzarella, cut into small cubes
1 medium egg beaten with 1 teaspoon water
1 recipe tomato sauce for Neapolitan Pizza (see page 42), heated,
    optional

1. Make the pastry: Combine the flour, salt, and sugar in a large bowl. Using fingertips, work the butter into the flour to a coarse crumble. Add the eggs and ½ cup water and knead quickly just until the pastry holds together; do not overwork the pastry. Divide the pastry into 2 pieces, one twice as large as the other, and shape each piece into a ball. Flatten each ball into a thick disk, wrap in plastic wrap, and refrigerate for 1 hour.

2. Make the sauce: Melt the butter in a saucepan over medium heat. Add the flour and whisk until well incorporated. Slowly add the milk and bring to a boil, whisking constantly. Whisk in the crème fraîche, return to a boil, and simmer for 3 minutes. Remove from the heat and set aside. Add the nutmeg and crushed pepper flakes.

3. Cook the tagliatelle in plenty of boiling salted water for a couple of minutes less than the package directions indicate. The pasta should be very al dente; it will finish cooking as the pie bakes. Drain the pasta well and transfer it to a large bowl. Add the 2 tablespoons butter and mix well. Pour in the reserved béchamel sauce and mix well, until the pasta is evenly coated with the sauce.

4. Preheat the oven to 400°F. Dust a work surface with flour and roll out the larger piece of pastry to a circle that will line the bottom and sides of a 10-inch round and 2½-inch-deep cake pan with a little overhang. Roll the circle of pastry over the rolling pin and then carefully unroll it over the cake pan. Gently

tuck in the corners. Spread half of the pasta mixture over the pastry. Sprinkle with half of the Parmesan, then with half of the Fontina and half of the mozzarella. Cover with the remaining pasta and then the remaining Parmesan, Fontina, and mozzarella.

5. Roll out the other piece of pastry to a diameter of about 10½ inches, to cover the filling with a little overhang. Pinch the pastries together to seal. Trim the edges with a knife, and pinch again tightly to ensure a good seal. Brush with the beaten egg.

6. Bake for 35 to 40 minutes, until the top crust is golden. Remove from the oven and let sit for 5 minutes. Unmold to a serving dish and serve immediately, accompanied, if you like, with the tomato sauce, or transfer to a wire rack to serve later warm.

⚡ Potato Pie

Torta di Patate

Here is the Italian version of the French tourte Bérrichonne, page 216. The French pie is a rather refined affair in which potatoes are sliced very thin and encased in puff pastry. By contrast, the Italian version is hearty peasant fare, with mashed potatoes and a simple dough. For an interesting variation on the filling here, dice the potatoes instead of mashing them and add fresh tomatoes, capers, and olives to the boiled potatoes.

SERVES 6 TO 8

2 pounds all-purpose potatoes

2 ounces bacon fat, chopped

1 tablespoon unsalted butter

1 tablespoon extra-virgin olive oil, plus more for greasing the pie plate

1 medium onion, finely chopped (about ½ cup)

1 medium leek, white part only, finely chopped (about 1½ cups)

1 tablespoon tomato paste

3 tablespoons beef stock

4 ounces freshly grated Parmigiano-Reggiano (about 2 cups)

¼ cup whole milk

Fine kosher salt or sea salt

2 recipes dough for Swiss Chard Pie (page 193)

Fine breadcrumbs

1. Place the potatoes in water to cover in a large saucepan over medium heat. Bring to a boil and cook for about 25 minutes, until tender.

2. Put the bacon fat, butter, and olive oil in a sauté pan over medium heat. When the fats have melted, add the onion and leek and cook until soft. Add the tomato paste and beef stock and cook, stirring frequently, until the tomato paste is completely diluted. This will be the soffritto.

3. Drain the potatoes, peel them, and put them through a potato ricer to mash them. Return them to the saucepan, and add the soffritto, Parmesan, milk, and salt to taste. Mix well, cover, and set aside.

4. Preheat the oven to 350°F. Brush a 10-inch round pie plate with a little olive oil. Divide the dough into 2 pieces, one slightly larger than the other. Roll out the larger piece of dough, sprinkling with flour every now and then, to a circle large enough to line the bottom and sides of the pie plate, with a little extra to hang over the edges. Sprinkle the bottom and sides of the pie plate lightly with breadcrumbs and place the rolled-out circle of dough over the plate. Carefully tuck the corners in. Spread the potato mixture evenly over the dough.

5. Roll out the other piece of dough to a circle large enough to cover the filling, with some overhang. Place over the potatoes, and press to seal the overhang.

6. Bake for 30 to 40 minutes, until crisp and golden all over. Serve hot or warm.

⚎ Radicchio Pie

Pizza di Verdura

I made this pie at a friend's house in Los Angeles one evening when we had Chinese friends coming over for dinner. Chinese people are accustomed to unusual tastes and textures, and so I thought that the slight bitterness of the radicchio filling would appeal to Mei, our friend, and Xiaoyin, her nanny. How wrong I was. Xaioyin took one bite of the pie, immediately pushed back her plate, and said that the pie was bitter enough to kill someone. Mei agreed with her, although she politely ate a little of the pie. Italians, in any case, are used to bitter tastes, and this pie, a specialty from Puglia, is quite unusual and certainly worth trying.

SERVES 4 TO 6

For the dough
4½ teaspoons (2 packages) active dry yeast
2⅔ cups unbleached all-purpose flour, plus extra for kneading and
    shaping
1½ teaspoons fine kosher salt or sea salt
¼ teaspoon freshly ground black pepper

For the filling

½ cup extra-virgin olive oil, plus extra for greasing the pie plate and
   drizzling over the pie

2½ pounds radicchio, trimmed and shredded

1 garlic clove

Fine kosher salt or sea salt

Freshly ground black pepper

Heaping ¼ cup salted capers, rinsed and drained

¾ cup black olives, pitted and halved

1 medium egg beaten with a pinch of salt

1. Dissolve the yeast in ½ cup warm water and stir until creamy. Combine the flour, salt, and pepper in a large bowl and make a well in the center. Add the yeast to the well and gradually add ½ cup warm water, bringing in the flour as you go along. Knead briefly to make a rough ball of dough.

2. Remove the dough to a lightly floured work surface. Knead for about 3 minutes. Invert the bowl over the dough and let rest for 15 minutes. Knead for 2 to 3 minutes more, until the dough is smooth and elastic. Shape the dough into a ball and place in a lightly floured clean bowl. Cover with plastic wrap and let rise in a warm, draft-free place for 1 hour. Fold the dough (see pages 6–7), cover again, and let rise for 1 hour more. The dough should have doubled in volume.

3. Put the oil, radicchio, and garlic in a large sauté pan over medium heat. Cook, stirring frequently, until the radicchio is wilted and very lightly golden, 20 to 30 minutes. Season with salt and pepper to taste. Remove from the heat and discard the garlic.

4. Return the dough to the work surface. Divide into 2 pieces, one slightly larger than the other. Shape each piece into a ball, cover with a damp kitchen towel, and let rest for 15 minutes.

5. Grease a 10-inch round pie plate with a little olive oil. Roll out the larger piece of dough, sprinkling with flour every now and then, to a circle large enough to

line the bottom and sides of the pie plate, with a little extra to hang over the edges. Place the circle of dough over the pie plate. Carefully tuck in the corners. Spread the radicchio evenly over the dough, and scatter the capers and olives over the radicchio. Roll out the second piece of dough to a circle large enough to cover the filling. Place over the filling, fold the loose dough over the top piece, and press to seal. Brush generously with olive oil, loosely cover with plastic wrap, and let rise for 45 minutes. Meanwhile, preheat the oven to 400°F.

6. Brush the top of the pie with the beaten egg. Bake the pie for about 30 minutes, until golden all over. Serve warm or at room temperature.

Salami, Ham, and Cheese Pie from Naples

Pizza Rustica Napoletana

The Neapolitan pizza rustica is far more elaborate, and rather more sophisticated, than the one from Abruzzo (see page 212). As it bakes, it rises a little like a soufflé, because of the egg whites in the filling; unfortunately, it collapses fairly quickly once it has been taken out of the oven. It is a good idea to serve it immediately, for it looks lovely while it's still puffed up.

SERVES 4 TO 6

For the pastry
2⅔ cups unbleached all-purpose flour, plus extra for kneading and
   shaping
1½ teaspoons fine kosher salt or sea salt
1 tablespoon sugar
9 tablespoons (1 stick plus 1 tablespoon) cold unsalted butter, cut into
   cubes
2 medium egg yolks beaten with ⅓ cup plus 1 tablespoon water

For the filling
4 egg yolks, beaten
4 egg whites, beaten into stiff peaks
12 ounces ricotta, mashed (about 1⅓ cups)
½ cup finely diced fresh mozzarella (about 2 ounces)
¾ cup finely diced smoked provola (about 3 ounces)

½ cup finely diced prosciutto (about 2 ounces)
½ cup finely diced Italian-style salami (about 2 ounces)
2 tablespoons freshly grated Parmigiano-Reggiano
Fine kosher salt or sea salt
Freshly ground black pepper

1 egg yolk beaten with 1 teaspoon milk

1. Make the pastry: Combine the flour, salt, and sugar in a large bowl and make a well in the center. Add the butter to the well and, with fingertips, rub it into the flour until well incorporated. Add the 2 beaten egg yolks and knead quickly to make a smooth dough; do not over-knead. Wrap in plastic wrap and place in the refrigerator while the filling is prepared.

2. Make the filling: Put the 4 beaten egg yolks in a large bowl and gradually fold in the stiff egg whites. Mix the remaining ingredients for the filling in another large bowl, then gently fold in the eggs.

3. Preheat the oven to 350°F. Grease an 8- or 9-inch round pie plate with a little butter. Divide the pastry into 2 pieces, one slightly larger than the other. Roll out the larger piece into a circle large enough to cover the bottom and sides of the pie plate, with a little overhang. Place the rolled-out pastry over the pie plate. Carefully tuck in the corners. Spread the filling evenly over the pastry.

4. Roll out the other piece of pastry into a circle large enough to cover the filling, with a little overhang. Place over the filling. Fold and seal the excess pastry all around in a fluted edge, by pressing on the edge and making small diagonal pleats all the way around. Prick with a fork here and there to let out steam during baking. Brush the top with the egg-milk mixture.

5. Bake for 50 minutes to 1 hour, until golden brown all over and slightly puffed up. Serve immediately.

✤ Sausage and Cheese Pie from Abruzzo

Pizza Rustica d'Abruzzo

Though it's called a pizza in Abruzzo, this is a filled pie with two crusts, not one. In Italy, fresh cow's-milk mozzarella is called *fior di latte,* meaning "flower of the milk." It is always better to use cow's-milk (as opposed to buffalo) mozzarella in cooking, because it is less watery.

SERVES 4 TO 6

For the pastry
2 cups unbleached all-purpose flour, plus extra if needed
½ teaspoon fine kosher salt or sea salt
⅓ cup plus 1 tablespoon lard or unsalted butter
2 medium eggs plus 1 medium egg yolk
Unsalted butter, for greasing the pie plate

For the filling
8 ounces fresh mozzarella, diced (about 2¼ cups)
½ pound Italian-style salami, diced (heaping 1 cup)
2 medium eggs, beaten
2 tablespoons freshly grated Parmigiano-Reggiano

1. Combine the flour and salt in a large bowl and make a well in the center. Add the lard to the well and, with fingertips, rub it into the flour until the mixture is crumbly. Add the 2 eggs and the egg yolk. Mix quickly to make a medium-soft pastry; do not over-knead the pastry.

2. Preheat the oven to 425°F. Grease an 8-inch round pie plate with a little butter, or use a nonstick one. Divide the pastry into 2 pieces, one slightly larger than the other, and transfer to a lightly floured work surface. Roll out the larger piece of pastry to a circle large enough to line the bottom and sides of the pie plate. Place the pastry in the pie plate and, with a fork, prick the bottom in a few places.

3. Scatter the mozzarella over the pastry. Arrange the salami all over the cheese and pour the beaten eggs evenly over the filling, reserving a little to brush the top of the pie. Sprinkle with the grated Parmesan.

4. Roll out the remaining pastry to a circle large enough to cover the filling and slightly overlap the bottom pastry. Cover the filling with this pastry, and press on the edges to seal. Brush with the reserved egg and, using a fork, make a few pricks here and there to allow steam to escape during baking.

5. Bake for 25 to 35 minutes, until the top is golden brown. Remove from the oven and let sit for about 5 minutes. Serve hot or warm.

❖ Calzone from Puglia

Calzone Pugliese

This Pugliese version of a calzone is made as a rectangle, instead of the more common crescent shape, and its large size means that you make one and serve it in slices, rather than spending more time making individual calzoni.

SERVES 4 TO 6

For the dough
2¼ teaspoons (1 package) active dry yeast
2⅔ cups unbleached all-purpose flour, plus extra for kneading and
    shaping
1½ teaspoons fine kosher salt or sea salt
2 tablespoons extra-virgin olive oil or lard

For the filling
2 tablespoons extra-virgin olive oil, plus extra for brushing the baking
    sheet and the calzone
1 pound onions, coarsely chopped
Fine kosher salt or sea salt
Freshly ground black pepper
10 cherry tomatoes, halved
1 cup black olives, pitted and halved
¼ cup salted capers, rinsed and drained (about 2 ounces)
3 salted anchovies, rinsed, filleted, and chopped
2 tablespoons finely chopped flat-leaf parsley
1 cup grated pecorino romano (about 3 ounces)

1. Make the dough: Dissolve the yeast in ¼ cup warm water and stir until creamy. Combine the flour and salt in a large bowl and make a well in the center. Add the olive oil to the well and, with fingertips, rub it into the flour until well incorporated. Add the yeast and gradually add ½ cup plus 1 tablespoon warm water, bringing in the flour as you go along. Knead briefly to make a rough ball of dough.

2. Remove the dough to a lightly floured work surface. Sprinkle with a little more flour and knead for about 3 minutes. Invert the bowl over the dough and let rest for 15 minutes. Knead for 2 to 3 minutes more, until the dough is smooth and elastic. Shape the dough into a ball and place in a lightly floured clean bowl. Cover with plastic wrap and let rise in a warm, draft-free place for 1 hour, until doubled in volume.

3. Make the filling: Put the olive oil and onions in a sauté pan over medium heat. Cook the onions, stirring occasionally, until soft and transparent. Season with salt and pepper to taste; do not oversalt, for the olives, capers, anchovies, and cheese will add salt as well. Add the tomatoes and olives and cook for about 5 minutes. Add the capers, anchovies, and parsley, and cook for about 2 minutes more. Remove from the heat to let cool slightly. Add the pecorino, and mix well.

4. With a fist, gently punch the dough down the middle. Fold one half over the other and remove to a work surface. Shape the dough into a ball, sprinkle with flour, and cover loosely with plastic wrap. Let rest for 15 minutes.

5. Preheat the oven to 450°F. Sprinkle the work surface with a little more flour. Place the dough on it and roll it out to a 15 by 15-inch square, sprinkling with flour every now and then. Spread the filling on one half of the square, leaving about ½ inch free around the edges. Fold the plain half of the dough over the filling, making a large rectangle. Transfer the calzone to a nonstick baking sheet, or to a baking sheet lined with parchment paper or a silicone pastry mat. Brush generously with oil, cover with plastic wrap, and let rise for 30 minutes.

6. Uncover the calzone and bake it for 25 to 30 minutes, until golden brown all over. Transfer to a wire rack to cool slightly. Serve hot or warm.

✛ French Potato Pie

Tourte Bérrichonne

Puff pastry is time-consuming to make because it has to be rolled out and then refrigerated several times to achieve the thin layers its French name indicates: *pâte feuilletée,* which means "many-leafed pastry." I usually buy puff pastry from a good baker. It is crucial that the puff pastry stay cold, so when rolling it out, work quickly on a cold surface—marble or granite, perhaps. As you roll it, flour the pastry regularly so that it doesn't stick to the work surface and rolls out evenly. If there's no good baker nearby, be sure to buy ready-made puff pastry made with all butter.

SERVES 6 TO 8

1 17.3-ounce package frozen puff pastry, thawed in the refrigerator

2 pounds all-purpose potatoes, thinly sliced

1½ tablespoons finely chopped flat-leaf parsley

1 medium shallot, finely chopped

2 garlic cloves, finely chopped

Fine kosher salt or sea salt

Freshly ground black pepper

5 ounces smoked bacon, finely diced

1 egg beaten with 1 teaspoon water

¼ cup crème fraîche

1. Place one sheet of puff pastry on a nonstick baking sheet, or on a baking sheet lined with parchment paper or a silicone pastry mat.

2. Combine the potatoes, parsley, shallot, and garlic in a bowl. Season with salt and pepper to taste. Spread the mixture over the pastry that is on the baking sheet, leaving about 1 inch free around the edges. Scatter the bacon over the potatoes. Brush the edges with a little of the beaten egg. Place the other pastry sheet over the filling, aligning the edges. Lightly press on the edges to seal.

3. Brush with the beaten egg, taking care not to let the egg dribble over the edges, which will inhibit the pastry from puffing. Let dry briefly, then brush again with egg. With a fork, prick the pastry in different places to let steam out. Loosely cover with plastic wrap and let rest in the refrigerator for 1 hour. Meanwhile, preheat the oven to 400°F.

4. Bake the tourte for 45 minutes to 1 hour, until well puffed up and golden all over. Remove from the oven, and cut out a circle in the middle of the top layer of pastry. Spoon the crème fraîche inside the tourte and replace the circle of pastry. Let sit for about 5 minutes, until the crème fraîche has seeped into the potatoes. Serve hot or warm.

French Pork, Chestnut, and Apple Pie

Tourte Cévenole

Here is a wonderfully warming pie for supper on a cold winter night, served with steamed green beans or broccoli or a simple salad. The combination of slightly sour apples with the sweet chestnuts and pork is very appealing inside the flaky short crust. Be sure, whenever making a short crust, to use the butter straight out of the refrigerator, cut into a medium dice, so that it doesn't become too soft as you incorporate it into the flour.

SERVES 6 TO 8

1 recipe short-crust pastry for Tian Pie (page 250), through step 2

10 ounces vacuum-packed (not canned) peeled whole chestnuts

2 sprigs fresh thyme

1 bay leaf

10 ounces trimmed pork meat, from pork chops, ground medium fine

10 ounces Granny Smith or other medium-tart apples, cored, peeled, quartered, and thinly sliced

2 medium eggs, beaten

Fine kosher salt or sea salt

Freshly ground black pepper

Unbleached all-purpose flour, for rolling the pastry

1 egg yolk beaten with 1 teaspoon water and a pinch of salt

I. Divide the pastry into 2 pieces, one slightly larger than the other. Pat into disks, wrap in plastic wrap, and refrigerate for 1 hour.

2. Poach the chestnuts in a little salted water with the thyme and bay leaf for about 10 minutes. Drain and chop coarse. Discard the thyme and bay leaf.

3. Put the pork, apples, chestnuts, and 2 beaten eggs in a large bowl. Season with salt and pepper to taste, and mix well.

4. Preheat the oven to 350°F. Place the larger piece of pastry on a lightly floured work surface (leaving the smaller piece in the refrigerator) and roll it out, sprinkling with flour every now and then, to a circle large enough to line the bottom and sides of a 9½-inch round nonstick pie plate or tourtière, with a little overhang. Roll the pastry circle onto the rolling pin and unroll it over the pie plate, taking care to center it well; it will be difficult to pick it up and reposition. Gently tuck in the corners. Spread the pork filling evenly over the pastry.

5. Roll out the other piece of pastry to a circle large enough to cover the filling. Place over the filling, bring the loose edges up over the top, and press to seal. Then cut out a small circle of pastry in the middle to insert a "chimney," by rolling a piece of cardboard and fitting it into the hole. Brush the top of the pie with the beaten egg yolk.

6. Bake for 60 to 70 minutes, until golden all over. Remove from the oven and discard the chimney. Let sit for a few minutes. Serve immediately.

✤ French Pâté in Short Crust

Pâté en Croûte

Pâtés en croûte are probably the most common of all French pies. This is not to say that they are ordinary. Quite the contrary; when well prepared, they are elegant creations made with a variety of fillings, including foie gras, chicken livers, different ground meats, and game. The pastry shell is usually made with short crust, which is made with more or less butter depending on the style and tastes of the charcutier or home cook. Pâtés en croûte are typically served at room temperature. They are eaten as snacks, starters, or main courses. The quatre-épices seasoning used here, a combination of black pepper with coriander, nutmeg, cinnamon, and cloves, is also used in civets, terrines, daubes, and a variety of charcuterie. If you cannot find the seasoning, use a pinch of each of the spices listed above. It is best not to refrigerate pâté en croûte, for the pastry will spoil. Instead, find the coolest place in your kitchen (or elsewhere in the home) and keep it there, with the filling part covered with foil or plastic wrap.

SERVES 8 TO 10

1 recipe short-crust pastry for Tian Pie (page 250), through step 2

14 ounces veal breast, finely ground

14 ounces pork shoulder, finely ground

2 shallots, finely chopped

2 tablespoons finely chopped flat-leaf parsley

2 tablespoons finely chopped chives

2 medium eggs, beaten

¼ teaspoon ground nutmeg

¼ teaspoon quatre-épices seasoning, optional

Fine kosher salt or sea salt

Freshly ground black pepper

1⅓ cups green olives, pitted and halved

¼ cup cognac

Unbleached all-purpose flour, for rolling the pastry

14 ounces thick-sliced cooked ham, cut into thin strips

1 egg yolk beaten with 1 teaspoon water

1. Divide the pastry into 2 pieces, one twice as large as the other. Pat each piece into a disk. Wrap in plastic wrap and refrigerate for 1 hour.

2. Put the veal and pork in a large bowl. Add the shallots, herbs, eggs, nutmeg, and, if using, quatre-épices. Season with salt and pepper to taste. Mix well. Add the olives and cognac and mix well again.

3. Preheat the oven to 400°F. Place the larger piece of pastry on a lightly floured work surface (leaving the smaller piece in the refrigerator) and, sprinkling with flour every now and then, roll it out into a circle large enough to line the bottom and sides of an 8 by 2½-inch round cake pan, with a little overhang. The pastry should be just over ¼ inch thick. Roll the pastry circle around a rolling pin and carefully unroll over the cake pan. Gently tuck in the corners, leaving a little overhang.

4. Layer one-fourth of the ham over the pastry. Spread one-third of the meat filling over the ham, cover with another one-fourth of the ham, and spread another one-third of the meat filling over the ham. Cover with another one-fourth of the ham, and then mound the remaining meat filling over. Cover with the last one-fourth of the ham.

5. Roll out the smaller piece of pastry to a circle large enough to cover the filling. Place it over the filling. Trim the loose edges to have enough extra pastry to make a ring border. Press to seal, and brush the top with the egg wash. Roll the

trimmed extra pastry into thin strands, and use these to decorate the top of the pie, brushing with additional egg wash.

6. Bake for 60 to 70 minutes, until crisp and golden all over; cover the top loosely with aluminum foil if the crust is browning too quickly as the end of the cooking time approaches. Remove from the oven, let rest for 5 minutes, and unmold onto a wire rack to let cool. Serve at room temperature.

✤ French Swiss Chard Pie

Tarte aux Blettes

Tarte aux blettes is one of Nice's great treasures. There are really two tartes aux blettes. One is a savory tart, made with an olive oil short crust filled with chard, olives, thyme, eggs, and cream. The other is a sweet-savory tart, made with a sweet short crust filled with chard, pine nuts, Parmesan, lemon zest, raisins, sugar, and rum. The recipe here is for the sweet-savory version. It is usually served as a dessert, but I like to serve it as an unusual lunch or supper.

SERVES 6

1 recipe short-crust pastry for Neapolitan Macaroni Pie (page 198), through step 1

Unsalted butter, for greasing the pie plate

2 medium eggs

⅓ cup sugar

Grated zest of 1 unwaxed lemon

1 cup grated Parmigiano-Reggiano (about 2 ounces)

1 pound Swiss chard leaves, very finely shredded

3 ounces raisins (about ¾ cup), soaked for 30 minutes in 2 tablespoons rum and drained

3 ounces pine nuts (about ¾ cup)

Fine kosher salt or sea salt

Freshly ground black pepper

Unbleached all-purpose flour, for rolling the pastry

1. Divide the pastry into 2 pieces, one slightly larger than the other. Pat each into a thick disk. Wrap it in plastic wrap and refrigerate for 1 hour.

2. Preheat the oven to 450°F. Grease a 9-inch round pie plate with a little butter. Beat 1 whole egg and 1 egg white (reserving the yolk for brushing the pie) with the sugar and lemon zest in a large bowl. Add the Parmesan, Swiss chard, raisins, and pine nuts. Season with salt and pepper to taste, and mix well.

3. Sprinkle a work surface with flour. Roll out the larger piece of dough (leaving the other in the refrigerator), sprinkling lightly with flour every now and then, to a circle large enough to line the bottom and sides of the pie plate, with a little overhang. Roll the circle of dough onto the rolling pin and unroll it over the pie plate. Carefully tuck in the corners. Spread the filling over the pastry. Roll out the other piece of dough to a circle large enough to cover the filling. Place over the filling. Fold the overhanging pastry up over the edge of the top pastry and press to seal.

4. Beat the reserved egg yolk with 1 teaspoon water and brush the top of the pie with it. Bake for 45 minutes, or until golden all over. Let cool for 5 to 10 minutes, then unmold to a wire rack to continue cooling. Serve warm or at room temperature.

❖ Spinach Pie

Spanakopittia

There are endless variations on spanakopita. It can be made in many shapes and sizes. The dough can be a bread dough, an olive oil short crust, or phyllo. The recipe here is my adaptation of an interesting version I once had while visiting Kassos, a wonderful and unspoiled island east of Crete. The islanders call the pie *spanakopittia*. This one was made by a woman named Mangafoula, who is known around the island by her nickname, "the captain's wife." Mangafoula makes her *pittia* with a bread dough; adds rice, tomatoes, onions, and cinnamon to the spinach; and omits the feta or myzithra cheese that is used elsewhere in Greece. This recipe is for one large *pittia* like Mangafoula's, but you can divide the dough into 8 to 10 equal pieces to make individual pies; simply roll out the pieces into thin circles, and fill and fold the dough in half-moons sealed with fluted borders.

SERVES 6 TO 8

For the dough
2¼ teaspoons (1 package) active dry yeast
3⅓ cups unbleached all-purpose flour, plus extra for kneading and
   shaping
1½ teaspoons fine kosher salt or sea salt
⅓ cup extra-virgin olive oil, plus extra for greasing and brushing

For the filling
1 pound fresh spinach, finely shredded (about 14 cups)
Fine kosher salt or sea salt
1 medium onion, very finely chopped (about ½ cup)
2 medium tomatoes, seeded and finely chopped (about ¾ cup)
3 tablespoons short-grain white rice, rinsed under cold water
¼ cup extra-virgin olive oil
¼ teaspoon ground cinnamon
Freshly ground black pepper

1. Dissolve the yeast in ¼ cup warm water and stir until creamy. Combine the
   flour and salt in a large bowl and make a well in the center. Add the olive oil to

the well and, with fingertips, rub the oil into the flour until well incorporated. Add the yeast and gradually add another ⅔ cup plus 1 tablespoon warm water, bringing in the flour as you go along. Mix briefly to make a rough ball of dough.

2. Remove the dough to a lightly floured work surface. Knead for about 3 minutes. Shape the dough into a ball. Invert the bowl over the dough and let rest for 15 minutes. Knead for 2 or 3 minutes more, until the dough is smooth and elastic. Shape into a ball again. Grease a bowl with a little olive oil and place the dough in the bowl, turning it to coat all over with oil. Cover with plastic wrap and let rise in a warm, draft-free place for 1 hour. Fold the dough (see pages 6–7), cover again, and let rise for 1 hour more. The dough should have doubled in volume.

3. Put the spinach in a large bowl and sprinkle with salt. With fingertips, rub the salt into the spinach until it wilts. Squeeze out the excess liquid. Transfer the spinach to a clean bowl and separate the leaves. Add the onion, tomatoes, rice, olive oil, cinnamon, and pepper to taste and mix well. Taste and adjust the seasoning, and set aside.

4. Return the dough to the work surface and divide the dough in half. Roll the halves into balls, cover with plastic wrap, and let rest for 15 minutes.

5. Roll out one ball of dough to a circle 12 to 13 inches in diameter, sprinkling with flour every now and then. Transfer to a nonstick baking sheet, or to a baking sheet lined with parchment paper or a silicone pastry mat. Spread the filling over the dough, leaving about ½ inch free around the edge. Roll out the other piece of dough to the same size and place it over the filling, aligning the edges. Flatten and flute the edges to seal. Brush the top with olive oil, cover loosely with plastic wrap, and let rest for 30 to 45 minutes. Meanwhile, preheat the oven to 375°F.

6. Bake the pie for 40 to 45 minutes, until golden brown all over. Remove from the oven and let sit for about 5 minutes, then slide the pie onto a wire rack to let cool. Serve at room temperature.

✢ Greek Meat Pie from Kefalonia

Kreatopitta Kefalonitiki

Kefalonia has long been the breadbasket of the Ionian Islands. Pies have always been considered festive fare there, especially those made with billy goat for August fifteenth to celebrate the feast of the Virgin Mary. This hearty pie from Kefalonia may be made with lamb or beef.

SERVES 4 TO 6

1 recipe short-crust pastry for Tian Pie (page 250), through step 1
1 pound lean beef or lamb, cut into bite-size pieces (about 2 cups)
Fine kosher salt or sea salt
12 peppercorns
3 tablespoons extra-virgin olive oil
1 medium onion, thinly sliced (about ¾ cup)
1 garlic clove, crushed
1 medium tomato, finely chopped (about ⅓ cup)
2 tablespoons white short-grain rice, rinsed
¼ teaspoon ground cinnamon
Freshly ground black pepper
1 medium egg
Heaping ¼ cup crumbled feta cheese
1 egg lightly beaten with 1 teaspoon water and a pinch of salt

1. Divide the pastry into 2 pieces, one slightly larger than the other. Pat the pieces into disks. Wrap in plastic wrap and refrigerate for 1 hour.

2. Put the meat in a saucepan and cover with water. Bring to a boil over medium heat; just as the water is about to boil, skim it clean. Add salt to taste and the peppercorns. Cover the pan and simmer for about 30 minutes, until the meat is tender. Drain the water and discard the peppercorns. Cover and set aside.

3. Put the olive oil and onion in a sauté pan over medium-high heat. Cook, stirring occasionally, until the onion is lightly golden. Add the garlic, cook for about 1 minute, and then add the tomato, rice, and meat. Stir for another minute or so, then add ⅓ cup water, and the cinnamon and pepper, and bring to a gentle boil. Cook, stirring occasionally, for about 10 minutes. Remove from the heat, cover with a clean kitchen towel, and let cool. Add the egg and feta and mix well. Cover with a kitchen towel and set aside.

4. On a lightly floured work surface, roll out the larger disk of dough to a circle large enough to line the bottom and sides of a 10-inch round pie plate, with a little overhang. Place the dough over the bottom of the pie plate. Carefully tuck in the corners. Spread the meat filling evenly over the dough.

5. Roll out the smaller disk of dough to a circle large enough to cover the filling. Place over the filling and bring up the overhang loosely over the edge of the top pastry. Cover with plastic wrap and refrigerate for 1 hour. Meanwhile, preheat the oven to 400°F.

6. Uncover the pie and brush twice with the beaten egg. Bake for 45 to 50 minutes, until crisp and golden all over. Serve immediately, or transfer to a wire rack to serve later warm.

Greek Meat and Potato Pie

Peta me Arni

This is a lighter version of the previous pie. It's made with phyllo instead of a short-crust pastry, and it has potatoes mixed in with the meat instead of rice.

SERVES 6

For the filling

3 tablespoons unsalted butter

1 pound 12 ounces lean lamb shoulder, cut into ½-inch cubes (about 3½ cups)

1 medium onion, very finely chopped (about ½ cup)

2 medium all-purpose potatoes, diced (about 1½ cups)

¾ cup crumbled feta cheese (about 3½ ounces)

¾ cup finely chopped flat-leaf parsley

½ teaspoon crushed dried mint leaves

½ teaspoon ground cinnamon

Fine kosher salt or sea salt

Freshly ground black pepper

¼ cup extra-virgin olive oil

½ cup (1 stick) unsalted butter, melted

12 sheets phyllo pastry, thawed if frozen

I. Melt the 3 tablespoons butter in a large sauté pan over medium-high heat. Add the lamb and cook, stirring occasionally, until browned. With a slotted spoon, transfer the lamb to a bowl, leaving the cooking juices in the pan.

2. Add the onion and potatoes to the pan and cook, stirring occasionally, until the potatoes are just done, 10 to 15 minutes. Return the lamb to the pan, and add the feta, parsley, mint, cinnamon, salt and pepper to taste, and the olive oil. Mix well and set aside.

3. Preheat the oven to 400°F. Brush a 10-inch round pie plate with a little of the melted butter. Place 1 sheet of phyllo in the pie plate and brush with melted butter. Lay down another 4 sheets, at different angles so that the pie plate is covered, and brush the top of each with butter. Trim the overhang; alternatively, brush the overhang with butter, which will make the pie look very pretty once it is baked but will make for a lot of crumbs when you come to cut it. Spread the filling evenly over the phyllo. Cover with the remaining sheets of phyllo, brushing each with butter. Pour any leftover butter all over the top and, using a very sharp knife, cut into the top layers of phyllo to make 6 triangles.

4. Bake the pie for 15 to 20 minutes, until golden brown all over. Serve hot.

Greek Zucchini Pie

Kolokythopitta

This pie comes from Syros, an island at the center of the Cyclades and the capital of the Cycladic Islands province. Some Greek cooks recommend grating the zucchini, but I prefer it sliced very thin, which makes it less mushy once it's cooked. The pale green zucchini sold in Middle Eastern markets are less watery and bland than the darker variety sold in supermarkets, and are worth seeking out if you get the chance.

SERVES 6 TO 8

For the filling
1 pound 14 ounces zucchini, very thinly sliced
Fine kosher salt or sea salt
6 medium eggs, beaten
6 scallions, white and green parts, thinly sliced (heaping ½ cup)
1½ cups crumbled feta cheese (about 6 ounces)
½ cup coarsely chopped fresh dill
Freshly ground black pepper

½ cup (1 stick) unsalted butter, melted
12 sheets phyllo pastry, thawed if frozen

1. Put the zucchini in a colander and sprinkle lightly with salt. (Bear in mind that the feta cheese will add additional salt.) Let sit for 30 minutes. Squeeze the zucchini to extract as much water as possible. Transfer to a large bowl; add the eggs, scallions, feta, dill, and salt and pepper to taste, and mix well.

2. Preheat the oven to 375°F. Brush a 10-inch round pie plate with a little of the melted butter. Place 1 sheet of phyllo in the pie plate and brush with melted butter. Lay down another 4 sheets at different angles so that the pie plate is covered, and brush the top of each with butter. Trim the overhang; alternatively, brush the overhang with butter, which will make the pie look very pretty once it is baked but will make for a lot of crumbs when you come to cut it. Spread the filling evenly over the phyllo. Cover with the remaining sheets of phyllo, brushing each with butter. Pour any leftover butter all over the top.

3. Bake for 50 minutes to 1 hour, until golden brown all over. Serve hot or warm.

⚏ Greek Leek Pie

Prasopita

P rasopita is a popular dish in Greece during Lent. It's often made with bécha-mel sauce, which nowadays is ubiquitous in Greek cooking. Béchamel was introduced to Greek cooks at the beginning of the twentieth century by the chef and food writer Nicholas Tselementes, who, having been trained in France, added béchamel to almost everything. Before him, no one in Greece used the sauce. I prefer the pie made with tomatoes instead of béchamel; it's lighter and it more truly reflects traditional Greek cooking.

SERVES 6 TO 8

For the filling
⅓ cup (⅔ stick) unsalted butter
10 medium leeks, trimmed and cut into 1-inch lengths
Fine kosher salt or sea salt
Freshly ground black pepper
8 medium tomatoes, seeded and finely chopped
¼ cup dry white wine
4 medium eggs, beaten
1 pound ricotta or myzithra cheese (about 4½ cups)
2 to 4 tablespoons chopped fresh dill

½ cup (1 stick) unsalted butter, melted
12 sheets phyllo pastry, thawed if frozen

1. Melt the ⅓ cup butter in a large sauté pan over medium heat. Add the leeks, season with salt and pepper to taste, and cook, stirring frequently, until the leeks are soft, 15 to 20 minutes.

2. Add the tomatoes and wine and cook, stirring frequently, until almost all of the liquid has evaporated. Remove from the heat and let cool slightly.

3. Mix the eggs with the cheese and dill in a large bowl. Season with salt and pepper to taste. Add the leeks and tomato mixture and combine well. Taste and adjust the seasoning if necessary.

4. Preheat the oven to 400°F. Brush a 9 by 14-inch baking dish with a little of the melted butter. Place 1 sheet of phyllo on the bottom. Brush with butter and lay down another 5 sheets of phyllo, brushing the top of each with butter and arranging them so that they cover the bottom of the dish. Spread the filling evenly over the pastry. Cover with the remaining phyllo sheets, brushing each with butter. Cut the top layers of phyllo into 14 squares.

5. Bake for 40 to 45 minutes, until crisp and golden brown all over. Remove from the oven and let cool slightly. Then cut all the way down the slits to yield 14 pieces of pie. Serve hot or warm.

❖ Cretan Easter Pie

Toúrta Paschalini

Here is a wonderful and rather unusual pie that is made for Easter on the western side of Crete. The dough is light and fluffy, a cross between bread and brioche, and the filling is soft and juicy with an exotic cinnamon flavor and a fresh taste of mint.

SERVES 6

For the filling
1 shoulder of lamb, about 3 pounds
Juice of 1 lemon
Fine kosher salt or sea salt
Freshly ground black pepper
2 bay leaves
¼ teaspoon ground cinnamon
½ teaspoon ground cumin
1 pound ricotta or myzithra cheese, crumbled (about 4½ cups)
½ pound mozzarella or malaka cheese, diced (about 4 cups)
5 tablespoons finely chopped fresh mint

For the dough
3 cups plus 2 tablespoons unbleached all-purpose flour, plus extra for
    kneading and shaping
2¼ teaspoons (1 package) active dry yeast
½ teaspoon fine kosher salt or sea salt

1 medium egg, beaten
1 cup whole milk, at room temperature

To finish
Unsalted butter, for greasing the pie plate
1 medium egg, beaten
2 tablespoons white sesame seeds

1. Rub the lamb shoulder with the lemon juice. Season with salt and pepper to taste and let sit, covered in plastic wrap, in the refrigerator for about 2 hours.

2. Place the shoulder in a large saucepan. Add the bay leaves and cover with water. Bring to a boil over medium-high heat; just as the water is coming to a boil, skim it clean. Cover the pan, reduce the heat to medium, and boil gently for 1 hour, or until the meat is very tender.

3. While the meat cooks, begin making the dough: Combine the flour, yeast, and salt in a large bowl and make a well in the center. Add the beaten egg to the well and gradually add the milk, bringing in the flour as you go along. Knead briefly to make a rough ball of dough.

4. Remove the dough to a floured work surface. Knead for about 3 minutes. Invert the bowl over the dough and let rest for 15 minutes. Knead for 2 to 3 minutes more, until the dough is smooth and elastic. Shape the dough into a ball and place in a lightly floured clean bowl. Cover with plastic wrap and let rise in a warm, draft-free place for 1 hour. Fold the dough (see pages 6–7), cover again, and let rise for 1 hour more.

5. Let the lamb shoulder cool slightly, then take the meat off the bone. Trim and discard the skin and fat. Cut the meat into bite-size cubes. Season with the cinnamon and cumin and with salt and pepper to taste. Mix the cheeses together in a large bowl.

6. Preheat the oven to 375°F. Grease a 1½-inch-deep 10- inch round pie plate with a little butter, or use a nonstick pie plate.

7. Return the dough to the work surface. Divide the dough into 2 pieces, one slightly larger than the other. Shape each into a ball. Roll out the bigger piece to a circle large enough to line the bottom and sides of the pie plate, with a little overhang. Place the circle in the pie plate. Carefully tuck in the corners. Spread half the cheese evenly over the dough. Spread the meat over the cheese in an even layer. Sprinkle the mint all over the meat and cover with the remaining cheese.

8. Roll out the other piece of dough to a circle large enough to cover the filling. Place over the filling, fold the overhang up over the top dough, and seal the edges by making small diagonal pleats all the way around, to create a fluted edge.

9. Brush the top of the pie with the beaten egg. Slash the dough in a couple of places, and sprinkle the pie with the sesame seeds. Bake for 35 to 45 minutes, until golden all over. Serve hot.

Cretan Liver and Rice Pie

Tzoulamás

Nevin Halici's *Turkish Cookbook,* published in 1989, has a recipe for a pie, with lamb liver instead of chicken livers, that is remarkably similar to this pie from Crete. Although Diana Farr Louis, an expert on Mediterranean cooking, surmises that tzoulamás is Cretan in origin, my guess is that the dish has its origins in the days of the far-flung Ottoman Empire. (My friend Charles Perry, leading historian of Islamic cuisine, confirms my suspicion about the origin of the Cretan pie tzoulamás. It's the Turkish word *çullama,* which comes from *cul,* which means "horse cloth," and the sense is "the thing that is covered." In the big Langenscheidt Turkish dictionary, çullama is defined as "food covered with dough and baked." In the Redhouse dictionary of Ottoman Turkish, it is defined as "food cooked in a closely covered vessel; dish of meat covered with dough.") I am indebted to Farr Louis, in any case, for allowing me to adapt her recipe.

SERVES 6 TO 8

½ cup (1 stick) unsalted butter

1 pound chicken livers, cut into bite-size pieces

1½ cups long-grain white rice

3½ cups chicken broth

1 cup seedless raisins

1 cup blanched almonds, finely chopped

½ teaspoon finely ground white pepper

Fine kosher salt or sea salt

3 tablespoons sugar

¾ teaspoon ground cinnamon

12 sheets phyllo pastry, thawed if frozen

1. Put 2 tablespoons of the butter in a medium saucepan over medium-high heat. When the butter is hot, add the livers. Sauté for about 2 minutes, until the surface of the meat no longer looks raw.

2. Add the rice and cook, stirring, for 2 minutes. Add the broth and bring to a boil. Reduce the heat and simmer, covered, for 10 minutes.

3. Stir in the raisins and almonds and season with the pepper and salt to taste. Cover and simmer for 5 to 10 minutes more, stirring occasionally, or until the broth is completely absorbed and the rice is cooked. Wrap the lid in a kitchen towel and replace over the pan. Let sit until the rice is just warm.

4. Preheat the oven to 375°F. Melt the remaining 6 tablespoons butter, and use some to brush the bottom and sides of a 14 by 9-inch baking dish. Place 1 sheet of phyllo over the bottom. Brush with butter and sprinkle with 1 tablespoon of the sugar and ¼ teaspoon of the cinnamon. Lay down another 4 sheets of phyllo, brushing each with butter.

5. Spread half the rice filling evenly over the phyllo. Cover with 3 layers of phyllo, brushing each with butter. Sprinkle 1 tablespoon of the sugar and ¼ teaspoon of the cinnamon over the phyllo, then spread the remaining filling. Cover with the remaining sheets of phyllo, brushing each with butter. Drizzle any remaining butter all over the top. Sprinkle with the remaining sugar and cinnamon.

6. Bake the pie for 35 to 45 minutes, until golden all over. Serve hot or warm.

✣ Turkish Pilaf Pie

Yufkali İç Pilavi

This is my adaptation of the rice and liver pie from Nevin Halici's *Turkish Cookbook*. It's a spicier dish than the Cretan Liver and Rice Pie on page 239, with a little less sweetness. But the link between them is undeniable.

SERVES 4 TO 6

10 tablespoons (1¼ sticks) unsalted butter, plus extra for brushing the
    baking dish
¼ cup pine nuts (about 1 ounce)
1 medium onion, finely chopped (about ½ cup)
7 ounces lamb's liver, diced
1 medium tomato, seeded and diced
¼ cup seedless raisins (about 1 ounce), soaked in water and drained
⅛ teaspoon cayenne pepper
¼ teaspoon ground cinnamon
¼ teaspoon ground allspice
¼ teaspoon ground cardamom
1 teaspoon fine kosher salt or sea salt
¼ teaspoon finely ground black pepper
1 teaspoon sugar
1½ cups long-grain white rice (about 11 ounces)
12 sheets phyllo pastry, thawed if frozen
½ cup (1 stick) unsalted butter, melted, for brushing the phyllo sheets

1. Melt 2 tablespoons of the butter in a large sauté pan over medium-high heat. Add the pine nuts and sauté for about 2 minutes, until they start to color. Add the onion and sauté for 3 to 4 minutes, until lightly golden. Add the liver and sauté for about 2 minutes more. Add the tomato, raisins, cayenne, cinnamon, allspice, cardamom, salt, pepper, and sugar. Add 2⅓ cups water, bring to a boil, turn off the heat, and set aside.

2. Put the remaining 8 tablespoons butter in a large saucepan over medium-high heat. When the butter is melted, add the rice and cook, stirring, for 3 to 4 minutes. Add the liver mixture and its cooking liquid, bring back to a boil, reduce the heat to low, and simmer, covered, for 15 to 20 minutes, or until the rice is cooked and the liquid is completely absorbed. Stir the rice to mix the ingredients well. Wrap the lid with a clean kitchen towel and replace over the saucepan. Set aside to let cool.

3. Preheat the oven to 500°F. Grease an 8-inch round, 3-inch-deep baking dish with a little butter. Spread 1 phyllo sheet over the bottom and side of the pan and brush with butter. Lay down another phyllo sheet at right angles to the first to cover all of the baking dish with some overhang, and brush with butter. Lay down 4 more sheets, crossing them over and brushing each with butter. Spread the rice mixture evenly over the phyllo. Flap the overhang up and over the filling. Lay down 6 more sheets, crossing them over and brushing each with butter, and trim them to just inside the baking dish.

4. Bake for 5 to 10 minutes, until golden brown. Invert the pie over a heat-proof serving dish, and serve immediately.

⚜ Spinach Böreks

Ispanakli Tepsi Böregi

öreks occupy an important place in Turkish cooking and are probably the most ancient of all Mediterranean savory pastries, brought by the Turks when they migrated westward from Central Asia. They are made with phyllo, yufka (see page 51), or a rough puff pastry, and they are eaten as a snack—at home or as street food—or as part of a meal. The filling often includes a meat or a cheese, but the variety is tremendous, from region to region and even from one family to another.

SERVES 4

For the filling
1 pound fresh spinach
1 tablespoon extra-virgin olive oil
1 tablespoon unsalted butter
2 medium onions, finely chopped (about 1 cup)
2 medium eggs
¼ cup crumbled feta cheese
Fine kosher salt or sea salt
Freshly ground black pepper

⅓ cup (⅔ stick) unsalted butter, melted, plus extra for greasing the pie
    plate
1½ tablespoons whole milk
1 medium egg
12 sheets phyllo pastry, thawed if frozen

1. Make the filling: Wash and drain the spinach and put it in a large stockpot over medium-high heat. Cook for 3 to 5 minutes, stirring frequently, until just wilted. Drain and let cool. Then squeeze the spinach by hand until it is very dry. Separate the leaves and set aside.

2. Put the olive oil, butter, and onions in a large sauté pan over medium-high heat. Cook, stirring occasionally, until the onions are lightly golden. Add the spinach and cook for another minute or two. Remove from the heat and stir in the 2 eggs and the feta. Season with salt and pepper to taste, return to the heat, and cook for about 2 minutes, stirring constantly, until the eggs are very softly scrambled. Set the filling aside.

3. Preheat the oven to 400°F. Mix the melted butter with the milk and 1 egg in a small bowl. Grease a 9-inch round and 1-inch-deep pie plate with a little melted butter.

4. Place 1 sheet of phyllo across the pie plate, leaving half the sheet hanging over the edge. Keep the remaining sheets of phyllo covered with plastic wrap or a damp kitchen towel so that they don't dry out. Brush the portion of the first sheet that is in the pie plate with the milk mixture and fold the overhanging half over it; if any part of the sheet still hangs over the edge, either leave it there or trim it (a pie made with untrimmed overhangs will look very appealing with, as it were, a crisp, golden skirt). Brush again with the milk mixture. Repeat the process with 4 more sheets of phyllo.

5. Spread the filling over the pastry. Cover with the remaining phyllo sheets, brushing each layer with the milk mixture and folding the overhangs over. Pour any remaining milk mixture over the top and cut the pie, all the way to the bottom, into 4 quarters.

6. Bake for 25 to 35 minutes, until golden all over. Serve hot or warm.

❖ Chorizo Pie

Empanada Asturiana

The dough for this pie is traditionally made with lard but you can use olive oil or butter. Lard will make the flakiest pastry, olive oil the least flaky.

SERVES 4

For the pastry
Heaping teaspoon (½ package) active dry yeast
1⅔ cups unbleached all-purpose flour, plus extra for kneading and
    shaping
¾ teaspoon fine kosher salt or sea salt
1½ tablespoons extra-virgin olive oil, plus extra for brushing the
    dough and baking dish
1 medium egg, lightly beaten
¼ cup warm milk

For the filling
1 tablespoon extra-virgin olive oil
1 medium onion, finely chopped (about ½ cup)
1 garlic clove, crushed
4 ounces lean pork, thinly sliced
4 ounces chorizo, skin removed and thinly sliced
1 large ripe tomato, peeled and finely chopped
1 fresh pimiento or jalapeño pepper, thinly sliced
Pinch of saffron threads
Fine kosher salt or sea salt
Freshly ground black pepper
1 medium hard-boiled egg, finely chopped

1 medium egg beaten with 1 teaspoon milk

1. Make the pastry: Dissolve the yeast in 2 tablespoons warm water and stir until creamy. Combine the flour and salt in a large bowl and make a well in the center. Add the oil to the well and, with fingertips, rub it into the flour until well incorporated. Add the yeast, egg, and milk and knead briefly to make a rough ball of dough.

2. Remove the dough to a work surface. Knead for about 3 minutes. Invert the bowl over it and let rest for 15 minutes. Knead for 2 to 3 minutes more, until the dough is smooth and elastic. Shape the dough into a ball. Brush lightly with olive oil and place in a clean bowl. Cover with plastic wrap and let rise in a warm, draft-free place for 1 hour. Fold the dough (see pages 6–7), cover again, and let rise for 1 hour more. The dough should have doubled in volume.

3. Make the filling: Put the oil and onion in a sauté pan over medium-high heat. Cook, stirring occasionally, until the onion is soft and translucent. Add the garlic and pork and cook, stirring occasionally, until the meat is cooked through. Add the chorizo and cook, stirring, for about 1 minute.

4. Add the tomato, pimiento, and saffron. Season with salt and pepper to taste. Reduce the heat and simmer, uncovered, for about 10 minutes. Remove from the heat, add the hard-boiled egg, and mix well. Set aside to let cool.

5. Preheat the oven to 350°F. Grease a 6-inch round pie plate with a little olive oil, or use a nonstick pie plate. Return the dough to the work surface. Divide the dough into 2 pieces, one slightly larger than the other. Roll out the larger piece into a very thin circle about 8 inches in diameter, sprinkling the work surface and dough with flour every now and then. Place the dough over the bottom and side of the pie plate, with a little overhang. Spread the filling evenly over the dough. Roll out the second ball of dough to a circle large enough to cover the filling, with a little overhang again. Place over the filling, and seal the edges into a fluted border by pressing on the edges and making small diagonal pleats all the way around.

6. Brush the top of the pie with the beaten egg. Let the pie sit for 5 to 10 minutes, then brush again with the egg. Bake for about 30 minutes, until golden brown. Remove from the oven and let rest for about 5 minutes. Serve hot.

Maltese Fish Pie

Torta tal-Lampuki

Maltese food has perhaps the worst reputation among Mediterranean cuisines. However, this pie challenges that reputation. It may not be perfectly exquisite, but it is good. I first tried making it with short-crust pastry, the authentic way I was told, but the pastry was soggy on the bottom and the pie was rather heavy. I then tried it with phyllo and the result, although less authentic, was much nicer. Maltese cooks make the pie with sea bream, but I used tuna steaks, which make a good substitute.

SERVES 6 TO 8

Vegetable oil, for pan-frying
2 medium tuna steaks, about ½ pound each
Fine kosher salt or sea salt
Freshly ground black pepper
2 pounds fresh spinach
3 tablespoons extra-virgin olive oil
1 medium onion, thinly sliced
1 14½-ounce can peeled plum tomatoes, drained and coarsely chopped
1 small to medium cauliflower, broken into small florets
¼ cup black olives, pitted
1 tablespoon raisins
¼ cup walnuts, coarsely chopped
⅓ cup (⅔ stick) butter, melted
12 sheets phyllo pastry, thawed if frozen

1. Brush the bottom of a large frying pan with vegetable oil. Place the pan over medium-high heat. When the pan is very hot, slide the fish steaks in and sear for a few seconds on each side. Remove the fish to a plate, season with salt and pepper to taste on both sides, and set aside.

2. Wash the spinach, drain it, and put it in a large saucepan over medium-high heat. Cook, turning often to ensure even doneness, until just wilted. Drain in a colander and, when cool enough to handle, squeeze it very dry by hand. Separate the leaves and set aside.

3. Put the olive oil and onion in a large saucepan over medium-high heat. Cook, stirring occasionally, until the onion is lightly golden. Add the tomatoes and cauliflower. Season with salt and pepper to taste, reduce the heat to medium-low, and simmer, covered, for 10 minutes, stirring occasionally, until the cauliflower is cooked al dente. Remove from the heat. Add the spinach, olives, raisins, and walnuts, and mix well. Taste and adjust the seasoning if necessary. Let cool.

4. Preheat the oven to 400°F. Brush the bottom and sides of a 9 by 14-inch rectangular baking dish with melted butter. Place a sheet of phyllo over the bottom. Brush with melted butter. Lay down another 5 sheets, brushing each with butter.

5. Spread half the vegetables on the bottom. Place the fish steaks over the vegetables. Cover with the remaining vegetables. Cover with the remaining sheets of phyllo, brushing each with butter.

6. Bake for about 30 minutes, until the top is crisp and golden brown all over. Serve hot or warm.

✠ Tian Pie

Tarte au Tian

Tian is the name of a deep earthenware dish used for gratins of zucchini or of other vegetables. I am not quite sure why this pie is called Tarte au Tian, unless it is simply because the main ingredient is zucchini. What is more important than the name is that the pie is perfectly scrumptious and ideal for a light summer lunch, served hot, warm, or at room temperature.

MAKES 2 PIES; SERVES 8

For the pastry

3⅓ cups unbleached all-purpose flour, plus extra for kneading and
   shaping
2 teaspoons fine kosher salt or sea salt
1 cup (2 sticks) unsalted cold butter, cut into medium dice
1 medium egg

For the filling

6 tablespoons extra-virgin olive oil
10 ounces red bell peppers (about 4), cored, seeded, halved lengthwise,
   and thinly sliced across
10 ounces onions (about 3 medium), thinly sliced
16 large garlic cloves, thinly sliced
Fine kosher salt or sea salt
Freshly ground black pepper
1 pound zucchini, thinly sliced

Handful of fresh basil leaves, finely chopped
14 ounces Gruyère, grated (about 6 cups)
20 ounces plum tomatoes (about 5), seeded and thinly sliced into
    circles

1. Make the pastry: Combine the flour and salt in a large bowl and make a well in the center. Add the butter to the well and, with fingertips, rub it into the flour to make a coarse crumble.

2. Add the egg and ⅓ cup plus 1 tablespoon water. Knead quickly just until the pastry is evenly mixed; don't overwork the pastry.

3. Divide the pastry in half. Pat each half into a disk, wrap in plastic wrap, and refrigerate for 1 hour.

4. Remove the pastry to a work surface. Roll out each disk to a circle large enough to line the bottom and side of an 8-inch pie plate. Transfer the circles to 2 pie plates, and trim the edges. Cover with plastic wrap and refrigerate for 1 hour. Meanwhile, make the filling and preheat the oven to 400°F.

5. Make the filling: Put 3 tablespoons of the olive oil and the peppers, onions, and garlic in a large sauté pan over medium heat. Cook, stirring frequently, until the onions are softened and lightly golden. Season with salt and pepper to taste. Remove with a slotted spoon to a dish. Set aside.

6. Add the remaining 3 tablespoons oil to the same pan and place over medium-high heat. Add the zucchini and sauté until lightly golden, about 10 minutes. Remove from the heat and set aside.

7. Take the pastry out of the refrigerator and remove the plastic wrap. Cover with parchment paper and weigh down with pie weights. Bake for 25 to 30 minutes, until lightly golden. Remove the pie plates from the oven and let the pastries cool for 15 minutes.

8. Remove the pie weights and parchment paper from the pie shells. Spread one-sixth of the zucchini over each. You are going to have basically three layers of zucchini in each pie. Season with salt and pepper to taste. Scatter one-fourth of the basil over each. Sprinkle each with 1 cup grated cheese. Cover the cheese in each pie with half the onion mixture. Season with salt and pepper again. Scatter half the remaining basil and one-fourth of the remaining cheese over each. Spread another sixth of the zucchini over each pie and top with one-fourth of the tomatoes, and then repeat these two layers. Sprinkle half of the remaining cheese over the top of each pie and drizzle with a little olive oil.

9. Bake for 25 to 30 minutes, until golden and slightly crisp all over. Serve hot or warm. This pie will be just as good, if not better, the next day, at room temperature or reheated.

✣ Watercress Pie

Tarte au Cresson

The dough for this pie is the same one that French bakers use for *pain de mie,* a soft sandwich bread that is a cross between plain white bread and brioche.

SERVES 8

For the dough

2¼ teaspoons (1 package) active dry yeast

3⅓ cups unbleached all-purpose flour, plus extra for kneading and
    shaping

2 teaspoons fine kosher salt or sea salt

5 teaspoons sugar

2 teaspoons powdered milk

3 tablespoons unsalted butter, softened

For the topping

1 pound watercress, thick stalks removed

1½ tablespoons kosher salt or sea salt

1½ tablespoons unsalted butter

5 ounces mushrooms, thinly sliced

1½ tablespoons fresh lemon juice

Heaping 1 cup grated Gruyère (about 2½ ounces)

For the béchamel sauce
3 tablespoons unsalted butter
⅓ cup unbleached all-purpose flour
1 cup whole milk
Fine kosher salt or sea salt
Freshly ground black pepper

1. Make the dough: Dissolve the yeast in ¼ cup warm water and stir until creamy. Combine the flour, salt, sugar, and powdered milk in a large bowl and make a well in the center. Add the yeast and the softened butter to the well. Gradually add ¾ cup warm water, bringing in the flour as you go along. Knead briefly to make a rough ball of dough.

2. Remove the dough to a lightly floured work surface. Knead for about 3 minutes. Invert the bowl over the dough and let rest for 15 minutes. Knead for 2 to 3 minutes more, until the dough is smooth, elastic, and slightly firm. Shape into a ball and place in a lightly floured clean bowl. Cover with plastic wrap and let rise in a warm, draft-free place for 1 hour. Fold the dough (see pages 6–7), cover again, and let rise for 1 hour more. The dough should have doubled in volume.

3. Make the topping: Bring 2 quarts of water to a boil in a large saucepan. As soon as the water boils, add the watercress. Add the 1½ tablespoons salt and boil for 3 minutes. Drain, reserving the cooking liquid, and immediately plunge the cooked watercress in ice water to preserve its bright green color. Measure out and set aside ¾ cup of the reserved cooking liquid, and discard any excess. Drain the watercress and squeeze it very dry by hand. Separate the leaves and set aside.

4. Melt the butter in a wide saucepan over medium heat. Add the mushrooms and lemon juice and sauté for about 2 minutes. Remove the mushrooms with a slotted spoon to a plate. Pour the cooking liquids into a bowl and set aside, and return the saucepan to the stove.

5. Make the béchamel sauce: Melt the 3 tablespoons butter over medium heat in the same saucepan that was used for the mushrooms. Whisk in the flour and cook, whisking constantly, until lightly golden. Slowly add the reserved cooking liquids from the watercress and the mushrooms, and the milk, whisking constantly to prevent lumps. Season with salt and pepper to taste and bring to a boil. Boil for 2 minutes. Remove from the heat.

7. Add the Gruyère and the watercress to the béchamel sauce, and mix well.

8. Return the dough to the work surface. Shape into a ball, cover with a damp kitchen towel, and let rest for 15 minutes.

9. Roll out the dough to a large rectangle about ⅛ inch thick. Transfer to a nonstick baking sheet, or to a baking sheet lined with parchment paper or a silicone pastry mat. Cover with a wet but not dripping kitchen towel and let rise for 1½ hours. Meanwhile, preheat the oven to 400°F.

10. Spread the watercress and sauce over the dough, leaving about ½ inch free around the edges. Scatter the mushrooms all over the top. Bake the pie for 20 to 30 minutes, until golden all over. Serve hot or warm.

Nena's Spinach Tart

Tarta me Lapatha kai Yaourti

I was shown how to make this pie by Nena Ismirnoglou, a Greek chef I first met at a Mediterranean culinary conference in California. Sometime later, as I was preparing to go to Greece to do research for this book, a friend gave me some brief contact information for a Greek chef he thought I should meet. Nena and I were both very amused when I walked through the door to her teaching kitchen in Athens, once we realized that we already knew each other. In our earlier encounter Nena had promised to send me a recipe, but she lost some data on her computer, including my address, and so she never did. She made serious amends by being very generous with her time and knowledge during our afternoon together. According to her, this pie is a specialty of the Christian Greeks who lived in Turkey until the "catastrophe," as they call it—the time in the early 1960s when Greeks were deported from Turkey. Nena's family had lived in Turkey prior to that, and her cooking reflects her ties with that country.

SERVES 6 TO 8

For the pastry
1½ cups cornmeal
1½ cup unbleached all-purpose flour
1 teaspoon baking powder
¾ teaspoon fine kosher salt or sea salt
½ teaspoon finely ground black pepper
½ cup whole milk, warmed
½ cup olive oil

For the filling

½ pound onions, thinly sliced

½ pound ground veal

½ pound ground lamb

1 pound fresh spinach, finely shredded, boiled in 1 inch of water,
    drained, and squeezed dry

½ teaspoon ground coriander

Fine kosher salt or sea salt

Freshly ground black pepper

2 tablespoons extra-virgin olive oil, plus extra for greasing the pie
    plate

1 cup finely chopped fresh mint leaves

½ tablespoon dried mint

For the topping

2⅓ cups strained yogurt (see page 296)

3 medium eggs

Fine kosher salt or sea salt

Freshly ground black pepper

2 tablespoons toasted white sesame seeds

1. Make the pastry: Combine the cornmeal, flour, baking powder, salt, and pepper in a large bowl and make a well in the center. Gradually add the milk, olive oil, and ½ cup water to the well, and bring in the flour as you go along. Knead briefly to make a rough ball of dough.

2. Remove the dough to a lightly floured work surface. Knead for about 3 minutes. Invert the bowl over the dough and let rest for 15 minutes. Knead for 2 to 3 minutes more, until the dough is smooth and elastic. Wrap with plastic wrap and let rest on the counter while the filling is made.

3. Put the onions in a heavy-bottomed saucepan over medium-low heat. Cook for 3 to 4 minutes, stirring frequently, until the onions have softened. Add the veal

and lamb and cook, stirring and pressing on the meat with the back of a wooden spoon to separate lumps, until the meat has lost all traces of pink.

4. Add the spinach and coriander, and season with salt and pepper to taste. Cook for 10 to 12 minutes more, until there is almost no liquid in the pan. Remove from the heat. Add the olive oil and fresh and dried mint. Mix well, and set aside.

5. Preheat the oven to 350°F. Grease an 11-inch round pie plate with a little olive oil, or use a nonstick pie plate. Roll out the dough to a circle large enough to line the bottom and side of the pie plate. Place the dough over the dish. Carefully tuck in the corners. Cut off any excess pastry to make the pastry level with the top of the pie dish. Spread the filling evenly inside the pastry.

6. Mix the strained yogurt and eggs in a bowl. Season with salt and pepper to taste, and spread all over the filling, leveling it with a spatula to make a smooth top. Sprinkle with the sesame seeds. Bake for 45 minutes to 1 hour, until crisp and golden brown all over. Serve immediately.

Pumpkin, Leek, Walnut, and Cheese Tart

Praso-Kolokythopita

Aglaia Kremezi, one of my favorite Greek authors and a great cook herself, invented this pie as a fall dish to use up her large supply of pumpkins. Aglaia lives on Kea, a beautiful island near Athens. The recipe for the phyllo pastry that I use here is not Aglaia's, however, but comes instead from another island, Kassos, and was given to me by Mrs. Bonaparte, a great baker from Kassos who also makes the best myzithra, a kind of Greek ricotta, that I have ever had.

Ouzo is an anise-flavored liqueur made by combining pressed grapes, herbs, and spices. The grapes are used to make the alcohol, which is then mixed with herbs and spices such as star anise, coriander, cloves, angelica root, liquorice, mint, wintergreen, fennel, cinnamon, and lime blossom. The mixture is boiled in a copper still and regulated by a taster, and the resulting liquid is cooled and stored for several months before it is diluted to about 40 percent alcohol.

Kopanisti is a sharp, creamy sheep's-milk cheese from the Cyclades that is similar to the ricotta forte of Puglia. If you can't find it, use Roquefort or any other sharp blue cheese, or ricotta forte as I did. You can replace the homemade phyllo with store-bought puff pastry, if you like. The resulting pie will be fluffier.

SERVES 6 TO 8

For the dough
3⅓ cups unbleached all-purpose flour, plus extra for kneading and
    shaping
1½ teaspoons fine kosher salt or sea salt
1 small egg beaten with 2 tablespoons ouzo
Few grains of mastic, ground (about ¼ teaspoon; see page 159), optional
Juice of 1 lemon
½ cup extra-virgin olive oil

For the filling

3 to 4 leeks, white parts and a little green, sliced in ¼-inch pieces,
   rinsed well, and drained

6 tablespoons extra-virgin olive oil

1 pound seeded and peeled pumpkin, or calabaza, cut into
   ½-inch cubes

2 cups crumbled feta cheese (about 10 ounces)

3 tablespoons kopanisti or other sharp blue-veined cheese, such as
   Roquefort

½ cup coarsely chopped walnuts (about 2 ounces)

1 cup strained yogurt (see page 296)

Freshly ground black pepper

Kosher salt or sea salt

2 large eggs

3 tablespoons whole milk

Walnut halves, for garnish, optional

1. Combine the flour and salt in a large bowl and make a well in the center. Add the egg mixture, the mastic, if using, and the lemon juice and olive oil to the well. Mix these together before bringing in the flour. Gradually add ⅓ cup water and knead quickly to make a manageable dough; do not overknead. Pat into a ball. Place in a lightly floured clean bowl, cover with plastic wrap, and let rest in the refrigerator while the filling is made.

2. Preheat the oven to 400°F. Put the leeks and 3 tablespoons of the olive oil in a large sauté pan over medium heat. Cook for about 15 minutes, stirring frequently, until the leeks have softened. Transfer the leeks to a large bowl, and set aside.

3. Put the pumpkin and the remaining 3 tablespoons olive oil in a bowl. Mix well to coat all the pumpkin pieces with oil. Spread the pumpkin in a single layer on a nonstick baking sheet, or on a baking sheet lined with parchment paper or a silicone pastry mat. Bake for about 15 to 20 minutes, until tender. Reduce the oven temperature to 375°F.

4. Add the pumpkin to the leeks. Add the cheeses, chopped walnuts, and all but 3 tablespoons of the yogurt, reserving the rest of the yogurt for the topping. Season with black pepper to taste. Mix well. Taste and add salt if needed, but note that the cheeses are quite salty. Separate one egg. Reserve the yolk and add the white and the other egg to the pumpkin mixture.

5. Remove the dough to a floured work surface. Roll out the dough to a circle 14 to 16 inches in diameter. Transfer the dough to a large nonstick baking sheet, or to a baking sheet lined with parchment paper or a silicone pastry mat. Spread the filling evenly all over the dough, leaving about 2 inches free around the edge. Flap the edge over to cover part of the filling.

6. With a small whisk, mix the reserved yogurt and egg yolk and the milk until creamy. Brush the pastry lightly with some of the mixture. Reserve the rest.

7. Bake the tart for 15 minutes. Then, wearing oven mitts, open the oven and, without taking the pie out, spread the remaining egg-yogurt mixture over the filling. Garnish with some walnut halves if you like. Bake for 30 to 35 minutes more, until golden brown. Transfer to a wire rack to cool for about 10 minutes. Serve hot or warm.

✣ Teresa's Ricotta Pie

La Torta di Ricotta di Teresa

Teresa Agnelli is a wonderful cook who has been with my friend Suni Agnelli in Porto Santo Stefano, on the Tuscan coast, for many years. Every time I go to stay with Suni, I spend time in the kitchen with Teresa to learn some of her secrets. She taught me how to make this delicious pie (and also the Pizza Campofranco, page 155).

SERVES 6

10 ounces ricotta
2 medium eggs, beaten
5 ounces prosciutto, thinly sliced
1½ cups grated Parmigiano-Reggiano (about 3 ounces)
1 cup grated pecorino romano (about 3 ounces)
Unsalted butter, for greasing the pie plate
1 17.3-ounce package frozen puff pastry, thawed in the refrigerator
1 egg beaten with 1 teaspoon water, for brushing the pastry

1. Put the ricotta in a bowl. Add the eggs and mix well. Add the prosciutto and half of the Parmesan and pecorino. Mix well.

2. Preheat the oven to 400°F. Grease a 10-inch round pie plate with a little butter, or use a nonstick pie plate. Divide the puff pastry into 2 pieces, one slightly larger than the other. Roll out the larger piece to a circle large enough to cover the bottom and side of the pie plate, with a little overhang. Line the pie plate with the pastry circle. Carefully tuck in the corners. Spread half the ricotta

mixture all over the pastry. Mix the remaining Parmesan and pecorino and sprinkle all over the filling. Cover with the remaining ricotta mixture.

3. Roll out the other piece of pastry to a circle large enough to cover the filling. Place loosely over the filling. Loosely fold the overhang over the top. Brush with the beaten egg. Bake for 45 minutes to 1 hour, until golden brown all over. Serve hot or warm.

Roquefort and Cherry Tomato Quiche

Quiche Roquefort et Tomates Cerises

There are all kinds of different quiches in France and not all are made with the dense egg custard of a quiche Lorraine. This Roquefort quiche is light and sophisticated, with a delicate sauce made with fewer eggs than usual. It makes a wonderful vegetarian meal, served with a green salad and grilled vegetables.

SERVES 4 TO 6

½ recipe (to make 1 pie shell) short-crust pastry for Tian Pie (page 250)
    through step 3
2 tablespoons Dijon mustard
2 ounces Roquefort cheese, diced (about ½ cup)
1 pound cherry tomatoes
Scant 1 cup crème fraîche
2 medium eggs
Fine kosher salt or sea salt
Freshly ground black pepper
2 tablespoons finely chopped flat-leaf parsley

1. Roll out the pastry to a circle large enough to line the bottom and side of a 10-inch round nonstick pie plate. Carefully roll up the pastry onto a rolling pin and unroll it into the pie plate. Gently tuck in the corners. Cover loosely with plastic wrap and let rest in the refrigerator for 1 hour. Meanwhile, preheat the oven to 400°F.

2. Uncover the pastry. Line it with parchment paper and weigh it down with pie weights. Bake for 20 to 25 minutes, or until just colored. Remove from the oven and let cool for 15 to 20 minutes. Remove the pie weights and parchment paper.

3. Spread the mustard all over the pastry. Scatter the Roquefort all over. Arrange the cherry tomatoes in an even layer. Beat the crème fraîche and eggs together, season with salt and pepper to taste, and pour over the cheese and tomatoes. Sprinkle with the chopped parsley.

4. Bake for 30 to 45 minutes, until the filling is set and both crust and filling are golden brown all over. Serve hot.

Spring Quiche

Quiche Printanière

This is an interesting and unusual quiche, in which the filling is a carrot mash with celeriac and Gruyère. Although there's plenty of butter in the pastry, it's a pretty healthy dish.

SERVES 4 TO 6

½ recipe (to make 1 pie shell) short-crust pastry for Tian Pie (page 250)

14 ounces (about 4 medium) carrots, 12 ounces diced and 2 ounces cut into thin rounds for garnish

Fine kosher salt or sea salt

½ lemon

3 ounces celeriac, peeled and diced (about 1½ cups)

⅓ cup crème fraîche

1 medium egg

Heaping ½ cup grated Gruyère (about 1¼ ounces)

2 tablespoons finely chopped flat-leaf parsley, plus extra for garnish

Freshly ground black pepper

1. Roll out the pastry to a circle large enough to line the bottom and sides of a 10-inch round nonstick pie plate, or a regular pie plate brushed with unsalted butter. Carefully roll up the pastry onto a rolling pin and unroll it into the pie plate. Gently tuck in the corners. Cover loosely with plastic wrap and let rest in the refrigerator for 1 hour.

2. Cook the diced carrots in boiling salted water for 8 to 10 minutes, until just soft. Drain and mash or purée them. Set aside. Boil the carrot rounds for 7 minutes, until just al dente. Drain and set aside.

3. Preheat the oven to 400°F. Bring a saucepan of salted water to a boil and squeeze the juice of the half lemon into it. Boil the celeriac for 10 to 15 minutes, until just soft. (The lemon juice keeps the celeriac from turning dark.) Drain and set aside.

4. Mix the crème fraîche, egg, Gruyère, and parsley in a bowl. Add the carrot purée and the celeriac, and mix well. Season with salt and pepper to taste. Cover and set aside.

5. Uncover the pastry. Line it with parchment paper and weigh it down with pie weights. Bake for about 20 minutes, or until just colored. Remove from the oven and let cool for 15 to 20 minutes. Remove the pie weights and parchment paper.

6. Spread the vegetable purée over the crust. Arrange the carrot rounds all around the edge of the pie and, if there are any left, make a rosette shape in the middle. Garnish with a little chopped parsley.

7. Bake the quiche for 20 to 30 minutes, until golden all over. Serve hot or warm.

⚟ Leek Pie

Tarte aux Poireaux

Leeks originated in the Mediterranean and were highly prized by the ancient Egyptians, Greeks, and Romans. In France the pie is made with poireaux de vignes, a small, wild variety that grows in the south. However, poireaux de vignes are not always available; the best substitute is "mini leeks," a common variety for gardeners that often appears on produce shelves. If you can't find these, simply use regular leeks. You can replace the leeks with sautéed mushrooms or blanched broccoli, or use sautéed bacon and peas. And the custard mix on its own makes for a scrumptious savory custard pie.

SERVES 6 TO 8

½ recipe (to make 1 pie shell) short-crust pastry for Tian Pie (page 250)
About 40 mini leeks or 8 medium leeks, trimmed and cut into ½-inch rings (about 6½ cups)
¼ cup (½ stick) unsalted butter
8 medium eggs, beaten
1½ cups crème fraîche
1½ cups whole milk
½ teaspoon ground nutmeg
Fine kosher salt or sea salt
Freshly ground black pepper

1. Roll out the pastry to a circle large enough to line the bottom and side of a 10-inch round and 2½-inch deep nonstick pie plate or tart pan, or a regular pie plate or tart pan brushed with unsalted butter. Carefully roll up the pastry onto

a rolling pin and unroll it into the plate or pan. Gently tuck in the corners. Cover loosely with plastic wrap and let rest in the refrigerator for 1 hour. Meanwhile, preheat the oven to 400°F.

2. Sauté the leeks in the butter over medium heat, stirring occasionally, until just tender, 15 to 20 minutes.

3. Line the pastry with parchment paper and weigh it down with pie weights. Bake for about 20 minutes, until just colored. Remove from the oven and let cool for 15 to 20 minutes. Remove the pie weights and parchment paper.

4. Arrange the leeks in an even layer all over the crust. Mix the eggs, crème fraîche, and milk in a bowl. Season with the nutmeg and salt and pepper to taste. Pour evenly over the leeks.

5. Bake for 35 to 40 minutes, until the pastry is golden and the filling is set. Remove from the oven and let rest for 5 to 10 minutes. Serve hot or warm.

Moroccan Pigeon Pie

Pastilla

The traditional way of preparing pastilla is in three layers—ground almonds, whole pieces of stewed pigeons (Moroccan pigeons are very small), and eggs scrambled in a pigeon sauce—with one or two sheets of warqa (see pages 289–90) between the layers. The whole thing is then wrapped in several more sheets of warqa to make a round, flat pie that is cooked on the stovetop in a *tobsil,* a large, flat beaten-iron pan. The crisp pie is then sprinkled with confectioners' sugar and decorated with crisscross lines of ground cinnamon. Moroccans eat pastilla with their hands. They first break open the edge of the crisp pastry to pull out a piece of pigeon. They suck the meat off the bone, then daintily pinch off more pastry, but this time with some of the almond and egg filling.

Today very few restaurants, whether in Morocco or elsewhere, make pastilla in the traditional manner. Most use chicken instead of pigeon; and the cooks usually take the meat off the bone and mix it in with the scrambled eggs and almonds to make the pastilla in one layer, as in the recipe here.

Ras el-hanout, which means "head of the shop" in Moroccan Arabic, is perhaps the most complex of all spice blends, made with about twenty-seven different spices—mace, nutmeg, ginger, coriander, cloves, and cinnamon, to name but a few. It used to contain Spanish fly, which is reputed to be an aphrodisiac, but that now is illegal. Ras el-hanout is available in many Middle Eastern markets and spice stores in the United States, although the blend isn't always the traditional Moroccan one.

SERVES 6 TO 8

For the filling

2 poussins (young chickens, about 1 pound each) or 3 squabs (about
¾ pound each), preferably, or 2 small Cornish hens (about
1¼ pounds each)

2 medium onions, finely chopped (about 1 cup)

½ cup finely chopped flat-leaf parsley

½ cup finely chopped fresh cilantro

1½ teaspoons ground cinnamon

1½ teaspoons ground ginger

1 teaspoon ground ras el-hanout

¼ teaspoon crushed red pepper flakes

2 pinches of saffron threads

Fine kosher salt or sea salt

½ cup (1 stick) unsalted butter, plus extra for greasing the baking dish

⅔ cup blanched almonds

10 medium eggs, lightly beaten

2 tablespoons confectioners' sugar

For the pie

16 sheets (1⅓ 1-pound packages) 11 by 18-inch phyllo pastry, thawed if
frozen, or 8 sheets warqa (see pages 289–90)

About ½ cup (1 stick) unsalted butter, melted, for brushing the phyllo

Confectioners' sugar

Ground cinnamon

1. Put the poussins in a large saucepan. Add the onions, parsley, cilantro, cinnamon, ginger, ras el-hanout, red pepper flakes, saffron, and a little salt. Add 1¾ cups water, place over medium-high heat, and bring to a boil. When the water begins to boil, add 5 tablespoons of the butter. Cover, and boil the birds for 20 minutes. Reduce the heat to medium-low, turn the birds in the sauce, and simmer for 10 minutes more, until the birds are done. Remove the birds to a plate and let cool, reserving the sauce.

2. Melt the remaining 3 tablespoons butter in a sauté pan over medium-high heat. Cook the almonds, stirring constantly, until golden brown. Remove from the heat and let cool. Grind the almonds coarse in a food processor.

3. If the sauce in which the birds cooked is not quite thick, bring it back to a boil over high heat and cook, stirring constantly, until it is very thick and unctuous.

4. Over low heat, whisk the eggs into the sauce and scramble them, whisking constantly, for about 5 minutes, until the eggs are set but still creamy. Remove from the heat.

5. When the poussins are cool enough to handle, remove the meat from the bone and discard the skin. Tear the meat into small pieces. Add to the egg mixture along with the almonds and the 2 tablespoons confectioners' sugar. Mix well. Taste and adjust the seasoning if necessary.

6. Preheat the oven to 450°F. Grease a shallow 11-inch round baking dish with a little butter.

7. Prepare the pie: Place 1 sheet of phyllo over the bottom of the baking dish. Brush with some of the melted butter and lay down another sheet perpendicular to the first one. Brush with butter and repeat with 4 more sheets, placing them at different angles so that there is pastry overhanging all around the edge of the baking dish. (If using warqa, cover the bottom of the dish with 1 sheet. Then fan 4 sheets in a rosette pattern, half inside the dish and half outside, and then place 1 sheet at the same orientation as the bottom sheet.)

8. Spread the filling evenly over the pastry and fold the loose pastry over the filling. Place the remaining 10 sheets of phyllo over the filling at different angles, brushing each with butter, and carefully tuck in the loose ends under the pie, as if tucking in a sheet under a mattress. If the tucking is too difficult, simply trim the top sheets of pastry to just inside the edge of the dish; the resulting pie will not look very traditional but it'll look very pretty with the crispy layers of pastry puffing up slightly. Brush the top with butter. (If using warqa, cover the

pie with the two remaining sheets, one on top of the other, tuck the edges under the pie, and brush with butter.)

9. Bake the pastilla for 20 to 30 minutes, until golden brown all over. Remove from the oven and let cool for 2 to 3 minutes. Lightly dust the top with confectioners' sugar, then make a checkerboard pattern by sprinkling thin lines of ground cinnamon at about 1-inch intervals. Serve immediately.

Savory Pastries

Turkish Meat Böreks

Baklava Yufkasiyla Kiymali Muska Böregi

Most people know baklava as a sweet pastry dripping in sugar syrup, made by layering ground nuts between sheets of phyllo. However, in Turkey "baklava" can also describe savory multilayered preparations, such as these böreks. Before the First World War, elegant households in Istanbul might have two phyllo makers in the kitchen, one to make thin sheets for the sweet baklava and the other to make stronger and thicker sheets for savory böreks. But it is not so common nowadays for phyllo to be made at home. Despite its strong associations with Greek cooking, phyllo is undoubtedly of Turkish origin.

MAKES 16 BÖREKS

1½ tablespoons extra-virgin olive oil

½ teaspoon cumin seeds

1 large onion, finely chopped (about ¾ cup)

2 tablespoons pine nuts

1 garlic clove, finely chopped

½ red bell pepper, trimmed and diced (about ½ cup)

1 tablespoon finely chopped chili pepper

½ pound lamb shoulder, trimmed of skin and fat and minced (about 1½ cups)

7 to 8 ounces canned peeled tomatoes, drained and finely chopped

1½ tablespoons raisins

¼ cup finely chopped flat-leaf parsley

2 tablespoons finely chopped fresh dill

½ teaspoon ground allspice

Fine sea salt or kosher salt

Freshly ground black pepper
8 sheets phyllo pastry, thawed if frozen
6 tablespoons unsalted butter, melted

1. Heat the oil in a large sauté pan over medium-high heat. Add the cumin seeds and stir until the aroma rises. Add the onion and pine nuts and cook, stirring constantly, until both are lightly golden.

2. Stir in the garlic, peppers, and lamb. Press on the meat with the back of a wooden spoon to break up lumps, and cook, stirring frequently, until the lamb is no longer pink. Stir in the tomatoes, raisins, parsley, dill, and allspice. Season with salt and pepper to taste. Cook, stirring occasionally, until the mixture is quite dry. Set aside to let cool.

3. Preheat the oven to 400°F. Divide the meat mixture into 16 equal portions. Cut the phyllo sheets in half lengthwise. Place 1 cut sheet on your work surface. (Keep the others covered with plastic wrap or a damp kitchen towel so that they do not dry out.) Brush the sheet with butter. Fold in half lengthwise to make a long strip. Put one portion of the meat filling near one end of the strip and fold the end of the pastry over the filling to form a triangle. Brush the top of the triangle with butter and fold again repeatedly along the length of the strip, keeping to the triangle shape, until the filling is entirely encased; brush with butter every two folds or so. Trim any loose ends from the finished triangle, brush it with butter on both sides, and transfer, loose side down, to a nonstick baking sheet, or to a baking sheet lined with parchment paper or a silicone pastry mat. Make the remaining triangles in the same way.

4. Bake for 20 to 25 minutes, until golden all over. Serve hot or warm.

⚏ Israeli Potato Böreks

Borekas Tapükhay Adama

Israeli borekas, probably an adaptation of Turkish böreks introduced to Israel by Turkish Jews, are made with puff pastry and can be savory or sweet with a variety of fillings. They are made as rectangles, squares, or, as in this recipe, triangles. Borekas are sold as street food; the vendor opens the boreka to add chopped eggs, tomatoes, and tahini to the filling, and pickles are served on the side. At the Arab stalls, borekas are sold with a garnish of za'atar (see page 35) and salt.

SERVES 6

1 tablespoon extra-virgin olive oil
1 medium onion, thinly sliced (about ½ cup)
2 medium potatoes, cooked and mashed
Fine kosher salt or sea salt
Freshly ground black pepper
3 to 4 tablespoons crumbled feta cheese, optional
¾ package (1½ sheets) frozen puff pastry, thawed in the refrigerator
1 large egg yolk beaten with 1 tablespoon water
2 tablespoons white sesame seeds

1. Heat the oil in a sauté pan over medium heat. Add the onion and cook until lightly golden.

2. Preheat the oven to 400°F. Place the potatoes in a bowl and season with salt and pepper to taste. Add the onion and, if using, the cheese, and mix well. Set aside.

3. Roll out the puff pastry very thin, ¼ inch or less, and cut into 6 squares approximately 5 by 5 inches each. Divide the filling into 6 equal portions and place a portion in the center of each pastry square. Fold each square once to make a triangle shape that encloses the filling. Press firmly to seal well. Transfer to a nonstick baking sheet, or to a baking sheet lined with parchment paper or a silicone pastry mat. Brush the tops with the egg yolk. Sprinkle with the sesame seeds.

4. Bake for 25 to 30 minutes, until crisp and golden brown. Transfer to a wire rack. Serve warm or at room temperature.

✤ Cretan Spinach Crescents

Krépes Sto Foúrno me Spanáki

On Crete these are eaten as *mezze,* or snacks. Although the yogurt in the dough makes it wet and quite soft, it still is manageable and the results are excellent. Note that if you do not have strained yogurt on hand, making it is simple but you will need to prepare it several hours in advance; see page 296 for instructions. I adapted this recipe from one recorded by Diana Farr Louis in her wonderful book, *Feasting and Fasting in Crete.*

SERVES 12

For the dough
1⅓ cups unbleached all-purpose flour, plus extra for kneading and
    shaping
½ teaspoon fine kosher salt or sea salt
Scant 1 teaspoon baking powder
7 ounces strained yogurt (see page 296; about ¾ cup plus 1 tablespoon)
¼ cup extra-virgin olive oil

For the filling

8 ounces fresh spinach, tough stalks removed, cut into thin strips
    (about 7 cups)

Kosher salt or sea salt

3½ ounces fresh ricotta or myzithra cheese (about ¾ cup)

2 scallions, thinly sliced

3 tablespoons finely chopped fresh mint

2 tablespoons extra-virgin olive oil

Freshly ground black pepper

Milk for brushing the crescents

1. Make the dough: Combine the flour, salt, and baking powder in a large bowl and make a well in the center. Add the strained yogurt and olive oil to the well and mix by hand. Bring in the flour and knead until you have a rough ball of dough.

2. Remove the dough to a lightly floured work surface. Knead for 3 minutes. Invert the bowl over the dough and let rest for 15 minutes. Knead for about 2 to 3 minutes more, to make a soft dough that is smooth and elastic. Wrap in plastic wrap and refrigerate for at least 1 hour, but not more than 2 hours.

3. Make the filling: Place the spinach in a bowl and sprinkle with a little salt. Rub salt into the spinach by hand, until the spinach is very wilted. Squeeze out excess liquid thoroughly and transfer to a clean bowl. Loosen up the squeezed spinach. Add the cheese, scallions, mint, and oil, and season with salt and pepper to taste. Mix well, cover, and set aside.

4. Preheat the oven to 375°F. Divide the dough into 12 equal pieces. Shape each piece into a ball. Cover the balls with plastic wrap and let rest for 5 minutes.

5. Roll out a ball of dough to a circle about 5 inches in diameter. Place 2 tablespoons spinach filling in the middle and fold the dough over to make a crescent

shape. Pinch the edges tightly to seal. Transfer to a nonstick baking sheet, or to a baking sheet lined with parchment paper or a silicone pastry mat. Brush with a little milk. Make the remaining crescents the same way.

6. Bake for 25 to 30 minutes, until the crescents are golden all over. Serve hot, or transfer to a wire rack to serve warm or at room temperature.

Greek Cheese Triangles

Tyropitta

These little cheese pies or pasties are popular in much of Greece, so much so that they are widely available in big frozen packages. Freshly made ones are better, of course, and are not much trouble to prepare.

SERVES 6

2 cups crumbled feta cheese (about 7 ounces)
¼ cup chopped flat-leaf parsley
⅛ teaspoon grated nutmeg
Freshly ground black pepper
Fine kosher salt or sea salt, if needed
2 medium eggs, beaten
6 11 by 18-inch sheets phyllo pastry, thawed if frozen
4 tablespoons (½ stick) unsalted butter, melted

1. Combine the feta, parsley, nutmeg, and pepper in a large bowl. Add salt to taste, if needed; there may be enough salt in the feta already. Stir in the eggs.

2. Preheat the oven to 350°F. Brush the long half of a phyllo sheet with melted butter. Fold the plain half over the buttered one. Place 2½ to 3 tablespoons filling near one end of the folded sheet. Fold the end of the pastry over the filling to make a triangle shape. Brush the top of the remaining, unfolded pastry with butter and continue folding along the sheet, keeping to the triangle shape, until the sheet is completely folded and the filling is completely enclosed in the pastry. Trim any loose ends with a sharp knife. Brush the triangle on all sides with

butter and place, loose side down, on a nonstick baking sheet, or on a baking sheet lined with parchment paper or a silicone pastry mat. Make the remaining triangles in the same way.

3. Bake for 35 to 40 minutes, until the triangles are crisp and golden. Serve hot or warm.

Moroccan Triangles with Chicken

Briouats au Poulet

These briouats are traditionally made with *warqa,* Arabic for "leaf," which is the North African equivalent of phyllo. Warqa is used to make pastillas and briouats, both savory and sweet, and also some other sweets. Making authentic warqa is quite difficult; see box, pages 289–90. Fortunately, phyllo makes a fine substitute. Traditionally briouats are deep-fried, but I prefer to bake them. It is a healthier option and you don't have to worry about disposing of the frying oil. Briouats are usually served as a first course in Morocco; I like them as well as hors d'oeuvres with drinks.

MAKES 24 SMALL TRIANGLES

⅓ cup extra-virgin olive oil

3 medium onions, finely chopped

3 tablespoons finely chopped flat-leaf parsley

2 teaspoons ground cinnamon

1 teaspoon ground ginger

1 teaspoon finely ground white pepper

Good pinch of saffron threads

1 tablespoon confectioners' sugar

Fine sea salt or kosher salt

1 chicken, cut into 8 pieces

6 medium eggs

12 sheets 11 × 18-inch phyllo pastry or 12 sheets warqa, thawed if
     frozen

½ cup (1 stick) unsalted butter, melted

1. Combine the oil, onions, parsley, spices, sugar, and a little salt in a large saucepan. Add the chicken pieces and 1½ cups water. Bring to a boil over medium-high heat. Reduce the heat to medium and cook, covered, for about 30 minutes, until the chicken is tender. Transfer the chicken with tongs or a slotted spoon to a plate to let cool. Let the sauce bubble uncovered, until it is thick and unctuous.

2. When the chicken is cool enough to handle, remove the meat from the bone, discarding the skin, and break the meat into bite-size pieces. Break the eggs into the sauce and scramble until just set. Stir in the chicken pieces.

3. Preheat the oven to 400°F. If using phyllo, cut the sheets in half lengthwise. Place 1 strip on a work surface and keep the others covered with a slightly damp

kitchen towel or plastic wrap so that they do not dry up. Brush the strip with butter. Fold in half lengthwise and place about a tablespoon of the chicken mixture near one end. Fold the end of the phyllo over the filling to form a triangle shape. Brush the remainder of the strip with butter and continue folding, keeping to the triangle shape, until the strip is completely folded and the filling is enclosed. Cut off and discard any excess pastry. Transfer loose side down to a nonstick baking sheet, or to a baking sheet lined with parchment paper or a silicone pastry mat. Brush the top of the briouat with butter. Make the remaining briouats in the same way. (If using warqa, cut the circular sheets in half, fold each half in two lengthwise, and fill and fold triangles as with phyllo. Because warqa is oiled as it is made, there is no need to brush warqa with butter.)

4. Bake for 15 to 20 minutes, until golden brown. Serve hot or warm.

I once tried making warqa under the guidance of Boujemaa Mars, the venerable head chef, now retired, at La Mamounia Hotel in Marrakech, Morocco. Although my first and only attempt was not an abject failure, it did demonstrate that it would take me very many more trials before I could make warqa like an expert. I decided it wasn't worth the trouble, especially since the commercial warqa I buy from Middle Eastern stores is perfectly fine. And whenever I go to Morocco or Tunisia, I buy excellent homemade warqa in the souks or at bakeries, and I freeze it as soon as I get home.

Here is a translation of Mohamed Kouki's method for making warqa, from his fine book, *La Cuisine et Pâtisserie Tunisiennes*, from 1997:

Make a dough without yeast using ½ pound fine semolina, a large pinch of salt, and enough water to produce a smooth but fairly firm dough. Let rest for 1 hour. Knead the dough for a long time, sprinkling it generously, although a little at a time, with water until you have a very soft dough that spreads.

Place a hand-beaten copper tray, a special utensil for cooking mal-süqa [malsüqa, meaning "glued," is a Tunisian name for warqa], upside down over low heat. Let it become hot. Then dip your fingers in water and tear off a ball of dough the size of an orange. Quickly let the dough drop without letting it go and pick it up as soon as it touches the hot metal, leaving a thin film of dough. Repeat the operation, letting the dough drop next to the first patch until you have covered the back of the tray. As soon as the layer of dough is dry, peel it off and place on a cloth. Continue in this manner until you have used up all the dough. Half a pound of fine semolina will produce 18 to 20 leaves. It must be very light and extremely thin.

This dough, the making of which, as we have seen, requires a very special skill, is often used in Tunisian cooking to make a number of dishes and sweet pastries: briks, tajine malsüqa, ourta, brikit hilib, zriga, and others.

At the wonderful Stylia restaurant in Marrakech, where I shot the accompanying photographs, the cooks who work for Mr. Chami, the owner, make warqa in much the same way that Kouki describes.

⚜ Moroccan Triangles with Minced Meat

Briouats de Boeuf Haché

These savory triangles are often served as a dinnertime first course in Morocco. But they are also wonderful as an accompaniment with cocktails.

MAKES 20 SMALL TRIANGLES

For the filling
1 tablespoon unsalted butter
1 small onion, very finely chopped (about ⅓ cup)
1 pound ground beef
Pinch of saffron threads
¼ teaspoon crushed red pepper flakes
Fine kosher salt or sea salt
Freshly ground black pepper
2 medium eggs, beaten
1 tablespoon finely chopped cilantro
10 sheets phyllo pastry or 10 sheets warqa (see pages 289–90), thawed
    if frozen
1 stick unsalted butter, melted

1. Heat the 1 tablespoon butter in a large sauté pan over medium heat. Add the onion, beef, and saffron, and cook, stirring occasionally and pressing the meat with the back of a wooden spoon to break up lumps, until the meat is no longer

pink. Add the red pepper flakes and season with salt and black pepper to taste. Set aside to let cool.

2. Preheat the oven to 400°F. Once the meat mixture has cooled to the point at which it will not cook the eggs, add the eggs and cilantro and mix well.

3. If using phyllo, cut the sheets in half lengthwise. Place 1 strip on a work surface and keep the others covered with plastic wrap or a slightly damp kitchen towel. Brush the strip with melted butter. Fold in half lengthwise and place about a tablespoon of the meat mixture near one end. Fold the end of the phyllo over the filling to form a triangle shape. Brush the remainder of the strip with butter and continue folding, keeping to the triangle shape, until the strip is completely folded and the filling is enclosed. Cut off any excess pastry. Transfer loose side down to a nonstick baking sheet, or to a baking sheet lined with parchment paper or a silicone pastry mat. Brush the top of the triangle with butter. Make the remaining triangles in the same way. (If using warqa, cut the circular sheets in half, fold each half in two lengthwise, and fill and fold triangles as with phyllo. There usually is no need to brush warqa with butter.)

4. Bake for 15 to 20 minutes, until golden brown. Serve hot or warm.

Lebanese Spinach Triangles

Fatayer bil-S'banegh

Fatayer are popular both in Syria and in Lebanon. Aside from spinach, other greens that cooks use for fillings include purslane leaves, sorrel, Swiss chard, dandelion, and wild thyme. These may be substituted in this recipe, according to your taste and what is available and fresh. Sumac, which has a lemony flavor, is available in Middle Eastern markets and some supermarkets, as well as from on-line spice merchants.

MAKES ABOUT 18 TO 20 SMALL TRIANGLES

For the dough
2 cups unbleached all-purpose flour, plus extra for kneading and
    shaping
1 teaspoon salt
¼ cup extra-virgin olive oil, plus extra for brushing the triangles

For the filling
1 medium onion, very finely chopped (about ½ cup)
Fine kosher salt or sea salt
½ teaspoon finely ground black pepper
2 tablespoons ground sumac
14 ounces spinach, cut into thin strips (about 12 cups)
2 tablespoons pine nuts
Juice of 1 lemon, or to taste
2 tablespoons extra-virgin olive oil

1. Combine the flour and salt in a medium bowl and make a well in the center. Add the ¼ cup oil to the well and, with fingertips, work it into the flour until well incorporated.

2. Gradually add ½ cup warm water and mix until you have a rough dough. Remove the dough to a lightly floured work surface and knead for 3 minutes. Shape into a ball, invert the bowl over the dough, and let rest for 15 minutes. Knead for about 2 to 3 minutes more, until the dough is smooth and elastic.

3. Divide the dough in two and shape the two halves into balls. Cover with a damp kitchen towel and let rest while the filling is made.

4. Place the onion in a medium bowl. Add a little salt and the pepper and sumac, and, with fingers, rub the seasonings into the onion to soften it.

5. Place the spinach in a large bowl, sprinkle with a little salt, and gently rub the salt in with fingers until the spinach is wilted. Squeeze the spinach very dry. Transfer to a clean large bowl. Loosen up the squeezed spinach, so that you can mix it with the other ingredients more easily.

6. Add the onion to the spinach. Add the pine nuts, the lemon juice, and the 2 tablespoons oil. Mix well. Taste and adjust the seasonings if necessary; the filling should be quite strongly flavored to offset the rather bland dough. Cover with a clean kitchen towel and set aside.

7. Roll out one ball of dough on a lightly floured surface as thin as possible; as thin as ¹⁄₁₀ inch is ideal. Use a 3½-inch round pastry cutter to cut as many circles of dough as possible. Pick up the extra dough and knead it back together into a ball; keep this ball under the damp cloth with the other ball of dough.

8. Preheat the oven to 450°F. Place a scant tablespoon of filling in the middle of a circle of dough. Gently pick up the left and right thirds of the circle and pinch them together two-thirds of the way down. Pick up the bottom third of the circle and pinch it in the middle to join it to the seam made when the left and right thirds were pinched together. Then press in from the edges and pinch all

the loose seams together, to form a triangle with raised seams; do so firmly to prevent opening during baking. Transfer to a nonstick baking sheet, or to a baking sheet lined with parchment paper or a silicone pastry mat. Cover with plastic wrap. Make the remaining triangles in the same way, using the remaining balls of dough as well. Brush the tops of the triangles with a little olive oil.

9. Bake for about 15 minutes, until the triangles are lightly golden. Serve warm or at room temperature.

Lebanese Strained Yogurt Triangles

Fatayer bil-Labneh

Labneh, which is strained yogurt, can be bought ready-made in Middle Eastern groceries and in some supermarkets. To make it at home: Line a colander with a double layer of cheesecloth and pour plain yogurt into it. Pick up the corners and tie them to make a sack. Hang over the sink. Let the yogurt drain for at least 4 hours, until it reduces to about half its original weight. It is still a good idea to drain store-bought labneh in cheesecloth for an hour or two, for it usually is wetter than when it is made at home.

SERVES 4

1 recipe dough for Lebanese Spinach Triangles, page 293, prepared
    through step 2
2 small onions, diced (about ¾ cup)
½ teaspoon ground cinnamon
½ teaspoon ground allspice
Fine kosher salt or sea salt
¼ teaspoon finely ground black pepper
Pinch of crushed red pepper flakes, optional
1½ cups strained yogurt (see head note)
1 medium tomato, seeded and diced (about ½ cup)
1 teaspoon unsalted butter, softened
Unbleached all-purpose flour, for rolling the dough
Extra-virgin olive oil, for brushing the triangles

1. Divide the dough into 4 equal pieces. Shape each piece into a ball. Cover with plastic wrap and let rest for 15 minutes.

2. Place the onions in a medium bowl. Add the cinnamon, allspice, salt to taste, and the pepper and, if using, pepper flakes. With fingers, rub the seasonings into the onions to soften them.

3. Add the yogurt, tomato, and butter and stir well. Taste and adjust the seasonings if necessary. Cover and set aside.

4. Preheat the oven to 450°F. Roll out 1 ball of dough on a lightly floured surface into a circle that is as thin as possible; as thin as $\frac{1}{10}$ inch is ideal. Spread one-fourth of the filling in the middle of the circle. Lift up the left and right thirds of the circle and, with thumb and index finger, pinch them together two-thirds of the way down, making a narrow raised seam or joint. Lift up the bottom third and pinch it together with the loose edges of the left and right thirds; the pastry now should look like a triangle with a raised inverted Y in the middle. Pinch the seams tightly together so that they do not open during baking.

5. Carefully transfer the filled pastry seam side up to a nonstick baking sheet, or to a baking sheet lined with parchment paper or a silicone pastry mat. Brush with a little olive oil and loosely cover with plastic wrap. Make the remaining 3 triangles in the same way.

6. Bake, uncovered, for 20 to 25 minutes, until golden. Serve hot or warm.

Cheese Triangles

Fatayer bil-Qarish

The filling for these triangles traditionally was made with a Lebanese-Syrian cheese called qarish. But qarish is no longer commonly available even in Lebanon and Syria, and it certainly isn't available in the West. To make enough qarish for this recipe, boil 1 quart plain yogurt with 1 tablespoon lemon juice until the yogurt separates. Pour the curdled yogurt into a colander lined with cheesecloth. When cool enough to handle, tie the corners of the cheesecloth into a sack. Hang the sack over the sink and let the cheese drain overnight. Once the cheese is ready, add 1 tablespoon salt, and use as directed, or store in the refrigerator for two days. A good substitute may be made by mixing equal quantities of feta and curd cheese, as in this recipe.

SERVES 4

1 recipe dough for Lebanese Spinach Triangles, page 293, prepared
    through step 2
2 tablespoons unsalted butter
1 medium egg, beaten
½ cup crumbled feta cheese
½ cup curd cheese
½ cup finely chopped flat-leaf parsley
¼ cup finely chopped mint
2 tablespoons finely chopped scallions
½ teaspoon ground cinnamon
½ teaspoon ground allspice
Fine kosher salt or sea salt
Freshly ground black pepper

Unbleached all-purpose flour, for rolling the dough
Extra-virgin olive oil, for brushing the triangles

1. Divide the dough into 4 equal pieces. Shape each piece into a ball. Cover with plastic wrap and let rest for 15 minutes.

2. Heat the butter in a sauté pan over medium heat. Scramble the egg lightly in the butter; do not cook until dry. Transfer the scrambled egg to a medium bowl. Add the cheeses, herbs, and scallions. Season with the spices and with salt and pepper to taste. Mix well. Taste and adjust seasoning if necessary. Set aside.

3. Preheat the oven to 450°F. Roll out 1 ball of dough on a lightly floured surface into a circle that is as thin as possible; as thin as $\frac{1}{10}$ inch is ideal. Spread one-quarter of the filling in the middle of the circle. Lift up the left and right thirds of the circle and, with thumb and index finger, pinch them together two-thirds of the way down, making a narrow raised seam or joint. Lift up the bottom third and pinch it together with the loose edges of the left and right thirds; the pastry now should look like a triangle with a raised inverted Y in the middle. Pinch the seams tightly together so that they do not open during baking.

4. Carefully transfer the filled pastry seam side up to a nonstick baking sheet, or to a baking sheet lined with parchment paper or a silicone pastry mat. Brush with a little olive oil and loosely cover with plastic wrap. Make the remaining 3 triangles in the same way.

5. Bake, uncovered, for 20 to 25 minutes, until lightly golden. Serve hot or warm.

Lebanese Square Meat Pies

Sreyjatt

These little pies are also called *sfiha,* in Baalbek and other parts of Lebanon as well as in Syria. I remember having them during a wonderful stay at the Palmyra Hotel in Baalbek soon after the civil war ended in 1992. At the time the hotel was pretty run-down, charmingly reminiscent of a seedy hotel in an old Hollywood film. I could picture Sidney Greenstreet sitting on the terrace closing a sleazy deal or plotting to get rid of a competitor. I don't recall the food in those old films, but nowadays a director would show a platter of these scrumptious pastries and a glass of arak, an anise-flavored drink akin to Turkish raki or Greek ouzo, on the table for an authentic touch.

Do work fairly quickly when shaping these pastries, so that the dough does not rise too much. If it does, the seams in the pies will open up during baking and the pastries will not retain their square cuplike shape.

MAKES ABOUT 26 SMALL PASTRIES

1 recipe dough for Pita Bread (page 71) through step 3 but with only a
1-hour rise

For the filling
1 pound finely ground lamb (about 3 cups)
1 small onion, diced (about ⅓ cup)
2 garlic cloves, crushed
⅓ cup pine nuts (about 3 ounces)
2 tablespoons tahini (sesame paste)
2 tablespoons pomegranate syrup

¼ teaspoon grated nutmeg
Fine kosher salt or sea salt to taste
Freshly ground black pepper to taste

Unbleached all-purpose flour, for rolling and kneading
½ cup fresh pomegranate seeds, optional

1. Prepare the dough, but let the dough rise for only 1 hour. Divide it into 4 equal pieces and shape each piece into a ball. Cover with a wet but not dripping kitchen towel and let rest for 30 minutes more.

2. Combine all of the filling ingredients in a large bowl and mix well. Set aside.

3. Roll out 1 ball of dough on a lightly floured surface to a large circle no more than ⅛ inch thick, sprinkling with flour every now and then. Cut out as many smaller circles as you can with a 4-inch round pastry cutter. Gather the extra dough, knead it back together, roll into a ball, and let rest under the kitchen towel next to the other balls of dough.

4. Preheat the oven to 450°F. Turn over the cut-out circles and place 2 teaspoons filling in the center of each. Pinch the edges together at 4 equal intervals to make a square cuplike pie with raised corners and an open top. Transfer to a nonstick baking sheet, or to a baking sheet lined with parchment paper or a silicone pastry mat. Cover loosely with plastic wrap. Roll out, cut out, fill, and shape the remaining pies in the same manner.

5. Pinch the corners of the pies again to make sure they do not open during baking. Bake for 12 to 15 minutes, until the dough is golden brown and the meat is crisp on top and cooked through. Serve hot or warm, perhaps with a garnish of pomegranate seeds.

Syrian Cheese Fatayer

Fatayer Jibneh Süriyeh

Fatayer are the quintessential street food in Syria. Bakeries that specialize in fatayer are common both in the souks and along major streets. The bakeries are manned by young men, and even boys, who spend the day flattening dough, filling it with an amazing variety of fillings, and baking the fatayer. With every trip I make to Syria, the list of fillings seems to grow longer.

The dough used in Syrian fatayer is quite different from that used in Lebanese ones. It is made with milk and with a touch of ground mahlep (see page 159)—a more exotic flavor to the Western palate. (I recommend using mahlep in this recipe, but you may omit it if you don't have any on hand.) It is a slightly sweet dough with a spongy and fluffy texture. The akkawi cheese I recommend using here is an Arab cheese that is softer and less salty than Halloumi cheese.

SERVES 8

For the dough
Heaping teaspoon (½ package) active dry yeast
1 teaspoon sugar
¼ cup whole milk, at room temperature
1½ cups unbleached all-purpose flour, plus extra for kneading and
 shaping
½ teaspoon fine kosher salt or sea salt
⅛ teaspoon ground mahlep (see page 159), optional
1 medium egg

For the filling
¾ cup finely chopped akkawi cheese or fresh mozzarella (about 9
    ounces)
1 medium egg, beaten
1 tablespoon unsalted butter
¼ cup finely chopped flat-leaf parsley
Fine kosher salt or sea salt to taste
Freshly ground black pepper to taste

1. Dissolve the yeast and sugar in 2 tablespoons warm water. Stir until creamy.
   Add the milk and mix well.

2. Combine the flour, salt, and, if using, mahlep in a large bowl and make a well
   in the center. Add the yeast mixture and the egg to the well and mix. Slowly
   bring in the flour. Knead until you have a rough ball of dough.

3. Remove the dough to a lightly floured work surface. Knead for about 3 minutes. Invert the bowl over the dough and let rest for 15 minutes. Knead for about 2 to 3 minutes more, until the dough is smooth and elastic. Shape the dough into a ball and place in a lightly floured clean bowl. Cover with plastic wrap and let rise in a warm, draft-free place for 1 hour. Fold the dough (see pages 6–7), cover again, and let rise for 1 hour more. The dough should have doubled in volume.

4. Return the dough to the work surface. Divide into 8 equal pieces and shape each piece into a ball. Cover the balls with a wet but not dripping kitchen towel and let rest for 30 minutes. Meanwhile, mix the filling ingredients together in a bowl and set aside.

5. Flatten and shape a ball by hand into a circle about 6 inches in diameter, then stretch the circle into an oval shape. Spread 1 tablespoon filling in the middle. Fold one third of the oval over the filling, and then fold the opposite third to slightly overlap the first. Press to seal the seams. Transfer, seam side up, to a large nonstick baking sheet, or to a baking sheet lined with parchment paper or

a silicone pastry mat. Make the remaining fatayer in the same way. Cover the fatayer with a damp kitchen towel and let rest for 20 minutes. Meanwhile, preheat the oven to 500°F.

6. Bake for 10 to 12 minutes, until golden brown all over. Serve hot, warm, or at room temperature.

❖ Tunisian Meat Crescents

Banadhej

Tunisians make these savory pastries for Eid el-Kebir, also known as Eid el-Adha, the Muslim feast that commemorates Abraham's willingness to sacrifice his son Ismael. The crescents have a very subtle flavor of rose due to the b'harat seasoning—a mixture of equal amounts of ground cinnamon and dried rose petals, which may sound exotic but is a common seasoning in Tunisia. If you do not want to spend the time making the fluted edge for the pastry, you can simply press on the edges to flatten and seal. The crescents will not be as pretty but they will still be very presentable and just as delicious.

MAKES 36 TO 40 SMALL PASTRIES

For the dough
3⅓ cups fine semolina or semolina flour
1½ teaspoons fine sea salt or kosher salt
⅓ cup extra-virgin olive oil
Unbleached all-purpose flour, for kneading and shaping

For the filling
3 tablespoons unsalted butter
14 ounces ground beef (about 2⅓ cups)
Heaping ½ teaspoon b'harat seasoning, if available, or ground
    cinnamon
Fine kosher salt or sea salt
Heaping ¼ teaspoon freshly ground black pepper

1. Make the dough: Combine the semolina and salt in a large bowl and make a well in the center. Add the oil and, with fingertips, work the oil into the semolina until well incorporated. Gradually add 1 cup plus 2 tablespoons warm water, bringing in the flour as you go along, and knead until you have a rough ball of dough.

2. Remove the dough to a lightly floured work surface. Knead for 3 minutes. Invert the bowl over the dough and let rest for 15 minutes. Knead for about 2 to 3 minutes more, until the dough is smooth and elastic. Shape the dough into a ball and place in a lightly floured clean bowl. Cover with plastic wrap and let rest in a warm, draft-free place for 1 hour.

3. Meanwhile, make the filling: Heat the butter in a sauté pan over medium heat. Add the beef and season with the b'harat, salt to taste, and the pepper. Cook until the beef has lost all traces of pink and the mixture is quite dry, stirring often so that the meat has no lumps. Set aside.

4. Divide the dough into 2 equal pieces. Shape each piece into a ball. Cover with plastic wrap and let rest for 15 minutes. Meanwhile, preheat the oven to 400°F.

5. Roll out a piece of dough on a lightly floured surface to a circle ¼ inch thick. Using a 3-inch round pastry cutter, cut out as many smaller circles as possible. Pick up the extra dough, knead it back together into another ball, and place this ball next to the other ball of dough under the plastic wrap. Turn over the cut-out circles of dough on the work surface and place 1 teaspoon meat filling in the middle of each. Fold the circles into half circles and press the edges to seal and flatten; then pick up each crescent and, with fingertips, pinch the edges further and make small diagonal folds to create a fluted edge. Transfer to a nonstick baking sheet, or to a baking sheet lined with parchment paper or a silicone pastry mat. Cover with plastic wrap. Shape and fill the rest of the dough, including additional cut-outs, in the same way.

6. Remove the plastic wrap and bake for 25 to 30 minutes, until golden all over. Transfer to a wire rack to cool. Serve hot or warm.

✛ Large Italian Crescents

Calzoni

A calzone is basically a covered pizza. Most of the time, calzones are made as small or medium individual crescents. But calzones can also be made large, for sharing, as in this recipe. I rather like the generous size of the large calzones; and it is far quicker to make just two rather than four, six, or more. Here I recommend making the calzones with Italian bread dough, but you can also use the pizza dough on page 42.

SERVES 4

½ cup diced salami (about 3 ounces)
¾ cup fresh ricotta, mashed with a fork
½ cup diced fresh mozzarella (about 3 ounces)
¼ cup grated Parmigiano-Reggiano (about ½ ounce)
Freshly ground black pepper
1 recipe dough for Regular Italian Bread, page 119, through step 4
1 medium egg

1. Combine the salami, ricotta, mozzarella, Parmesan, and pepper to taste in a large bowl. Set aside.

2. Divide the dough into 2 equal pieces. Roll out each piece on a lightly floured work surface to a large circle about ¼ inch thick. Spread half the filling on one half of each circle to about 1 inch from the edge. Fold the uncovered half of the dough over the filling. Pinch with fingers to seal and flute the edges.

3. Preheat the oven to 450°F. Carefully transfer the calzones to a nonstick baking sheet, or to a baking sheet lined with parchment paper or a silicone pastry mat. Cover with a damp kitchen towel and let rest for 15 to 20 minutes.

4. Uncover and bake for 25 to 30 minutes, until crisp and golden all over. Serve immediately.

❖ Italian Onion Biscuits

Biscotti all Cipolla

These savory biscuits are often served as one among a selection of *stuzzichini,* which are *fuori menu* (outside the menu), salty nibbles usually served with drinks. In traditional restaurants, the waiter will bring you a small plate of stuzzichini, along with a glass of prosecco, to enjoy while you are deciding what to order. In bars, stuzzichini and canapés are lined up along the bar for customers to nibble on with their drinks.

MAKES 20 TO 25 BISCUITS

2 tablespoons extra-virgin olive oil

½ pound red onions, very thinly sliced

Fine kosher salt or sea salt

1⅔ cups unbleached all-purpose flour, plus extra for kneading and shaping

1½ teaspoons baking powder

3 tablespoons cold unsalted butter, diced into small cubes

1 medium egg

¼ cup milk

1. Heat the oil in a sauté pan over medium-low heat. Add the onions, sprinkle with a little salt, and cook, stirring occasionally, until the onions are very soft but have not darkened, about 20 minutes. Let cool.

2. Combine the flour, baking powder, and 1 teaspoon salt in a large bowl. Add the butter and, using fingertips, rub the butter into the flour until incorporated.

3. Beat the egg and milk together. Add to the flour and, working quickly, mix them into the flour and shape into a ball. Wrap the dough in plastic wrap and refrigerate for 30 minutes.

4. Preheat the oven to 375°F. Sprinkle a work surface and a rolling pin with flour. Roll out the pastry to a large circle about ½ inch thick. Use a 2-inch round pastry cutter to cut as many biscuits as possible. Transfer these to a nonstick baking sheet, or to a baking sheet lined with parchment paper or a silicone pastry mat. Spread a little onion over each circle. Working quickly, knead together the extra dough and roll out to make more biscuits. Again, spread a little onion over each circle.

5. Bake for 15 to 20 minutes, until lightly golden. Transfer to a wire rack to cool. Serve warm or at room temperature.

✣ Foie Gras Nibbles

Bouchées au Foie Gras

Here is a very elegant appetizer to serve with champagne. I adapted the recipe from one I found in an early number of *Pot-au-Feu*, an old French food magazine that started appearing near the end of the nineteenth century. The perfect time to make these is when you have broken up leftover foie gras that is no longer fit to serve at table, but still very good to eat. You can also use good pâté de foie gras from a jar or a tin.

MAKES 20 TO 25 SMALL PASTRIES

For the choux pastries
5 tablespoons unsalted butter, cut into small cubes
Scant teaspoon fine kosher salt or sea salt
⅔ cup unbleached all-purpose flour, sifted onto a piece of parchment
    paper
2 large eggs
1 medium egg, beaten, for brushing the pastry

For the filling
7 ounces foie gras
¼ cup (½ stick) unsalted butter, softened
3 tablespoons crème fraîche
Fine kosher salt or sea salt
Freshly ground black pepper

1. Make the pastry: Add the butter and salt to ½ cup water in a medium saucepan. Bring to a boil over medium heat. As soon as the water boils, remove the pan from the heat, add the flour all at once, and quickly begin stirring in the flour with a heat-proof spatula. Continue stirring until the mixture is very smooth.

2. Return the pan to medium heat and stir constantly until the pastry comes away from the sides of the pan and falls off the spatula. Stopping before this point will yield a pastry that is too moist; but do not keep the pan over the heat much beyond this point either. Remove the pan from the heat.

3. Preheat the oven to 350°F. Stir the 2 large eggs into the pastry one after the other, making sure the first is mixed in well before adding the second.

4. Fit a 1-inch funnel to a pastry bag and spoon the choux pastry into the bag. Squeeze out small dollops, ½ to ⅔ inch in diameter, onto a nonstick baking sheet, or onto a baking sheet lined with parchment paper or a silicone pastry mat. Place them about 1 inch apart to give them room to expand during baking. Brush them with the beaten egg.

5. Bake the choux for 25 to 30 minutes, until well puffed up, dry to the touch, and golden. Transfer to a wire rack to cool so that the bottoms don't soften.

6. Make the filling: Press the foie gras through a very fine sieve and into a medium bowl. Add the softened butter and crème fraîche, season with salt and pepper to taste, and mix well. Taste and adjust the seasoning. Fit a small funnel onto a clean pastry bag and spoon the foie gras mixture into the bag.

7. Make a small slit on the bottom of each pastry. Insert the funnel into the opening and pipe in as much filling as the pastry will take. Transfer to a baking sheet to keep hot (the open door of the oven may work for this). Fill the remaining choux in the same manner, and serve immediately.

Gougères from Burgundy

Gougères Bourguignonnes

Agougère is a choux pastry with added Gruyère cheese. Gougères are often made in a ring shape: spoonfuls of pastry are dropped onto a baking sheet right next to each other, where they join into a ring as they expand while baking. I like making them in ramekins, as they are in this recipe. They are great appetizers to serve with cocktails, but you can also serve them as a pastry alongside a meat dish—a little like Yorkshire pudding with roast beef.

MAKES 12 MEDIUM PASTRIES

2 cups milk
½ cup (1 stick) unsalted butter, plus extra for greasing the ramekins
1 teaspoon fine kosher salt or sea salt
½ teaspoon freshly ground black pepper
1⅓ cups unbleached all-purpose flour
8 medium eggs
6 ounces Gruyère cheese, cut into small cubes (1 heaping cup)
2 tablespoons crème fraîche
Twelve 2¾-inch-round by 1¼ inch-deep ramekins

1. Pour the milk into a large saucepan. Add the butter, salt, and pepper and place over medium heat. Bring to a boil, then remove immediately from the heat.

2. Gradually stir in the flour, using a whisk to start with and then a heat-proof spatula as the mixture starts to thicken. Return to medium heat and continue stirring for about 2 minutes. Set aside for 10 to 15 minutes, until slightly cooled.

3. Stir in 7 of the eggs, one at a time; continue stirring until the batter is thick, smooth, and shiny. Add the cheese and crème fraîche and mix well.

4. Preheat the oven to 350°F. Butter the ramekins and place them on a baking sheet. Spoon enough batter into each ramekin to fill halfway up. Press on the batter with the back of the spoon to eliminate air pockets. Beat the remaining egg and brush the tops of the gougères with it.

5. Bake for 40 to 45 minutes, until golden brown and well risen (to the top rim of the ramekins and slightly over). Do not open the oven to check; this may cause the gougères to collapse. Serve immediately.

✦ Anchovy Sticks

Allumettes aux Anchois

Puff pastry is rather difficult to make successfully from scratch at home. Bakeries sometimes have fresh puff pastry available for sale; you may need to order it a day ahead. There also are good brands of frozen puff pastry at the supermarket. Read the ingredients lists and choose one that is made with butter; it is far superior to one made with margarine.

MAKES ABOUT 24 STICKS

14 to 16 salted anchovies, rinsed well, boned, and separated into fillets
7 ounces fillet of a white fish, boned
½ cup crème fraîche
Freshly ground black pepper
2 pounds puff pastry, fresh or frozen and thawed in the refrigerator
1 egg beaten with 1 tablespoon water and a pinch of salt

1. Put 6 of the anchovy fillets, the fish fillet, and the crème fraîche in a food processor. Season with pepper to taste and process to a smooth paste. Set aside.

2. Divide the puff pastry into 2 equal parts. On a surface that can be cut with a knife, roll out each to a large rectangle just under ¼ inch thick.

3. Fit a ½-inch funnel onto a pastry bag and spoon the fish paste into the bag. Squeeze out onto one of the rectangles 3-inch-long lines of filling parallel to the short sides of the rectangle, keeping the lines about 1 inch apart from each

other and stopping about 1 inch short of the edges. Place an anchovy fillet on each line of filling.

4. Preheat the oven to 400°F. Dip a pastry brush into water and lightly brush the uncovered areas of the garnished rectangle. Carefully lay the other rectangle over the garnished one. Lightly press with fingertips between the lines of filling and all around the edges. With the back of a knife, make an incision to mark the divisions. Now using a sharp knife, trim the edges neatly, then cut between the bands of filled pastry; it is essential to cut sharply and neatly so that the pastry puffs up during baking. The result should be about 24 rectangles, each about 4 or 5 inches long. Transfer to a nonstick baking sheet, or to a baking sheet lined with parchment paper or a silicone pastry mat.

5. Brush the top of the allumettes with the beaten egg. Try not to let the egg dribble over the sides, which will inhibit the puffing of the pastry during baking. You can, if you like, cut a decorative shape or pattern on top of each allumette, using the back of a knife.

6. Bake for 10 to 15 minutes, until the pastry is all puffed up and golden. Serve immediately, or transfer to a wire rack to serve warm.

✤ Cheese Sticks

Allumettes au Fromage

My method for making these cheese sticks follows the *quatre pliages*—four folds—technique that French bakers use with puff pastry, to create lightly layered pastries. But for this recipe I start with a simple pastry dough rather than with puff pastry.

MAKES 30 TO 35 STICKS

1⅓ cups unbleached all-purpose flour, plus extra for shaping the dough
1 teaspoon fine kosher salt or sea salt
½ teaspoon powdered mustard
½ cup (1 stick) unsalted butter, at room temperature
Heaping 1 cup very finely grated Gruyère (about 2½ ounces)
Whole milk, for brushing the pastry

1. Put the flour in a medium bowl and make a well in the center. Add the salt and mustard to the well. Add 1 tablespoon warm water to the well and mix until the salt and mustard are dissolved.

2. Add the butter to the well and, with folded fingers, flatten the butter to a round cake-like shape. Pour ⅓ cup warm water on the butter and, with fingertips, mix the butter with the water. Bring in the flour to mix with the butter and water, working quickly so as not to develop the gluten.

3. Sprinkle a little flour onto a plate and place the dough on it. Sprinkle the dough lightly with more flour, and let rest for 15 minutes.

4. Sprinkle a work surface with a little flour and Gruyère and place the dough on it. Sprinkle the dough with a little more flour and Gruyère and, with a rolling pin, roll out the dough away from you (so that the long side is perpendicular to the front of the work surface) to a rectangle about 18 inches by 8 inches, sprinkling with more Gruyère as the dough is stretched out.

5. Fold one short third of the dough over, and give the fold a light roll with the rolling pin to fix it in place. Fold the opposite short third over, and again roll lightly to fix. Remove the dough from the work surface and sprinkle a little more Gruyère on the surface. Rotate the dough 90 degrees so that the line of the fold is perpendicular to the front of the work surface, and place the dough over the Gruyère. Roll out the dough to an 18 by 8-inch rectangle again, and fold again in thirds, sprinkling with more cheese as the dough is stretched out. Repeat the process twice more, for a total of 4 folds.

6. Preheat the oven to 400°F. Roll out the dough to a large rectangle and cut the rectangle in half. Sprinkle any remaining Gruyère on both halves. Roll out one half to a long rectangle about 5 inches wide and just under ½ inch thick. Brush the pastry lightly with milk and cut crosswise into ½-inch-wide strips. As you cut the strips, transfer them to a nonstick baking sheet, or a baking sheet lined with parchment paper or a silicone pastry mat. Roll out, brush, cut, and transfer the second half of the pastry in the same way.

7. Bake for 12 to 15 minutes, or until golden and puffed up to about 3 times their starting thickness. Serve immediately, or transfer to a wire rack to serve warm.

✦ Bibliography ✦

General

Alford, Jeffrey, and Naomi Duguid. *Flatbreads & Flavors*. New York: William Morrow and Company, Inc., 1995.

———. *HomeBaking*. New York: Artisan, 2004.

Andrews, Colman. *Flavors of the Riviera*. New York: Bantam Books, 1996.

Bolens, Lucie. *La cuisine Andalouse, Un Art de Vivre, XIe–XIIIe Siècle*. Paris: Albin Michel, 1990.

Boxer, Arabella. *Mediterranean Cookbook*. London: Penguin, 1983.

Calvel, Professeur Raymond. *Le Goût du Pain*. Les Lilas: Éditions Jérôme Villette, 1990.

Davidson, Alan. *Oxford Companion to Food*. Oxford: Oxford University Press, 2000.

Dupaigne, Bernard. *Le Pain de l'Homme*. Paris: Éditions de la Martinière, 1999.

Favre, Joseph. *Dictionnaire Universel de Cuisine Pratique*. Paris: Corbeil—Imprimerie ed. Crété, 1902.

Hamelman, Jeffrey. *Bread: A Bakers's Book of Techniques and Recipes*. Hoboken, NJ: Wiley, 2004.

Helou, Anissa. *Mediterranean Street Food*. New York: HarperCollins, 2002.

Jones, Judith, and Evan Jones. *The Book of Bread*. New York: Harper & Row, 1982.

Kleiman, Evan. *Angeli Caffè Pizza, Pasta, Panini*. New York: Morrow, 1997.

Larousse gastronomique. Paris: Larousse, 1932.

Lepard, Dan, and Richard Whittington. *Baking with Passion*. London: Quadrille, 1999.

Perry, Charles. *Medieval Arab Cookery*. London: Prospect Books, 2001.

Pot-au-feu, Le. 1900–1912.

Sluimer, Piet. *Principles of Breadmaking*. St. Paul, MN: American Association of Cereal Chemists, 2005.

Sokolov, Raymond. *The Cook's Canon*. New York: HarperCollins, 2003.

Qarooni, Jalal. *Flat Bread Technology*. New York: Chapman & Hall, 1996.

Balkans

Kaneva-Johnson, Maria. *The Melting Pot: Balkan Food & Cookery*. London: Prospect Books, 1995.

Egypt

Abdennour, Samia. *Egyptian Cooking*. Cairo: The American University in Cairo Press, 1984.

Aït Mohamed, Salima. *La cuisine Égyptienne*. Marseille: Temps Gourmands Éditions, 1997.

Darby, William J., Paul Ghalioungui, and Louis Grivetti. *Food: The Gift of Osiris*. New York: Academic Press, 1971.

France

Chamberlain, Samuel. *Bouquet de France*. New York: Gourmet Distributing Corporation, 1952.

Courtine, Robert. *The Hundred Glories of French Cooking*. London: Robert Hale & Company, 1976.

Sailland, Maurice Edmond. *Traditional Recipes of the Provinces of France, selected by Curnonsky* [pseud.]. London: W. H. Allen, 1961.

Darenne and Duval. *Traité de Pâtisserie Moderne*. Paris: self-published, 1909.

Escudier, Jean-Noel. *La Véritable Cuisine Provençale et Niçoise*. Toulon: Les Éditions Provencia-Toulon, 1964.

Guinet, Roland. *Les Pains de France*. Paris: Éditions Jacques Lanore, 2002.

Institut National de la Boulangerie-Pâtisserie. *Les Croc' midi*. Les Lilas: Éditions Jérôme Villette, 1999.

Kamir, Basile. *La Journée du Pain*. Paris: Hachette, 1999.

Lalos, Frédérique. *Le Pain, l'Envers du Décor*. Paris: Les Éditions de l'If, 2003.

Lheureux, Simone. *La Cuisine du Soleil entre Provence et Languedoc*. Nîmes: Éditions Lacour, 1986.

Olney, Richard. *Simple French Food*. London: Penguin, 1983.

Rousseau, Marguerite. *Pains de Tradition*. Paris: Flammarion, 2001.

Saint-Ange, E. *La Bonne Cuisine*. Paris: Larousse, 1995.

Vabret, Christian. *Tours de Main, Pains Speciaux et Recettes Regionales*. Les Lilas: Éditions Jérôme Villette, 2002.

Greece

Farr Louis, Diana. *Feasting and Fasting in Crete*. Athens: Kedros Publications, 2001.

Hoffman, Susanna. *The Olive and the Caper: Adventures in Greek Cooking*. New York: Workman Publishing Company, Inc., 2004.

Kochilas, Diane. *The Food and Wine of Greece*. New York: St. Martin's Press, 1990.

Kremezi, Aglaia. *The Foods of Greece*. New York: Stewart, Tabori & Chang, 1999.

———. *The Foods of the Greek Islands*. Boston: Houghton Mifflin, 2000.

Psilakis, Maria, and N. Psilakis. *La Cuisine Crétoise*. Heraklion: Karmanor, 1996.

The Recipe Club of Saint Paul's Greek Orthodox Cathedral. *The Complete Book of Greek Cooking*. New York: Harper Perennial, 1991.

Salaman, Rena. *Greek Food*. London: HarperCollins, 1993.

———. *Greek Island Cookery*. London: Ebury Press, 1987.

Souli, Sofia. *Grèce, Cuisine & Vins*. Athens: Editions Toubis, 1997.

Yianilos, Theresa Karas. *The Complete Greek Cookbook*. La Jolla: La Jolla Book Publishing, 2000.

Israel

Abu-Ghosh, Nawal. *The Arab-Israeli Cuisine*. Israel: Cater Publishing House, 1996.

Ganor, Avi, and Ron Maiberg. *Taste of Israel*. New York: Rizzoli, 1990.

Nathan, Joan. *The Foods of Israel Today*. New York: Knopf, 2001.

Tower of David Museum. *Eating in Jerusalem*. Israel: Moden, 1992.

Valero, Rina. *Delights of Jerusalem*. Israel: Nahar Publishing House and Steimatsky, 1985.

Italy

Accame, Franco, Silvio Torre, and Virgilio Pronzati. *Il Grande Libro dell Cucina Ligure*. Genoa: De Ferrari Editore, 1997.

Anonymous. *Millericette*. Milan: Avallardi, 1998.

Bugialli, Giuliano. *The Fine Art of Italian Cooking*. New York: Times Books, 1977.

———. *Foods of Naples and Campania*. New York: Stewart, Tabori & Chang, 2003.

D'Alba, Tommaso. *La Cucina Siciliana di Derivazione Araba*. Palermo: self-published, 1980.

Del Conte, Anna. *The Classic Food of Northern Italy*. London: Pavilion, 1995.

———. *Gastronomy of Italy*. London: Pavilion, 2001.

Della Croce, Julia. *Umbria*. San Francisco: Chronicle Books, 2002.

Ebla Studio Editoriale, ed. *Pane e Torte Salate*. Florence: Demetra, 2002.

Field, Carol. *The Italian Baker*. New York: HarperCollins, 1985.

Francesconi, Jeanne Caròla. *La Cucina Napoletana*. Roma: Newton Compton Editori, 2002.

Giorilli, Piergiorgio. *Pane & Pani*. Saviglia: Il Gusto Gribaudo, 2003.

Harmon Jenkins, Nancy. *The Flavors of Puglia*. New York: Broadway Books, 1997.

———. *Flavors of Tuscany*. New York: Broadway Books, 1998.

Lanza, Anna Tasca. *The Heart of Sicily*. New York: Clarkson Potter, 1993.

———. *The Flavors of Sicily*. New York: Clarkson Potter, 1996.

Lo Monte, Mimmetta. *Classic Sicilian Cooking*. New York: Simon and Schuster, 1990.

Medici, Lorenza de'. *The Heritage of Italian Cooking*. New York: Random House, 1995.

Michini, Vincenzo. *L'Eternità del Pane, Picola Storia dell'Alimento più Antico*. Naples: Tullio Pironti Editore, 2002.

Negrin, Micol. *Rustico: Regional Italian Country Cooking*. New York: Clarkson Potter, 2002.

Pradelli, Alessandro Molinari. *La Cucina Ligure*. Rome: Newton & Compton Editori, 1996.

Randazzo, Giuseppina. *La Cucina Siciliana*. Palermo: S.A.S., 1992.

Ricciardi, Massimo. *Pizza Napoletana*.

Salda, Anna Gosetti della. *Le Ricette Regionali Italiane*. Milan: Solares, 1980.

Simeti, Mary Taylor. *Pomp and Sustenance: Twenty-five Centuries of Sicilian Food*. New York: Henry Holt & Co., 1991.

Santasilia, Franco. *La Cucina Aristocratica Napoletana*. Naples: Mario Guida Editori.

Lebanon/Syria

Choueiri, Ramzi N. *Le patrimoine culturel du Liban*. Beirut: Ramzi N. Doueiri, 2002.

Corey, Helen. *The Art of Syrian Cookery*. New York: Doubleday, 1962.

Helou, Anissa. *Lebanese Cuisine*. New York: St. Martin's Press, 1995.

Khayat, Marie Karam, and Margaret Clark Keatinge. *Food from the Arab World*. Beirut: Khayats, 1959.

Mouzannar, Ibrahim. *La cuisine Libanaise*. Beirut: Librairie du Liban, 1981.

Malta

Caruana Galizia, Anne, and Helen Caruana Galizia. *The Food and Cookery of Malta*. London: Prospect Books, 1997.

Morocco

Benani Smires, Latifa. *La Cuisine Marocaine*. Paris: J. P. Taillandier, 1971.

Guineaudau Franc, Zette. *Les Secrets des Cuisines en Terre Marocaine*. Paris: J. P. Taillandier, 1981.

Helou, Anissa. *Café Morocco*. Lincolnwood, IL: Contemporary Books, 1999.

Jaouhari, Alain. *Maroc, La Cuisine de ma Mère*. Geneva: Minerva, 2002.

Spain

Andrews, Colman. *Catalan Cuisine*. London: Grub Street, 1997.

Domingo, Xavier, and Pierre Hussenot. *Le Goût de l'Espagne*. Paris: Flammarion, 1992.

Luard, Elisabeth. *The Flavours of Andalucia*. London: Collins & Brown, 1991.

Mendel, Janet. *Traditional Spanish Cooking*. London: Garnet, 1996.

———. *My Kitchen in Spain*. New York: HarperCollins, 2002.

Sevilla, Maria José. *Life and Food in the Basque Country*. London: Weidenfeld & Nicholson, 1989.

Tunisia

Kaak, Zeinab. *La Sofra*. Tunis: Cérès Éditions, 1995.

Kouki, Mohamed. *La Cuisine et Pâtisserie Tunisiennes*. Tunis: Dar el-Türath el-Tünssi, 1997.

———. *La Cuisine Tunisienne d'Ommok Sannafa*. Tunis: Presses de l'Imprimerie Wafa, 1998.

Various authors. *Fann al-Tabkh el-Tunssi, Sofrat ben Ayyad*. Tunis: Dar el-Shabab lil-Nashr wa al-Tawzi'.

Turkey

Algar, Ayla. *Classical Turkish Cooking*. New York: HarperCollins, 1991.

Ertürk, Ilyas. *Turkish Kitchen Today*. Istanbul: Istanbul Mastabaasi, 1967.

Halici, Nevin. *Turkish Cookbook*. London: Dorling Kindersley, 1989.

———. *Classical Turkish Cuisine*. Istanbul: Gategourmet, 1999.

———. *Sufi Cuisine*. London: Saki Books, 2005.

✤ Index ✤

Note: *Italicized* page references indicate recipe photographs.